Lukas Leys

# Bitcoin and Cryptographic Finance. Technology, Shortcomings and Alternative Cryptocurrencies

**Bibliografische Information der Deutschen Nationalbibliothek:**

Die Deutsche Nationalbibliothek verzeichnet diese Publikation in der Deutschen Nationalbibliografie; detaillierte bibliografische Daten sind im Internet über http://dnb.d-nb.de abrufbar.

**Impressum:**



Ein Imprint der GRIN Verlag, Open Publishing GmbH

Druck und Bindung: Books on Demand GmbH, Norderstedt, Germany

Coverbild: GRIN | Freepik.com | Flaticon.com | ei8htz

# Table of Contents

## Abstract

Designed by an anonymous creator, Bitcoin is an intriguing to modern technology and payment transaction infrastructure that has the potential to become a game changer within the sector of virtual payments. But as with any new technology, there are many obstacles and threats on the path towards mainstream acceptance. In this thesis we analyze key shortcomings of the Bitcoin protocol and Bitcoin as a currency. Moreover, we explore competitors that may one day be able surpass Bitcoin and even make it obsolete. The key question we as is if a suitable competitor can replace Bitcoin or can the open source virtual currency be improved itself in other to make competition obsolete.

## Acknowledgement

My gratefulness goes first and foremost to the people who supported me during the research and writing phases of this diploma thesis. Getting a closer look at the technological innovation that Bitcoin represents and the potential benefits that it could offer was a very valuable experience that guided me through the process of creating this thesis.

Furthermore, I want to thank Univ.-Prof. DDr. Jürgen Huber for his continuing support and his enthusiasm for the topic of my diploma thesis during the entire time of researching and writing it. Likewise, I want to thank Univ.-Prof. Dr. Matthias Bank, CFA for his support and input during the Diplomanden AG at the University of Innsbruck.

Next, I want to acknowledge the outstanding work that MMag. Matthias Korp has provided with his diploma thesis about Bitcoin in 2012, which represented the basis for my thesis.

Additional thanks and appreciation go to family and friends who kept me motivated and provided me with valuable input during this phase of my life.

## List of Abbreviations

| | |
|---|---|
| AML | Anti-Money Laundering |
| AMLD | Anti-Money Laundering Directive |
| API | Application Programming Interface |
| ARS | Argentine Peso |
| ASIC | Application Specific Integrated Circuit |
| ATM | Automated Teller Machine |
| BET | Binominal Expansion Technique |
| BRL | Brazilian Real |
| BSAM | Bear Stearns Asset Management |
| BTC | Bitcoin |
| CFT | Combating of Financing of Terrorism |
| CISO | Constrained Input Small Output |
| CPI | Consumer Price Index |
| CPU | Central Processing Unit |
| CTR | Currency Transaction Reports |
| DGW | Dark Gravity Wave |
| DNS | Domain Name System |
| DoS | Denial-of-Service |
| DRK | Darkcoin |
| DOGE | Dogecoin |
| ECB | European Central Bank |
| ECC | Elliptic Curve Cryptography |
| ECDSA | Elliptic Curve Digital Signature Algorithm |
| EUR | Euro |
| EXIM | Exclusively Informational Money |
| FED | Federal Reserve System |
| FCC | Federal Communications Commission |

| | |
|---|---|
| FPGA | Field Programmable Gate Array |
| FX | Foreign Exchange |
| GB | Gigabyte |
| GBP | British Pound |
| GHOST | Greedy Heaviest Observed Sub-Tree protocol |
| GPU | Graphic Processing Unit |
| GS GIR | Goldman Sachs Global Investment Research |
| IOM | International Organization for Migration |
| JPY | Japanese Yen |
| KB | Kilobyte |
| KYC | Know Your Customer |
| LTC | Litecoin |
| MB | Megabyte |
| MSC | Mastercoin |
| NFC | Near-field Communication Feature |
| NMC | Namecoin |
| OFAC | Office of Foreign Asset Control |
| OTC | Over the Counter |
| PPC | Peercoin |
| P2P | Peer-to-peer |
| RPCA | Ripple protocol consensus algorithm |
| RTGS | Real Time Gross Settlement Payment System |
| SAR | Suspicious Activity Reporting |
| SMTP | Simple Mail Transfer Protocol |
| SPOF | Single Point of Failure |
| SPV | Simplified Payment Verification |
| TOR | The Onion Router |
| TPS | Transactions per Second |

| | |
|---|---|
| UNL | Unique Node List |
| VoIP | Voice over Internet Protocol |
| TIM | Technically Informational Money |
| XPM | Primecoin |
| XRP | Ripple |
| ZAR | South African Rand |

## List of Images

# List of Tables

I'm sure that in 20 years there will either be very large (bitcoin) transaction volume or no volume.

Satoshi Nakamoto

# 1 Executive Summary

This thesis aims to look at the virtual currency Bitcoin in order to investigate some of the potential of cryptocurrencies. Traditional classifications for currencies do not adequately apply to Bitcoin. Regulators and banks currently share this view on cryptocurrencies. Existing currencies have certain common characteristics that Bitcoin does not share. It is a new type of financial technology that entered the global market in 2008 and has since been able to draw the attention of investors, business leaders, regulators and politicians.

Whereas a Dollar, Yen, Yuan or Euro can be hold like a currency, they cannot be secured and transacted simply by itself. Individuals have to rely on third party intermediaries in order to transfer funds for them and in order to store them securely. Contrary to that, one cannot focus on Bitcoin as a currency without acknowledging that it is also a transaction system in itself and would not be able to function is one part of this duality is gone. In fact it is even more precise to look at Bitcoin as a decentralized transaction and financial services system, with a currency function being only one aspect of the technology. In this thesis, we evaluate not only the technological characteristics of decentralized, cryptographic currencies, but also the current applications that are in development and which can result into a number of decentralized financial services that are not subject to financial institutions.

Third party intermediaries, such as banks and payment providers and other non-bank entities all essentially rely on trust. They provide security, confidentiality, fraud protection, transaction infrastructure, payment disputes and reversals, access to financial products and services, international money transfers and the like. In order to be able to provide these services, they have to charge fees and interest from customers. In many cases, these customers must meet a set of criteria in order to have access to banking services. Moreover, they have to provide institutions with a significant amount of personal information, private information and confidential data about them and their financial characteristics. Thus customers have to enter a costly, trust-based relationship with institutions in order to engage into financial activities and benefit from financial services.

So what are the prospects of a technology that was invented and designed in order to provide most of these services at a low-cost, trust-less basis? Do financial intermediaries have reasons to ignore this technology and expect that cryptocurrencies will remain only present within niche markets for nerdy or technologically savvy people, or should they make use of the open-source code and incorporate some of its features into their systems? Or could cryptocurrencies themselves evolve into new type of financial market – "decentralized finance" or "cryptographic finance".

This thesis attempts to provide some answers to these questions and give an outlook for what can potentially be expected by cryptocurrencies.

In chapters two and three we will provide a detailed overview of Bitcoin's technology and the necessary infrastructure that it is based on. We discuss how cryptography is employed by the system as well as how it facilitates secure transactions. We explain the significance of the solution to the Byzantine Generals problem that the cryptocurrency represents and that of decentralized networks.

Chapter four goes into detail about current and persistent shortcomings that can be identified. We discuss issues concerning network delay, incentive schemes of the decentralized network, transaction confirmation delays, energy consumption and the like. Furthermore, we discuss whether these imperfections are likely to be permanent issues or can be mitigated by improving Bitcoin's current technology.

In chapter five we discuss a number of alternative cryptocurrencies that emerged after Bitcoin was developed and discuss some of their features that address certain weaknesses of Bitcoin that we discussed in chapter four. We list alternative options to Bitcoin's current technology and discuss how they could mitigate the shortcomings that are present within Bitcoin. Moreover, the question whether there is a Bitcoin 2.0 version foreseeable within the current alternative cryptocurrency market.

Chapter six details a special type of cryptocurrency that is already in use within a few banks. Ripple is a network, a distributed exchange and a cryptocurrency that is very akin to Bitcoin, but differs in some key aspects. It provides a different solution to the Byzantine Generals problem and is specifically targeted towards being used as a transaction system for banks and financial institutions.

Chapter seven gives an outlook on a proposal made by key people within the cryptography scene that is currently in development. Bitcoin side chains are alternative block chains that give Bitcoin additional features. These could incorporate features of alternative cryptocurrencies without altering the Bitcoin protocol itself. We discuss the influence that side chains could have on the cryptographic currency market.

## 2 Definition of Bitcoin

Bitcoin is a peer-to-peer version of electronic currency that allows direct payments between two parties without a financial intermediary. It is based on a decentralized network that facilitates and verifies transactions. It allows users to verify valid transactions and generate bitcoins by solving complex mathematical puzzles, which are based on a proof-of-work (PoW) concept.[1] It has become characteristic to refer to the network protocol as "Bitcoin" with a capital "B" and to the unit of currency as "bitcoin" in its lowercase form.

Bitcoin is both a special type of virtual currency and a peer-to-peer transaction system. It is based on a network of nodes that all share data and hardware resources in order to form a chain of transactions that are stored on the so-called block chain.

Goldman Sachs Global Investment Research (GS GIR) defined Bitcoin as "Bitcoin is a decentralized, peer-to-peer network that allows for the proof and transfer of ownership without the need for a trusted third party. The unit of the network is bitcoin (with a little "b"), or BTC, which many consider a currency or internet cash."[2]

The concept was initially proposed by an anonymous individual or group that operates under the alias 'Satoshi Nakamoto' and who published the concept in form of a white paper called "Bitcoin: A Peer-to-Peer Electronic Cash System" in October 2008. Nakamoto (2008) described Bitcoin as a purely peer-to-peer version of electronic cash which allows sending transactions from one person to another without relying on a third party payment transmitter. The first bitcoins were created on January 3rd 2009 by solving the so-called genesis block, which was accomplished by Satoshi Nakamoto.[3] The genesis block is the first block in the block chain – a non-alterable, majority consensus based public ledger that records and publishes the entire transaction history of Bitcoin.

What makes Bitcoin a significant innovation are two main reasons. First, it is the first successful attempt to establishing a cryptocurrency which has managed to gather a significant following behind it. Secondly, Bitcoin offers important technological innovations to the field of financial transactions that were previously inexistent. It solves the so-called Byzantine Generals problem in a way that enables the

---

1 c.p. Karame et al. (2012), p.1

2 GoldmanSachs (2014), p. 3

3 c.p. Barber et al. (2012), p.1

creation of a payment transaction system that does not rely on trust and therefore does not require a number of services that traditional financial intermediaries provide, as the software itself is designed to provide these functions. It is a decentralized, global means of payment that does not require financial intermediaries in order to conduct them.

Bitcoin transactions are significantly less expensive than currently existing payment transaction services. Wingfield (2013) compared Bitcoin transactions with credit card, PayPal or other transaction methods, which charge about 2-3% transaction fees. These forms of transactions rely on financial intermediaries and provide services to customers, such as security, facilitation, verification. Many of these services are, however, necessary to provide the current electronic payment infrastructure. Financial intermediaries are also present within the Bitcoin ecosystem. Examples such as Coinbase or Bitpay provide wallets services to securely store bitcoins or facilitate instant fiat conversion of received bitcoin transactions in order to hedge against price volatility. With these intermediaries present, transaction fees are still considerably lower than those of almost all current transaction services providers, which would broadly require 0.5-2.5% or fixed transaction fees to cover expenses and generate profit.[4]

Bitcoin must be seen as both a type of virtual currency and a decentralized transaction system. A clear differentiation from either use is not a simple task. GoldmanSachs (2014) argued that Bitcoin's future lies within the payment transaction infrastructure, but it will not be used as a currency or store of value. Central banks of several countries have already stated that Bitcoin cannot be defined as a currency but rather resembles a commodity.[5]

Contrary to what is often believed, bitcoins are not simply ordinary computer files that are stored on a hard drive and can thus be treated like any other data. Bitcoins exist in a shared, globally networked database, which is stored simultaneously on a great many of servers across the world. All of these network nodes maintain identical copies of the same database. Bitcoins therefore exist in many locations simultaneously and can by itself be moved between locations or exchanged between peers. Ownership of bitcoins is represented by possessing the knowledge about a

4 c.p. Henderson (2014), http://www.coindesk.com/bitcoin-solving-double-spending-problem/, 20.02.2014

5 c.p. Pohjanpalo (2014), http://www.bloomberg.com/news/2014-01-19/bitcoin-becomes-commodity-in-finlandafter-failing-currency-test.html, 19.03.2014

cryptographic key that allows access to bitcoin funds and enables transactions of bitcoins between Bitcoin addresses. Cryptographic keys are strings of alphanumeric characters that allow users to edit the shared database, e.g. when sending BTC from one address to another. Nakamoto (2008) described how Bitcoin relies on a peer-to-peer decentralized network that enables verifying transactions with a proof-of-work (PoW) method. PoW is used as a verifier to ensure that a enough computational effort has been performed in order to enable secure payments. [6] Traditional transaction processes require a trusted intermediary that verifies transactions and prevents funds from being counterfeited or subject to malicious attacks.

A simple peer-to-peer financial payment network would still be vulnerable to malicious attacks and theft. In fact, it would be very easy to do so within decentralized networks. The key innovation about Bitcoin that it provides security to the network and also provides similar benefits that financial intermediaries offer to financial networks. Transactions are verified based on a proof-ofwork (PoW) concept that distributes financial funds and prevents manipulation of the financial network. PoW imposes costs and resource requirements that prevent malicious attacks due to making them very resource-intensive and therefore unprofitable.

Bitcoins are not centrally issued but are created by a process referred to as "mining", which is the process of solving complex mathematical computations (solving blocks) in order to receive bitcoins (block rewards) and at the same time verifying valid transactions. Bitcoin is based on a SHA-256 algorithm and designed to create new blocks every 10 minutes for which miners are competing against each other in order to solve a block and broadcast it to the remaining network first.

Citing the director of the Financial Crimes Enforcement Network Jennifer Calvery in a hearing in front of the United States Senate, as well as Gup (2014), Rogojanu & Badea (2014) and Barber et al. (2012) – among others – list the following advantages that Bitcoin offers:

---

6 c.p. Tromp (2014), p.1-2

Table 1: Bitcoin Specific Benefits

| Benefit | Description |
|---|---|
| Users remain largely anonymous | Bitcoin transactions are publicly broadcasted, traceable and accessible but do not contain information about the parties involved with conducting the transaction. |
| Global accessibility | The Bitcoin network and services are basically accessible from any location with Internet connection. Global transactions can be conducted without international barriers. |
| Ease of Use | Transactions require simple inputs, are user-friendly and can be automated or scripted. |
| Low fees | Transactions are fee-less or have optional, insignificant fees, which are attributed to the transaction verifiers. |
| Few transaction limits | Digital currency does not require financial intermediaries, are non-impedimental and can be used simply by using software. |
| Irreversible transactions | Completed transactions are not reversible. This eliminates chargeback options and complicates payment fraud. |
| Decentralized, no central administrator to maintain records | Bitcoin nodes and databases are completely decentralized and therefore do not require customers to enter trust-based relationships with intermediaries. |
| Versatility, openness, and vibrancy | Open source technology that allows development of new applications, services and additions without impediments. |
| Predictable money supply | Total supply of bitcoins is capped at a maximum number of about 21 million BTC, money supply is algorithmically predefined and inalterable. |
| Divisibility and fungibility | Bitcoin transaction amounts can be divided into a minimum amount of 0.00000001 BTC, and bitcoins are potentially infinitely divisible. |
| Scripting | Bitcoin allows embedded scripts or additional protocol layers that add additional features to transactions. (deposits, escrow, dispute mediation, assurance contracts, etc.) |

Bitcoin and many other virtual currencies are, however, also subject to features that are less desirable and could cause them to fall under intense scrutiny by regulators, politics and law enforcement. Virtual currencies can also be misused to facilitate tax avoidance, money laundering, illegal goods purchases, fraud, and terrorism finance.[7] As such, it is logical to assume that Bitcoin and other virtual currencies will face regulatory uncertainty and political risk, and specific cryptocurrency-specific regulation will be in place at some time in the future.

Gup (2014) also noted that Bitcoin could be used as a secure store of value. This, however, is currently very questionable, as virtual currencies are still unregulated, highly speculative assets that are subject to limited liquidity, intense volatility and considerable operational risk (theft, business failure, hacking, etc.). Levin (2014) found an average daily price volatility of around 5%, which he compares to one of the most volatile currency pairs – ZAR:JPY (South African Rand : Japanese Yen) – which has a daily volatility close to 1%. In Bitcoin's relatively short history there have been a number of intense price fluctuations.[8] Figure 1 provides an overview of the historical bitcoin price in USD, beginning at the time bitcoins were actively traded against the US Dollar on dedicated bitcoin exchanges.

Figure 1: Historical Bitcoin Price in USD

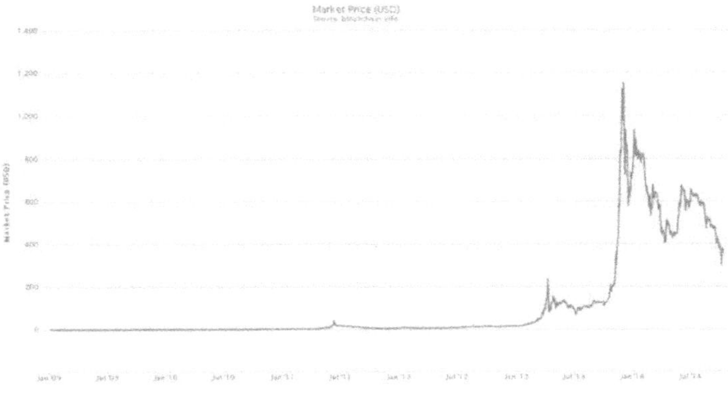


Source: Blockchain (2014), blockchain.info, 12.10.2014

Nobel Prize laureate Milton Friedman is said to have predicted the development of 'internet money' in 1998, by stating: "So that I think that the Internet is going to be one of the major forces for reducing the role of government. The one thing that's missing, but that will soon be developed, is a reliable e-cash, a method whereby on

---

7 c.p. Bryans (2014), p.442-443

8 c.p. GoldmanSachs (2014), p.610

the Internet you can transfer funds from A to B, without A knowing B or B knowing A."[9] Friedman, however, went on to also note the negative implications of such an invention, noting that illegal activities, such as illegal transactions and tax evasion will also be easier to conduct.[10]

Bergstra & de Leeuw (2013) proposed to classify Bitcoin as a hybrid form of money that falls under the definition of technically informational money (TIM). Money can be distinguished into informational and non-informational depending on e.g. its capacities to store, access and exchange informational value. They acknowledged that Bitcoin could also be a hybrid class of informational money that exhibits aspects of both technically informational money (TIM) and exclusively informational money (EXIM).

When attempting to analyze Bitcoin, it is fundamentally important to understand that the underlying technology. Digital currencies have been proposed and developed long before the invention of Bitcoin. Tanaka (1996) described the different aspects of digital cash just two years after the first online shops were opened and internet banking was still in its infancy.

Tanaka (1996) argued that the key benefits of digital cash would be

1. Cost Reduction: transferring funds through the internet is significantly less expensive when compared to the traditional banking system, as online payments do not, or only to a very limited extend, require physical presences, human resources and electronic transaction systems. Moreover, digital cash payments can be done through already existing internet infrastructure, such as personal computers and already active online presences.
2. Cross-country money transfers: In the absence of national borders in the Internet, money can be transferred across countries without international money transfer infrastructure. Digital cash eliminates transfer fees as well as currency exchange fees. Moreover, in certain aspects of cross-country money transfers, digital cash would eliminate currency exchange risks.
3. Accessibility: Digital cash systems could be accessed and used by anyone who is connected to the internet, whereas conventional banking and non-bank financial service providers limit accessibility of their services. Limits

9 Gustafsson (2013)

10 c.p. Gustafsson (2013)

as to who can use credit card payments or from which region in the world the payment can originate are not present with digital currency payments.

Due to these reasons digital cash certainly offers the potential for more efficient and broader financial services that are not present within the walled-garden architecture of the global financial market.

Tanaka (1996), however, also points out obvious drawbacks for digital cash. Internet currencies, due to its anonymity and the potential for untraceable money transfers could facilitate tax evasion and money laundering. Moreover, due to the absence of a central bank or institution backing the value of digital cash the exchange rate of digital currencies would be inherently unstable and there is a potential for financial crises as operations on the internet are subject to the thread of power outages, theft and malicious software.

The European Central Bank (ECB) provided a clear distinction between electronic money systems and virtual currency systems. They emphasize that virtual currency schemes do fulfill some of the criteria but remain a distinct category. Electronic money schemes have a link to traditional money and as such are connected to regulated currencies with a legal foundation. The unit of account are fiat currencies, and as such fall within the frameworks of electronic mine institutions and prudential supervisory requirements. As of yet, virtual currencies are privately generated and can be distinguished by whether they can be exchanged for virtual as well as real goods and services.

Figure 2: Differences between Electronic Money and Virtual Currency

| | Electronic money schemes | Virtual currency schemes |
|---|---|---|
| Money format | Digital | Digital |
| Unit of account | Traditional currency (euro, US dollars, pounds, etc.) with legal tender status | Invented currency (Linden Dollars, Bitcoins, etc.) without legal tender status |
| Acceptance | By undertakings other than the issuer | Usually within a specific virtual community |
| Legal status | Regulated | Unregulated |
| Issuer | Legally established electronic money institution | Non-financial private company |
| Supply of money | Fixed | Not fixed (depends on issuer's decisions) |
| Possibility of redeeming funds | Guaranteed (and at par value) | Not guaranteed |
| Supervision | Yes | No |
| Type(s) of risk | Mainly operational | Legal, credit, liquidity and operational |

Source: ECB.

Source: European Central Bank (2012), p. 16

They fundamental difference between both categories is that electronic money schemes refer to units of account that are regulated and issued by sovereign entities, such as the ECB or the Federal Reserve System (Fed). They are digital equivalents of Euro, Dollars, or Yuan. As such, they are legal tender within their jurisdictions that have to be redeemed at par value. Contrary to that, virtual currencies are private inventions that are unregulated and do not qualify as legal tender.

Early research in the field of digital cash payment systems repeatedly pointed out the potential for money laundering and tax evasion. This was due to the assumption that digital currencies would be untraceable and anonym. Despite being citizen for similar reasons, Bitcoin is in fact neither untraceable nor is its use as a payment system truly anonymous. The peer-to-peer based proof-ofwork concept of Bitcoin allows it to trace and publicly show every single payment that has been conducted in the network over the entire history of Bitcoin. All valid transactions are broadcasted publicly across the entire networked Bitcoin system and the data about these transactions will be stored and preserved inalterable within the public block chain ledger.

The monetary supply is defined by the protocol which imposes a fixed cap of about 21 million bitcoins. The precise reason why 21.000.000 was chosen to be the maximum amount of Bitcoin in existence is subject to discussion.[11]

The term "Bitcoin" is somewhat misleading for most individuals. Bergstra & de Leeuw (2013) argued that "Bitcash" would be a more adequate term. The term "coin" is commonly associated with a non-divisible unit of value consisting of valuable metals. Contrary to that, Bitcoin is designed to be highly divisible, with its base units commonly referred to as "satoshi" (0.00000001 BTC, or $10^{-8}$), in reference to the alias of Bitcoin's inventor. Over time many major Bitcoin proponents began popularizing the term "bits" instead of "satoshis" for its base value in order to facilitate ease of use.[12]

11 c.p. Bitcoin Wiki. Controlled supply, 10.10.2014

12 Coinbase (2014), http://blog.coinbase.com/post/89405189782/its-bits, 21.07.2014

Table 2: Bitcoin Units

| Unit | Subunit |
|---|---|
| 1 BTC | 100,000,000 satoshis |
| 1 BTC | 1000 mBTC (millibitcoin) |
| 1 mBTC | 100,000 satoshis |
| 1 μBTC | 100 satoshis / 100 bits |

Source: Bitcoin Wiki. Units, 09.07.2014

Thus the total amount of Bitcoin base units is 2,100,000,000,000,000 (21 quadrillion) bits.

In this thesis, we focus on Bitcoin primarily as a transaction system and discuss the details of its underlying technology that enables high-speed, low-cost, secure payments across the globe. Aspects concerning the question whether Bitcoin can be defined as a currency or an alternative monetary system are not within the focus of this thesis, and as such are discussed only incidental, wherever such discussion is deemed necessary.

## 2.1 Technical Description of Bitcoin Transaction

While a Bitcoin transaction is very simple to conduct and the process of transacting bitcoins is rather straightforward, the technological process underlying to it is complex and full understanding requires some relevant knowledge in the field of cryptography. More details about public keys, private keys, processing, mining and the block chain is provided in subsequent chapters of this thesis.

In order to transfer bitcoins from sender $P^0$to receiver $P^1$, the sender must know the public key of the receiver. Transactions are sent to and received from Bitcoin addresses. Addresses are derived from public keys and vary in length but tend to be around 31 characters long. An address is a hash containing 160 bits and a checksum that provides error-detection. Transacting the cryptographic currency requires a hash value, which is the value that the SHA-256 algorithm produces in order to map larger data sets to smaller, fixed-length data sets. Notably, this process requires that that the code of the bitcoins includes and stores information about which public addresses where involved in the transaction. $P^0$ digitally signs the hash with his secret private key in order to transmit the transaction. Thereby he broadcasts the transaction to the decentralized peer-to-peer

Bitcoin network, where all other nodes receive and rebroadcast the transaction.[13]

Figure 3: Bitcoin Transaction

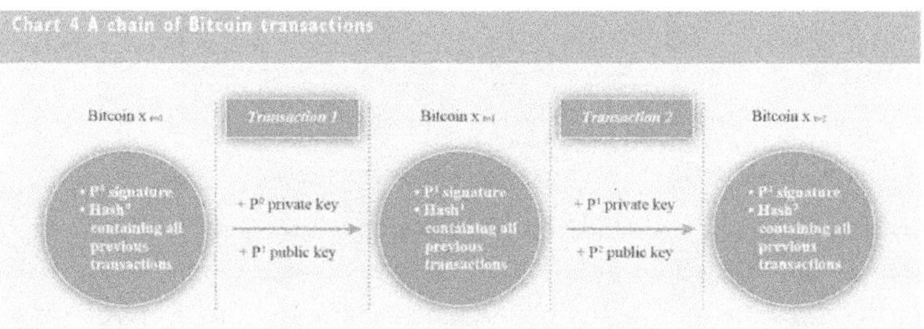


Source: European Central Bank (2012), p. 23

After a valid transaction is sent to the Bitcoin network it is included into the currently calculated block within the block chain. The block chain is a decentralized, consensus-driven public ledger that includes every valid transaction and archives them. [14] It timestamps and records valid transactions and shares this data with all nodes within the network. Stored information includes public addresses of sender and receiver, transaction key, transaction size, fees, timestamp and network propagation (number and location of nodes that received the broadcast about the transaction). It does not include identities of the payee and receiver, the IP addresses of their devices, or purpose of the transaction.

A transaction remains unverified until a valid block is found, verified by the network and linked to the longest chain of blocks within the Bitcoin block chain. If the transaction is included in the data set of the most recent block, and not fraudulent activity was detected, it will be verified by the network and confirmed. As new blocks are generated every 10 minutes, the first confirmation of the transaction should be obtained within these 10 minutes or less, depending on the progression of the current block period. For each subsequent block that is added to the block chain another confirmation is obtained. The number of confirmations can be seen as a measure of confidence that the transaction is valid.

---

13 c.p. European Central Bank (2012), p. 23

14 c.p. Harrigan (2014), http://www.coindesk.com/network-analysts-view-block-chain/, 20.05.2014

Figure 4: Schematic Bitcoin Block Chain

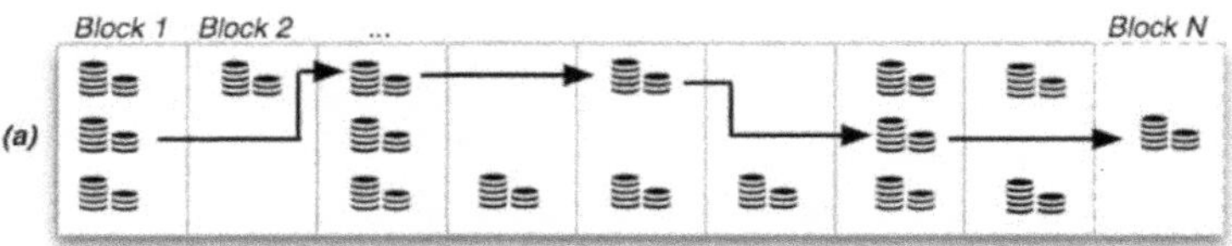


Source: Green (2013) blog.cryptographyengineering.com, 05.05.2014

Confirmations act as a verification that bitcoins have actually been successfully transferred and e.g. no double-speding of bitcoins has occurred. This represents one of the key functions of the public block chain and the proof-of-work mining process.

Meiklejohn et al. (2013) explained that in each transaction the previous owner signs with his private key a hash of the received transaction and the public key of the new owner, thus forming a chain. This chain is used to verify the validity of a Bitcoin transaction and also allows to track the history of the received bitcoins.

Nakamoto (2008) argued that in order to achieve a decentralized payment network that does not require a trusted intermediary, transactions must be publicly announced and all participants in the network must agree on a single history of transactions. Without consensus of the network, it could be possible to send the same bitcoins from one address to more than one receiver, thus doublespending them. As only one of those can be validated by the block chain, the other one would be classified as double-spent and rejected by the network.

Transactions of bitcoins are not reversible. As all transactions with bitcoins require to be signed with a cryptographic private key, there is no technical method built-in the protocol to reverse transaction from the sender's perspective once they are completed and added to the public block chain ledger.

Bitcoin transactions are verified and broadcasted by Bitcoin miners, who provide the necessary network that enables transactions between peers. In order for miners to identify valid transactions and propagate them, transactions are included into a 'block'.

## 2.2 Blocks

A block is a set of data that contains all transaction data that was created since validation of the previous block.[15] Blocks contain meta data, the block header and a reference to the previous block. Blocks are created by finding the correct nonce that results into a hash that meets certain criteria (see chapter 3.8). A valid block is then broadcasted to the network and verified by the network peers. Once a valid block is found by a process called 'mining' and validated by the network, it is added to the block chain that records all transactions, stores the date and prevents anyone from manipulating it in retrospect through hash-based proof-of-work technology. The first transaction of each block is designed to be a block reward. Miners who successfully validated a block first, propagated it to the network and added successfully it to the block chain receive a predefined number of newly created BTC for each block as well as transaction fees added to the transactions within the block.

Figure 5: Illustrative Bitcoin Block

**Hash:** 000000000043a8c0fd1d6f726790caa2a406010d19efd2780db27bdbbd93baf6
**Previous block:** 00000000001937917bd2caba204bb1aa530ec1de9d0f6736e5d85d96da9c8bba
**Next block:** 00000000000036312a44ab7711afa46f475913fbd9727cf508ed4af3bc933d16
**Time:** 2010-09-16 05:03:47
**Difficulty:** 712.884864
**Transactions:** 2
**Total BTC:** 100
**Size:** 373 bytes
**Merkle root:** 8fb300e3fdb6f30a4c67233b997f99fdd518b968b9a3fd65857bfe78b2600719
**Nonce:** 1462756097

| Input/Previous Output | Source & Amount | Recipient & Amount |
|---|---|---|
| N/A | Generation: 50 + 0 total fees | Generation: 50 + 0 total fees |
| f5d8ee39a430...:0 | 1JBSCVF6VM6QjFZyTnbpLjoCJ...: 50 | 16ro3Jptwo4asSevZnsRX6vf...: 50 |

Source: Karame et al. (2012), p. 3

Figure 5 illustrates an exemplified Bitcoin block that contains data about which nonce was correct to result into a hash of data that met certain criteria in order to classify it as valid. One of the key criteria for a valid block is that the resulting hash begins with a certain number of zeros. Rosenfeld (2014) noted that blocks are groups of transactions that are about acknowledging a single history of transactions that when linked together in a form of a chain and requiring proof-of-work would result into prohibiting difficulty against conflicting transactions. Each block references an earlier block by including a uniquely identifying hash of the previous

15 c.p. Decker & Wattenhofer (2013), p. 10

block in its header. Furthermore, a block contains a number of relevant and transparently displayed data about e.g. the number of transactions, transaction volume, block reward, data size, and a timestamp.

Table 3: Block Term Description

| Term | Description |
|---|---|
| Hash | A hash algorithm transforms an arbitrarily large amount of data and produces a fixed-length output data hash. |
| Previous Block | The hash of the previous block that is already validated and which will be linked to the current block within the block chain. |
| Time | Timestamp to proof that the data existed at a certain point in time. Approximate time when the block was created. |
| Difficulty | Moving average level of complexity to solve a block for the miner network that is periodically adjusted according to network hash power. |
| Transactions | Number of transactions contained within the block. |
| Total BTC | Amount of bitcoins that were transacted within the block. |
| Size | The resulting data size of the block. |
| Merkle root | The hash that is obtained by hashing all transaction hashes in the block. Instead of storing the Merkle tree (hashes of all transactions) in the block header only the Merkle root is stored. It verifies the integrity of all transactions in the block. |
| Nonce | A random 32-bit number that is used as input data to alter the outcome of a hash. Finding the correct nonce will result into that hash that validates the block. |

Source: Karame et al. (2012), p.3

A SHA-256 hash algorithm is employed in order to turn arbitrary data into fixed-length hashes that are written in hexadecimal form. Bitcoin's SHA-256 algorithm thereby produces hashes that if the input data is altered even slightly, the hash obtained would differ completely. [16]

Example: [17]

16 c.p. Bitcoin Wiki. Hash, 03.04.2014

17 c.p. N.N. http://www.xorbin.com/tools/sha256-hash-calculator (01.06.2014)

Table 4: Input – Output Differences of SHA-256 Hashes

| Input | SHA-256 Hash |
|---|---|
| 1.000.000,01 | 71800e2e937e7dd04774e5c9a9edfc371a3f3e781c4d70252eb4b100e8eee54a |
| 1.000.000,02 | 5ff06cdba807e519ed96330b88691ceb7b6022c1039d36ba7e954ad9da966572 |

Source: Xorbin (2014). www.xorbin.com, 01.06.2014

As can be observed, even a minimal alteration of the input data results into a completely different hash value. This can be used to check for integrity of the input data, as each alteration will be recognized. Within the block each transaction is hashed pair wise until only a root hash remains, which is included in the block header as the Merkle root. As such, if any portion of any transaction is altered or manipulated the resulting root hash would differ significantly and indicate loss of data integrity.

Figure 6: Merke Tree Root Hash

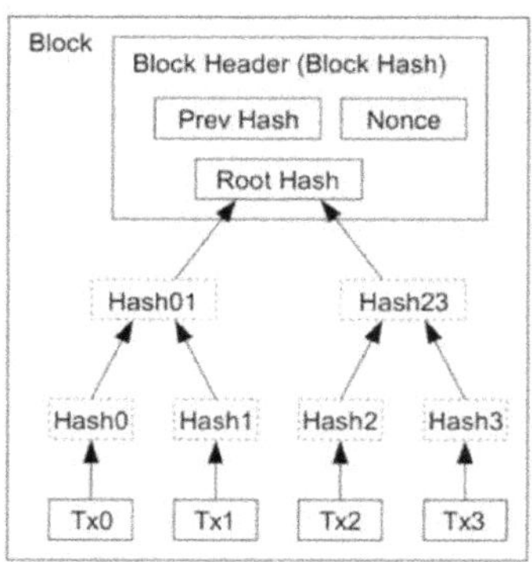


Source: Nakamoto (2008), p. 4

A Merkle tree is a type of binary tree in which a set of nodes are connected to each other on a multi-level basis. Transactions are hashed from leaf nodes to a single root node, which is formed by the underlying nodes. By doing so, an attempt to include a fraudulent transaction will influence the tree structure in an upward fashion, resulting in a different root node. This root node represents the hash of the block whose header is downloaded by other nodes, whilst the underlying tree is not. The Merkle tree guarantees that if a fraudulent transaction is included in the block, the resulting block hash is identified as an invalid proof-of-work.[18]

It is possible for two nodes to create a block at the same time that both satisfy the conditions to be added to the longest chain in the block chain. These blocks may be consistent but mutually conflicting. Each one would be a possible addition to the same sub-chain. This implies that at certain points of time, a number correct blocks could propagate the network that are mutually conflicting. The network assures that only one block is eventually validated and added to the longest chain of blocks.[19]

## 2.3 The Byzantine Generals Problem

One of the key characteristics of Bitcoin is that it provides a solution to the Byzantine Generals problem. This problem is an abstractly expressed form of an agreement problem in the context of geographical remoteness, communication by messengers and presence of traitors within the ranks of the Byzantine Empire's army.[20] A reliable system must cope with conflicting information of its parts in order to avoid malfunction. The question at hand is how to establish trust between unrelated parties within an untrusted network.

---

18 c.p. Buterin (2014a), http://bitcoinmagazine.com/14282/mining-2/, 07.07.2014

19 c.p. Sompolinsky & Zohar (2013), p.3

20 c.p. Pease et al. (1980)

Figure 7: Byzantine Generals Problem

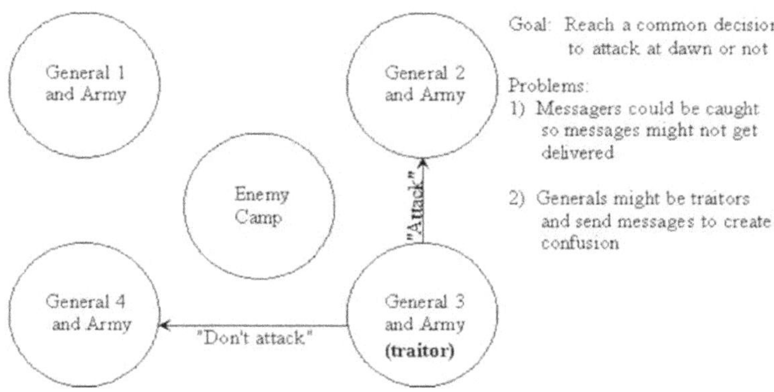


Source: Fieneup (2001), www.cs.uni.edu, 07. 04.2014

The Byzantine Generals problem is exemplified by a thought experiment, in which the fortified city-state Byzantinum is surrounded by ten smaller city-states.[21] Hypothetically, all surrounding city-states plan to invade Byzantinum in order to obtain its wealth but none of them is strong enough to do so on its own. Moreover, any uncoordinated attack would fail and result into the annihilation of the attacking city-state. In order to successfully invade Byzantinum the majority of city-states must invade simultaneously. The major problem that the attacking city-states face is that if one or more of the attackers betray the other city-states, they and the remaining non-attacking neighbors will be able to pillage the annihilated city-states. The problems faced by the city-states are based on trust and communication. Each individual city has an incentive to betray the next and all generals must decide unanimously whether to attack at certain times.

Moreover, their means of communication are limited, as none of the generals can leave the city to meet with other generals as they cannot trust that the other generals will not harm them. As such, their only way to communicate is sending messengers. They are not limited as to how many messengers they send or at which time they send messengers. When messengers of general 1 reach the other nine generals they hand them a sealed letter. The letter informs the other generals about the time general 1 plans to attack and requests to know which of the other generals will join him. As a response, each of the nine generals attaches his response to the

21 c.p. Lamport et al. (1982)

original letter and hands the sealed response letter to the messenger. At the same time, the other generals each also send nine individual copies of both the sealed letter and the attached response letter to the other generals.

Each city-state sends messengers and all letters combined equal 90 messages sent to the city-states, where each general receives nine messages with different indications about the time of attack. As such, the generals agree to more than one possible attack time, thereby betraying those generals who attack during other times. Those that betray others will send messengers across the city states indicating different times for the attack. The system is now subject to many different possible attack times and messengers' letters are untrustworthy.

Lamport et al. (1982) described the Byzantine Generals problem within the context of computer systems when a failed component is sending conflicting information to other parts of the system. Their version of the Byzantine Generals problem is conceptualized by the example of several Byzantine army division that are camping outside an enemy city. Generals of those army divisions can only communicate by messenger. Again, only a combined attack can be successful against the enemy city but generals cannot meet to discuss a common attack plan and some of the generals are not loyal and might betray the others. The problem is that communication is not instantaneous and if generals communicate different attack times, other generals may receive conflicting messages. Lamport et al. (1982) proposed a solution to the problem by designing algorithms that largely solves the problem, but only if certain assumptions are met and two-thirds of the generals are trustworthy. When messages are not corruptible or forgeable, there is a solution for any number of trustworthy generals.

Bitcoin solves this problem by using a proof-of-work chain that imposes a 10 minute time horizon in which all generals would be required to work on a difficult mathematical problem and only if one general finds a solution to the problem the information is broadcasted to the other generals, who in turn must use this information. They then go on to extend that solution by solving another, directly related puzzle and broadcasting it once a general finds a solution thereby forming a chain of solutions. After enough repetitions all generals can be certain that no other general could have been able to secretly create another chain of solutions that would be longer than the chain the he knows of. As a result, all generals have now ascertained that there is consensus about the longest chain of solutions without having to trust any of the other generals.[22]

## 2.4 Double Spending Solution

The concept of Bitcoin transactions includes that senders of bitcoins are not able to simultaneously broadcast conflicting messages to the block chain or reversing the transaction. The receiver of bitcoins must able to verify that he is in fact the possessor of the coins received by the recently completed Bitcoin transaction so that the sender may not redirect the coins to a third party. Double-spending is a common issue among digital transaction methods, as electronic files can be duplicated without effort, and ownership of data is not easily verifiable. Dion (2013) noted that double-spending can be seen as an equivalent to counterfeiting money within the Bitcoin universe. A double spending attack is successful when a malicious peer convinces another peer that he has transferred ownership of bitcoins to the peer, but simultaneously conducts a mutually conflicting transaction, leaving the malicious peer with both the bitcoins and the exchanged goods or services.[23] There is a number of different ways how a double-spending attack can be conducted with Bitcoin.[24] Nakamoto (2008) stated that the most common method to solve this issue is a central authority or intermediary that prevents double-spending and proposed Bitcoin as a peerto-peer based alternative solution to the double-spending problem.

A double spending attack includes several steps, as explained by Rosenfeld (2014):

- Step 1: Broadcast a transaction between payer and receiver to the network.
- Step 2: Before the transaction is included in a block, the payer mines an undisclosed branch of the current block and includes a conflicting transaction that acknowledges the payer as the recipient.
- Step 3: Wait until the receiver has obtained enough confirmations in order to be convinced that the transaction is valid.

22 c.p. Mayyasi (2013), http://blog.priceonomics.com/post/47135650437/are-bitcoins-the-future, 28.04.2014

23 c.p. Rosenfeld (2014), p.2

24 c.p. Bitcoin Wiki. Double-spending, 26.04.2014

- Step 4: Continue mining the undisclosed branch until the contradicting transaction of the undisclosed branch exceeds the public branch which includes the transaction.
- Step 5: Broadcast the undisclosed branch to the network, which will accept the longer branch as valid and discards the former public branch which included the transaction. The conflicting transaction will be validated by the network and replace the original transaction. The confirmed transaction that the receiver was convinced of will vanish.

A system that would rely on an intermediary to provide the costly and time-intensive process of preventing double-spending would also represent a single point of failure (SPOF). Nakamoto's solution is to make transactions public and create a decentralized network that finds consensus and agrees on a single history of transactions, which would also make double-spending extremely difficult and therefore very unlikely.

Figure 8: Double Spending Schematic

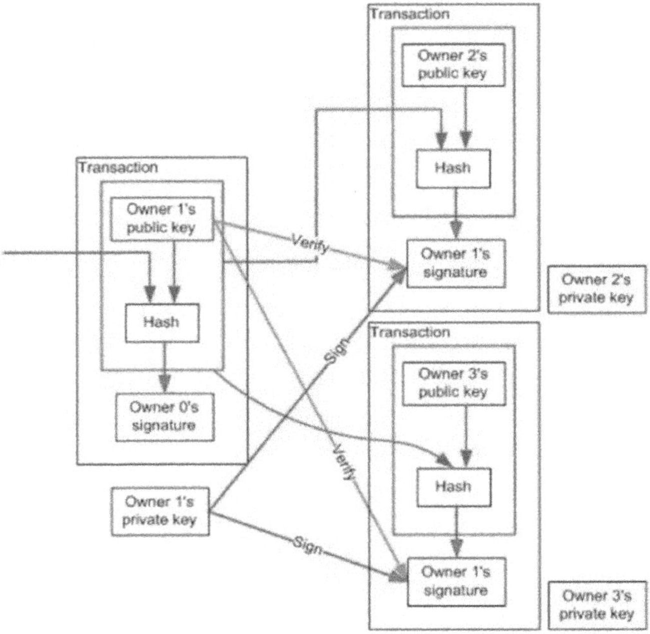

Source: Skudnov (2012), p.7

Skudnov (2012) argued that propagation delays and connectivity issues make it impossible to inform all nodes about the same transaction at the same time and therefore double spending could still occur. The solution to this problem is that a majority of peers have to agree on a common transaction history. The network does so by providing confirmations after solving a block. Karame et al. (2012) emphasized that Bitcoin is increasingly used in payment scenarios that make in impracticable or impossible to allow waiting for a secure number of confirmations by the network. For transactions to be validated by the network, users have to wait up to ten minutes for the first confirmation. Furthermore, Karame et al. (2012) underlined that double-spending would require significant effort and hashing power. For an undetected double-spend the malicious peers would not only have to redo all the work required to create the block where the illicit transaction occurred, but also recomputed all the subsequent blocks in the block chain. In theory, such effort would be computationally infeasible as long as the honest nodes are stronger than colluding, dishonest peers. Nakamoto (2008) acknowledged that there is a certain time frame given, where an attacker could create a fork in the block chain and maintain it for a certain amount of time, in which the attacker could attempt double-spending. Attackers would have to be at least one block ahead of the honest nodes, which can however only be done for a very limited time, as the attacker's chance to maintain a fork diminishes exponentially as long as the network majority is comprised of honest nodes.

## 2.5 Decentralization

Bitcoin is designed to function as a decentralized network underlying a virtual currency. As such it does not require a financial intermediary to conduct transactions or provide payment infrastructure. They can join and leave the network at will and provide their service at any point in time without compulsion to do so. Moreover, bitcoins are not centrally issued but are created by the network at a pre-specified rate. Sterner (2013) explained that with respect to centralized systems, decentralized systems are more flexible, more able to adapt do local conditions, more resilient and less vulnerable. Moreover, decentralized systems are significantly less expensive, as centralization results into the necessity to also concentrate expert organizational structures and capital within central hubs or institutions. Baran (1962) assessed centralized, decentralized and distributed communications systems with respect to their vulnerability against foreign attacks. His results also indicated that less centralized systems are preferable due to their resilient properties and architecture.

Figure 9: Centralization vs. Decentralization vs. Distributed Networks

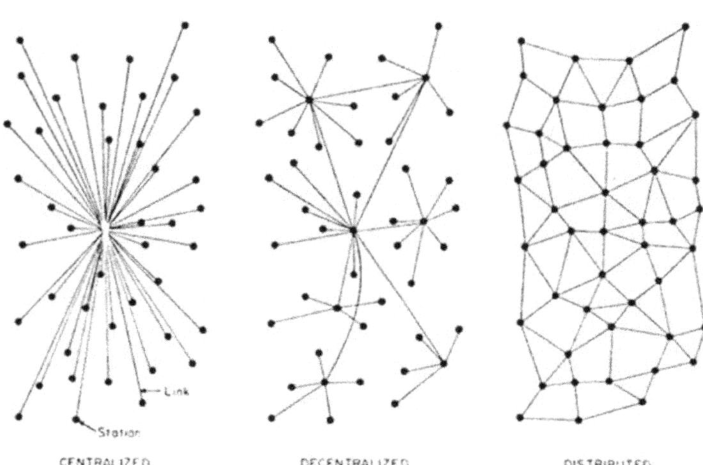


Source: Sterner (2013). www.carlsterner.com, 12.05.2014

Bitcoin is designed to be a decentralized system by necessity in order to perform its functions. It consists of connected nodes that form a single consensus system known as the block chain. Barber et al. (2012) argued that Bitcoin's decentralized nodes can be divided broadly into two classes – verifiers and clients. Verifiers are Bitcoin miners that use specialized computer hardware in order to solve cryptographic problems and identify valid blocks, which are linked to the block chain every 10 minutes. By doing so, they earn newly mined bitcoins and transaction fees. Miners timestamp valid transactions and add them and the data contained in them to the public ledger. Clients are participants in the network that are not contributing hardware to the mining process, such as PCs or smartphones of users. Decker & Wattenhofer (2013) explained how one decentralized node sends a block with transactions it included into the block to the network, in which all other nodes will receive the block and agree on it if certain criteria are met. Essentially, one node proposes its solution and other nodes accept it if it is valid, thus forming a single truth that the network agrees upon.

Cawrey (2014c) pointed out the lack of incentives for client nodes to participate in the network and maintain it, as they do not receive any rewards for the provision of their resources. Moreover, decreasing numbers of fully complete nodes and geographical concentration threatens the security of the network. As Nakamoto (2008) showed, the Bitcoin system is only secure as long as honest nodes collectively control more computational power than dishonest notes. Overpowering the honest nodes could allow dishonest nodes to fabricate transactions and create a centrally controlled block chain fork owned by the majority that imposes its view on the network. Barber et al. (2012) noted that as Bitcoin nodes cryptographically verify the authentic of all blocks and transactions, its network bandwidth and computational overhead will become an issue at some point in the future. Decentralization is therefore the key requirement for the network in order to maintain security of the system and prevent powerful colluding nodes to overpower the rest of the nodes.

Within the context of Bitcoin decentralization also refers to the fact that no necessity for a financial intermediary or other third parties. Nakamoto (2008) proposed Bitcoin as a system for virtual, global transactions that do not require trusted third parties in order to process these payments. Likewise, if seen as from a monetary system point of view, Bitcoin has no central issuer and does not require a central bank in order to function. Citing from various sources, Lerner (2013) also made the case that centralized systems also centralize costs and benefits, as well as concentrating capital. He intriguingly relates centralized systems to a "too big to fail" scenario, in which costs accrue downstream and benefits accrue upstream, thereby centralizing power within the centralized system. A recent software glitch that interrupted the clearinghouse automated payment system of the Bank of England serves as an example for the shortcomings of centralized systems. The bank's Real Time Gross Settlement Payment System (RTGS), which processes 140,000 transactions a day, worth on average £277bn, had shut down from 6am to 3.30pm.[25]

Decentralization also implies that the Bitcoin network can perform financial services without a central institution providing them. These applications can be built on top of the Bitcoin protocol on an open-source basis. Sompolinsky & Zohar (2013) argued that the core idea of the Bitcoin protocol is to enable money transmissions in a non-centralized fashion. This implies that no central institution, such

[25] c.p. Treanor et al. (2014), http://www.theguardian.com/business/2014/oct/20/bank-of-england-paymentsystem-crashes, 20.10.2014

as a central bank, is responsible for the money supply. There are no banks, credit card companies, non-bank entities or other financial institutions necessary in order to form the Bitcoin network. Accordingly, there is no intervention into the system by any entity that the network comprises of. Funds cannot be frozen, misconducted, seized or transactions reversed. The network is voluntary and as such does not impose any barriers to entry other than the costs of obtaining the necessary hardware and software that is physically required for participating in the network. Bitcoin thus represents a decentralized financial network.

# 3 Technology of Bitcoin

Bitcoin is often referred to as a 'cryptocurrency' because cryptography is core to its technology. Cryptography in general refers to the practice and study of techniques that create secure transfers of information in the presence of adversaries.[26] Mathematical cryptology refers to the encryption of messages in order to hide the information contained within the message from third parties. The sender of a message encrypts the message by using an encryption key, while the receiver must be able to decrypt the message with his decryption key. Encryption can be conducted through a continuous stream of symbols (stream encryption) or by dividing in into a number of blocks (block encryption). In what follows, we describe how cryptography can be utilized to form a secure means of transacting value between peers.

## 3.1 Method of Operating

Nakamoto (2008) defined Bitcoin as a chain of digital signatures. Bitcoins are transferred by signing a hash of the previous transaction and the public key of the following owner. Both will then be added to the end of the Bitcoin and the receiver verifies the signature in order to confirm ownership.

Figure 10: Simple Bitcoin Transactions

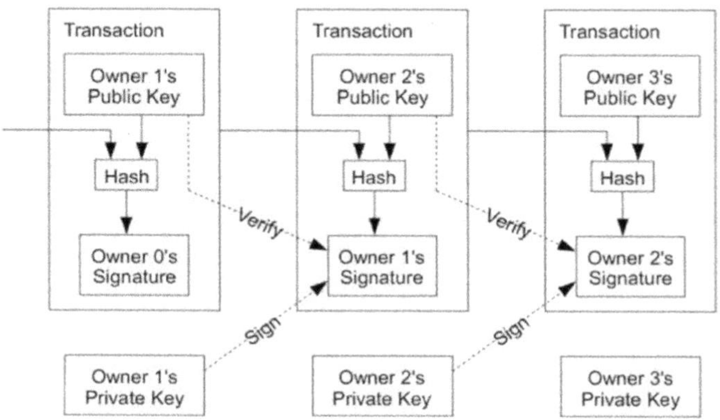


Source: Nakamoto (2008), p. 2

26 c.p. Bellare & Rogaway (2005), p.7-15

Transferring ownership of bitcoins from user A to user B is realized by attaching a digital signature (using user A's private key) of the hash of the previous transaction and information about the public key of user B at the end of a new transaction. The signature can be verified with the help of user A's public key from the previous transaction.[27] As a result, a chain of ownership is created. This basic building block of Bitcoin transactions is, however not protected against counterfeiting BTC by means of double-spending the same Bitcoin.

Therefore Nakamoto (2008) explained how a timestamp server uses the hash of a block in order to 'proof' that the data has existed at this time. In order to create a single history of the order in which transactions happened, a timestamp server is necessary. Each individual timestamp includes the previous timestamp in its hash and thereby links them together.

Figure 11: Timestamp Server

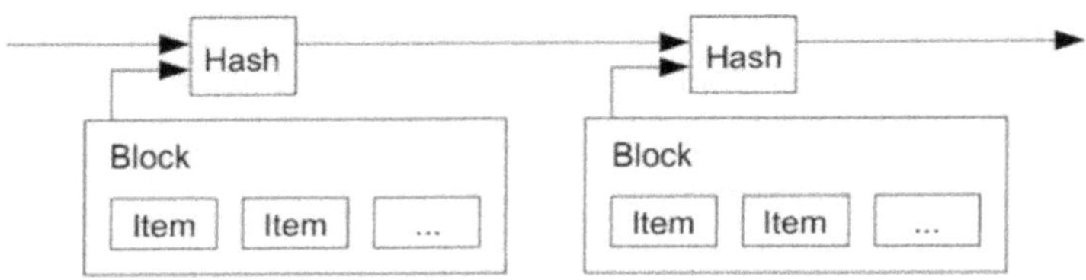


Source: Nakamoto (2008), p. 2

This implies that each consecutive timestamp reinforces the timestamps that were created before them.

Bitcoin bases much of its underlying technology on Hashcash – a proof-of-work based system designed to prevent Denial-of-Service (DoS) attacks and certain techniques relating to Email spam.[28] Proof-of-Work (PoW) is also employed in Bitcoin, in order to create a system that requires resources in order to mine bitcoins. PoW is used as a verifier to ensure that a required amount of computational effort in form of calculating hashes has been performed in order to create a block.[29] Without such a system in place, secure transactions could not be conducted as the system

27 c.p. Bos et al. (2013), p.5

28 c.p. Back (2002), p.3

29 c.p. Tromp (2014), p.1-2

would be vulnerable to a variety of attacks, e.g. pretending to represent a huge number of nodes in order to overpower the network. Moreover, requiring resources ensures that no one in the network can alter the already existing blocks without significant resource requirements that make such attempts not worthwhile. Nakamoto (2008) emphasized that PoW represents a one-CPU-one-vote system, in which the majority decision about the linked blocks is if found by the greatest resources and effort invested in it. As such, as long as the majority of the network is comprised of honest peers, a malicious attacker faces intense computational resource requirements in order to do damage to the system.

Figure 12: Proof-of-Work

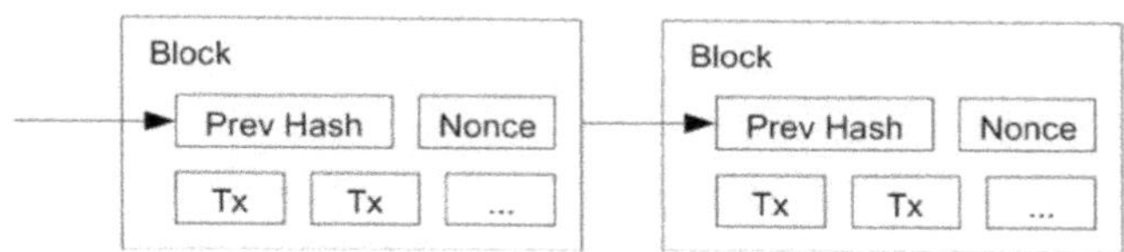


Source: Nakamoto (2008), p. 3

Proof-of-work is implemented by incrementing a nonce, that when hashed with the SHA-256 algorithm results into a hash with the required number of zeroes at the beginning of the hash. This guarantees that the majority of the network agrees on the block with the right nonce.

In an effort to enhance Bitcoin's scalability and reduce data storage requirements, Nakamoto (2008) designed the protocol in a way that after the latest transaction of a Bitcoin is followed by enough blocks, realized transactions before it will be discarded. Therefore all transactions are hashed in a Merkle tree[30] and only the Merkle Root hash is included into the block.

---

[30] c.p. Becker (2008), p.8-10

Figure 13: Merkle Tree Block Implementation

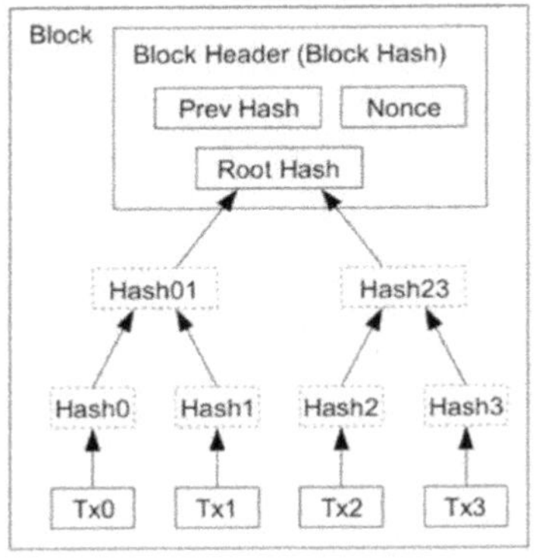


Transactions Hashed in a Merkle Tree

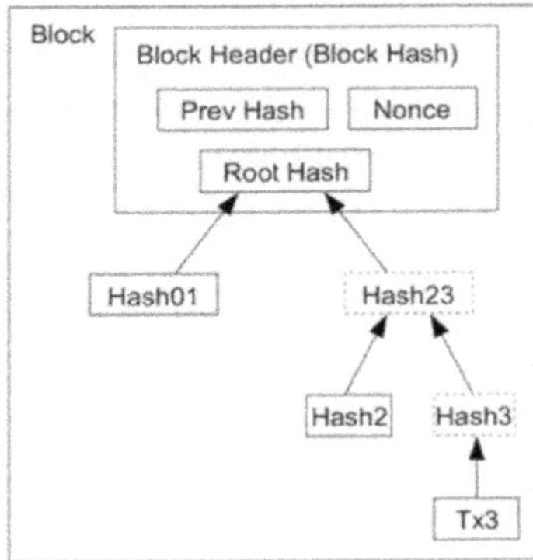


After Pruning Tx0-2 from the Block

Source: Nakamoto (2008), p. 4

Nodes that form the Bitcoin network verify these transactions. Approximately every ten minutes a new block is created, all the transactions it contains are validated and the block added to the chain of blocks. It is possible for more than one valid block circulating in the network. In such a case a fork in the chain of blocks may be created as nodes have not yet found consensus about which block to include in the longest chain of blocks. As there is only one possible transaction history that the network agrees upon, only one of these blocks can be included in the longest chain and forks will be discontinued. As it can be assumed that there are dishonest as well as honest nodes, this system works without threat of double-spending or other frauds as long as the majority consists of honest nodes.

Figure 14: Longest Proof-of-Work Chain of Blocks

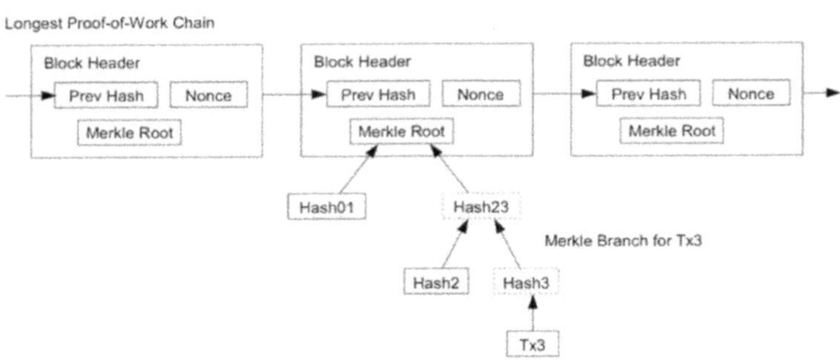


Source: Nakamoto (2008), p. 5

This process illustrates how bitcoins can be transferred from person A to B and how transactions are verified by a decentralized network that agrees on a single longest chain of blocks that include all agreed-upon transactions.

Figure 15: Bitcoin Transfer Inputs and Outputs

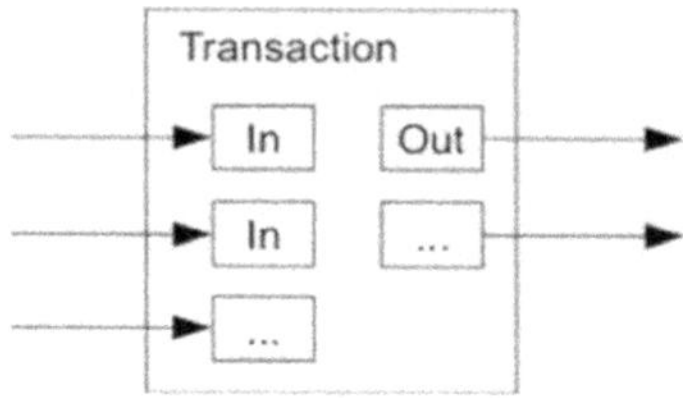


Source: Nakamoto (2008), p. 5

Received transactions themselves are not divisible, and therefore if a user received 10 BTC to an address and wants to send 2 BTC to another address, the transactions that the user is generating must also be 10 BTC. The protocol will assure that of this transaction 2 BTC will be sent to the intended address and 8 BTC will be transacted back to the address holding the initial amount.

Nakamoto (2008) judged that handling bitcoins individually would be less desirable as it would result into separate transactions for every cent in a transfer.

## 3.2 Network

In order to achieve a decentralized payment transaction system, Nakamoto (2008) proposed creating a network that finds a consensus on transaction data. The network consists of nodes, in which each node contributes a fraction of its computational power to the network.[31]

$$p_v \geq 0.0 \text{ of} \textstyle\sum_{v \in V} p_v = 1$$

Skudnov (2012) distinguished between five different types of clients that form the bitcoin network. Clients are software platforms that offer different kinds of services

[31] c.p. Sompolinsky & Zohar (2013), p.5

to users, such as private key generation, syndication of peer clients, sending/receiving transactions, security services, communication within the network, client application programming interfaces (API), etc.

Table 5: Client Description

| Type | Description |
|---|---|
| Full client | Implement the full Bitcoin client and hold a copy of the entire block chain.<br>Function: Sending/Receiving blocks, saving valid blocks, verifying all legitimate transactions, communicating with other nodes, storing all transaction data. |
| Header-only client | Keep only block headers of the block chain. Only downloads full blocks when payments are incoming or keys are needed. Cannot verify transactions at this moment<br>Function: Allow Bitcoin transactions on devices with limited storage capacity, such as smartphones. |
| Signing-only client | Focus on the incoming/outgoing transactions of the node itself and connected wallets of the client only. Do not provide services to the block chain.<br>Function: Simple desktop or web applications for sending and receiving bitcoins, minimal storage requirements. |
| Thin client | Send commands to remote servers on behalf of Bitcoin users. Private keys and signing transactions are not required. Thin clients do not engage with the block chain, nor do they sign transactions.<br>Function: Provide easy-to-use third-party services for users, without requiring much knowledge about Bitcoin functions. |
| Mining client | Specialized clients that compete against each other in order to find valid blocks and mine new bitcoins at a prespecified pace. Miners create new blocks for the block chain but do not actively send or receive information about transactions (see Full client).<br>Function: Provide constant money supply, find valid blocks that meet certain criteria, add verified blocks containing all valid transactions within the block to the block chain, and prevent alterations of historical transaction data. |

Source: Skundov (2012), p.12-17

Decker & Wattenhofer (2013) explained that the Bitcoin network consists of a network of homogeneous nodes that store a complete copy of the block chain (full client). Its typology is random and based on DNS (Domain Name System) servers, in which new nodes can join and receive information about the addresses of other nodes. Notably, not all nodes are connected with each other and each node attempts to keep a minimum number of nodes connected to it. Karame et al. (2012) stated that the network resembles a memory pool, in which all peers receive information about transactions that are not yet confirmed. If a transaction in this pool is confirmed elsewhere by another peer, it will be removed from the pool.

Figure 16: Network Message Propagation

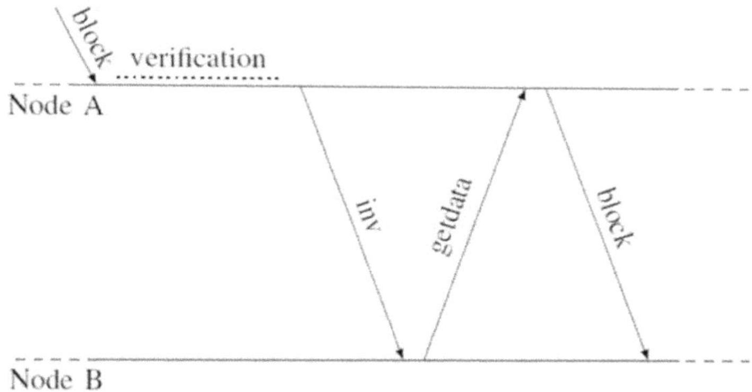


Source: Decker & Wattenhofer (2013), p. 4

Information propagation consists of updating and synchronizing the block chain copies of all nodes by transmitting information about transactions and blocks. Information is not propagated directly to nodes as this would be an inefficient network propagation method. Instead, the availability of information is broadcasted to other nodes and data is only transmitted if a node requests it. Availability is broadcasted via *inv* message and requests are conducted by *getdata* messages in the network. This method prevents sending transactions to nodes that have already received it. Nodes will issue getdata messages when they receive inv messages that contain block or transaction hashes that it has not stored locally. This ensures that each block and each transaction are introduced to the network by a one origin node within the network. Local verification of blocks and transactions at other nodes as well as transmission time messages and hash data causes the decentralized network to always experience a certain network delay.

As mentioned before, it is possible for two or more nodes to create a block at the same time that both satisfy the conditions to be added to the longest chain in the block chain, but are mutually conflicting. In order to mitigate this problem, Bitcoin makes block creation difficult as it requires proof-of-work and significant computational resources. Conflicting blocks that are broadcasted to nodes simultaneously enter a "race" in which two forks are created and eventually only one of the blocks succeeds. The network is designed to prefer the block that has a higher degree of proof-ofwork included into it. Forks can be prolonged for several blocks and the network can build on both of them, while essentially disagreeing about which block should be linked to the block chain as long as the race persists. Eventually one fork will become longer than the conflicting branch and the conflict will be dissolved, as the network agrees on the longest chain of blocks and all block chain ledger replicas are synchronized again. The discontinued fork will persist as a branch of disregarded blocks, which are referred to as "orphaned blocks". This can result into transactions becoming invalidated if they were only included in the discontinued fork.[32] The network can however only function correctly if there is no majority of nodes that build a cartel. If any party could obtain the majority of the network power, they could decide about a

Based on Decker & Wattenhofer (2013), Sompolinsky & Zohar (2013) explored network propagation further. They showed that blocks are created through a Poisson process in the network with a rate of $p_v \times$, where $\lambda$ denotes the rate of block creation. Each individual node $v$ that creates a block immediately broadcasts it to its neighbors within their network, which will further propagate it to their neighbors throughout the decentralized network. This process is repeated until all nodes are reached.

The time it takes for a block to reach 50% of the network nodes depends linearly on the size of the block.

$$D\,50\%(b) = D\,p\,r\,o\,p + D\,b\,w * b$$

For each KB of data, the delay to reach a majority of the network is a result of both propagation delay ($D_{prop}$) and bandwidth delay ($D_{bw}$).

The typology and architecture of Bitcoin's network is a fundamentally important issue to the technology. Network delay is a significant issue for the decentralized network of the cryptocurrency, as its main purpose is to agree on a single database for all nodes. Nodes verify each other's work to ensure that no node is working against the network. By doing so, each node becomes an operational part of the

32 c.p. Decker & Wattenhofer (2013), p.3

money transmission system. The network replicates all data at all nodes and thus form a data base together in which no single node can manipulate data that the majority of other nodes have agreed on.

## 3.3 The Block Chain

Bitcoin's block chain is a 'journal ledger' of all the transactions ever executed in the Bitcoin network. It acts as both a transaction database and a transaction processing system. The block chain stores all historical transactions indefinitely and provides public access to addresses, transaction size, timestamps, hash values and other relevant data.

As the name suggests, the block chain consists of a series of blocks that are linked together from the first block ('genesis block') to the most recent one. As each consecutive block must contain the hash of its predecessor it is designed to form a single history of all transactions since inception of the Bitcoin technology. The genesis block was the initial block that was solved by Satoshi Nakamoto himself on January 3rd 2008.[33] Each block in this chain contains the SHA-256-based hash of the previous block, which allows verifying that no previous block has been modified. The decentralized Bitcoin network is chaining each newly created block together with the previous blocks by a process referred to as mining.[34]

---

33 c.p. Bitcoin Wiki. Genesis block, 08.04.2014

34 c.p. Bos et al. (2013), p.5

Figure 17: Schematic Bitcoin Block


```
{"hash":"00000000000000f38...",
 "prev_block":"00000000000000c6d...",
 "time":1354114900,
 "difficulty":436527338,
 "nonce":282240624,
 "tx":[
   {"hash":"5ca...",
     "in":[
      {"prev_out":
        {"hash":"000...",},
      }
     ],
     "out":[
       {"value":"50.53620000",
        "scriptPubKey":"27a1..."
       }
     ]
   },
   ...
 ]
}
```


Source: Kroll et al.(2013), p. 4

Decker & Wattenhofer (2013) noted that blocks are created by one of the nodes in the network and contain a set of all the transactions that the node has committed since the validation of the previous block. Nodes agree on the validity of transactions in the network and discard those transactions that conflict with transactions that are committed as part of the block.

The Bitcoin protocol is designed to incentivize miners to work together and provide resources for the necessary network. Therefore, miners simultaneously provide two services for which they are rewarded: Relaying transactions and verifying transactions, and are thus working on continually expanding the chain of blocks. By doing so, Nakamoto (2008) argued that double-spending of bitcoins can be prevented by providing a peer-to-peer solution to the Byzantine Generals problem.

Figure 18: Schematic Bitcoin Block Chain

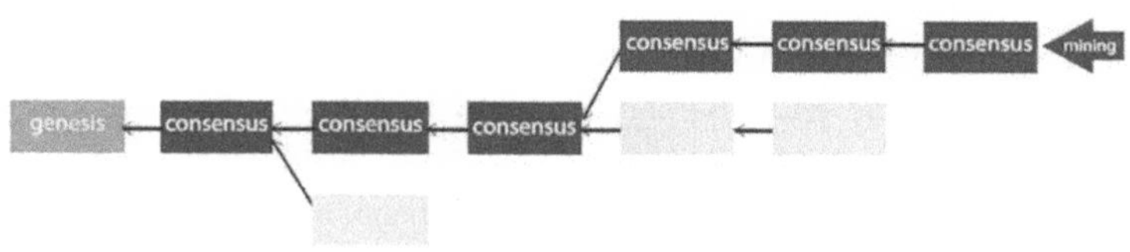


Source: Kroll et al.(2013), p. 4

The combined block chain provides one unique link back to the genesis block which is theoretically not falsifiable. Proof-of-work (PoW) technology employed in Bitcoin requires anyone who wants to manipulate transactions in an already verified block to redo the entire work that was necessary to create this block. Figure 18 illustrates the block chain and shows that it forms a tree of blocks that can have several branches. The illustration also depicts orphaned blocks of discontinued Bitcoin forks. Barber et al. (2012) illustrated how all Bitcoin transactions are essentially valid indefinitely, but only as long as they are not included in a discarded branch of a fork. Proof-ofwork guarantees that only the conflicting blocks with the larger difficulty will be linked to the block chain. Transactions that have only been included in the orphaned blocks typically will be delayed until resolved, meaning that the block chain disregards alternative forks and eventually includes transactions of the discontinued blocks into the prevailing chain.[35] Courtois (2014) evaluated the "Longest Chain Rule" of the block chain technology that is the assurance that only the longest chain is agreed upon and in case a fork is created by peers in the network, the longest chain rule would cause the network to switch to the longer chain. The broadcasting network, that relays transactions and new blocks within the block chain, is based on peers. When a peer broadcasts a transaction to the network, all peers will request data about the transaction, validate it and broadcast the valid transaction to all peers and save the information that this transaction was already validated. Trasnsactions can be included in

Miers et al. (2013) stated that the core of the Bitcoin protocol is essentially the block chain, as it enables the decentralized storage of information and processing

35 c.p. Decker & Wattenhofer (2013), p.2

of transactions. They define it as an "append-only bulletin board maintained in a distributed fashion by the Bitcoin peers."[36] The block chain is maintained by a peer-to-peer network of nodes that distribute and record all Bitcoin transactions. The block chain described as a significant technological achievement that could have numerous additional field of application. Cawrey (2014b) reported how Bitcoin's technology is developed into decentralized digital verification services ('Proof of Existence'). As the block chain is a public database, it can also serve as a secure verification service for authorship and intellectual property.

Aside from recording and archiving transaction data, it is also a sophisticated data base.[37] All complete nodes in the Bitcoin network need to download and store the full block chain history in order to function as a consensus-driven network. The block chain acts as a shared database for all nodes participating and thereby forming the network. Spagnuolo et al. (2013) parsed the block chain in order to utilize its data to cluster addresses, as well as graph, visualize and export data about the Bitcoin network and its users.

The block chain is often described as a remarkable technological innovation. Not only does it solve the Byzantine Generals problem. The Economist (2014) argued that it represents a disruptive financial innovation that may change the way financial sectors are organized. Most financial organizations are concerned with maintaining systems that track assets from one ledger to another. The block chain is a transparent, distributed ledger that exists in millions of computers simultaneously and operates on very low cost. A decentralized system, it offered a myriad of applications that can be built on top of it while benefiting from the advantages of decentralized networks.[38]

## 3.4 Wallets

Within the context of Bitcoin, wallets represent digital storage methods of bitcoins. Bitcoin wallets are based on public-key cryptography, which interlinks a pair of encryption keys to each other that allows creating addresses. The encryption pair consists of a private key and a public key that refer to each other through a cryptographic hash function. Private and public keys are (pseudo)randomly generated

---

36 c.p. Miers et al. (2013), p.3

37 c.p. Bitcoin Wiki. Block chain, 19.04.2014

38 c.p. N.N. (2014), http://www.economistinsights.com/technology-innovation/analysis/money-nomiddleman/tab/1, 14.10.2014

strings of letters and numbers that allow encrypted transactions. Each wallet holds a combination of a unique public key and its corresponding private key. Public keys are necessary to create 'addresses' at which Bitcoin can be stored and from which they can be transferred to other addresses. In order to transact bitcoins between different addresses, one must possess the corresponding private key that allows signing the transaction. Whereas public keys are freely accessible on Bitcoin's public ledger – the block chain – private keys must be protected in order to prevent theft.

Wallets are an essential part of the Bitcoin technology and therefore several versions of wallet types and wallet software providers have been developed.

Table 6: Types of Wallets

| | |
|---|---|
| **Desktop wallets** | Original Bitcoin wallet type, which was provided by the Bitcoin-Qt client. Addresses can be created by the client and private keys are stored on the computer on which the client is installed.<br>Individual service providers provide additional desktop wallets outside the bitcoin client, such as Multibit, Electrum, Armory, etc. |
| **Mobile wallets** | Smartphone apps that allow users to store Bitcoin on a mobile phone and conduct transactions using the smartphone's near-field communication feature (NFC). Mobile wallets do not require the Bitcoin-Qt client in order to save data storage capacities on smartphones. Their transaction method requires simplified payment verification (SPV). Private keys are stored in encrypted form on the mobile phone and are backed up on web-based servers. |
| **Online wallets** | Online- or web-based wallets are third-party providers of wallets that store private keys online on servers. As such, Bitcoin transactions can be conducted whenever connected to the Internet.<br>Online wallets require trust into a third party that effectively owns the private keys. They are commonly used when bitcoins are stored on exchanges in order to trade or exchange them. |
| **Hardware wallets** | Dedicated, physical devices that hold private keys electronically and facilitate payments through a third party. They are single-purpose electronic devices that store the private keys of users and are often used for offline transactions or as a secure storing method. |

| | |
|---|---|
| **Paper wallets** | Paper wallets are offline versions of wallets that are – as the name suggests – pieces of paper that display both the public and the private key, with the private key commonly being hidden on the back or by folding the paper. Paper wallet keys can be created completely offline and are therefore never exposed to the Internet. As Bitcoin must be transferred to the printed wallet, its address will still be recorded on the network, even if the wallet was created entirely offline. Paper wallets resemble traditional cash or debit cards in their application. |
| **Brain wallets** | Brain wallets are an exotic type of wallets as they imply memorizing certain passphrases in one's mind that are recorded nowhere else. Suitable phrases can be converted into a 256-bit private key through hashing or algorithms in order to compute a public key. Passphrases must be long enough and should contain intentional errors or grammar mistakes in order to prevent brute force hacking attempts.<br>Example:<br>Passphrase: "My friend I sure do like pancakes." Private Key:<br>5JZDUzvxkSi89rWRVUrgC3FUgovSc3AQXJujjyENcdLr4TmJvLu<br>Public Key: 12BFqkuMoDCr6neFqKSZUt7dBCG7mutYF4<br>(Source: http://brainwallet.org/) |

Source: Coindesk (2014), www.coindesk.com, 23.06.2014

Most wallet types contain cryptographic key pairs, transaction history, user preferences, default key, reserve keys, accounts, and the version number.[39] As the possession of both the private and the public key is the core requirement to Bitcoin transactions, it is essential to protect private keys. Wallet files can be stolen by malicious peers, but will still require private keys in order to access the funds in it.

Litke & Stewart (2014) analyzed the different wallet options for bitcoin funds and created a best practice recommendations list. They find a number of weaknesses and wallet risks for each wallet type. Wallet risks can be broadly distinguished into physical loss or theft, hard drive failure or theft by malware. Their recommendations include backups, encryption of wallet files, cold storage and access controls. Cold storage wallets are never connected to a network and thus prevent access to

[39] c.p. Bitcoin Wiki. Wallet, 27.04.2014

them. They are a means of securely storing bitcoins that are not actively needed, thus they act in similarity to vaults of safes storing financial funds and other assets. Hot wallets store private keys within online devices and are necessary for e.g. businesses that repeatedly transact bitcoins.[40]

Wallets are very sensible and need proper encryption and protection concerning their access controls. With the emergence of third party wallet systems there are also more points of failure introduced to Bitcoin users that do require trusted relationships.

## 3.5 Bitcoin Addresses

A full of understanding of the technical background to public/private key pairs and the creation of addresses requires relevant knowledge in the field of cryptography. Therefore the following subchapters will only focus on certain aspects of cryptography, as a full understanding is not relevant to this thesis.

Bitcoin is based on public-key cryptography, which is a class of cryptographic algorithms that are asymmetric in nature. This implies that two keys are utilized – one public verification key and one private signing key. Symmetric key algorithms use a single key that must be known to and kept secret by both the sender and the receiver of data. Naturally, this type of encryption cannot be securely utilized in a monetary transaction scenario. Asymmetric key algorithms allow for one publicly known key that encrypts data and can be distributed without risking access to the encrypted data by anyone. A private key is used to sign and decrypt data. Public key and private key are mathematically strictly related to each other, as the public key is derived from the private key. Elliptic Curve Cryptography (ECC) enables creation of a key pair in which calculating the public key from a known private key relatively easy but makes calculating the private key when a public key is known mathematically infeasible or exceedingly difficult.[41]

---

40 c.p. Goldfeder et al. (2014), p.1

41 c.p. Bellare & Rogaway (2005), p.211-214

Figure 19: Public-Private Key Schematic
Source: Bellare & Rogaway (2005), p.12-13

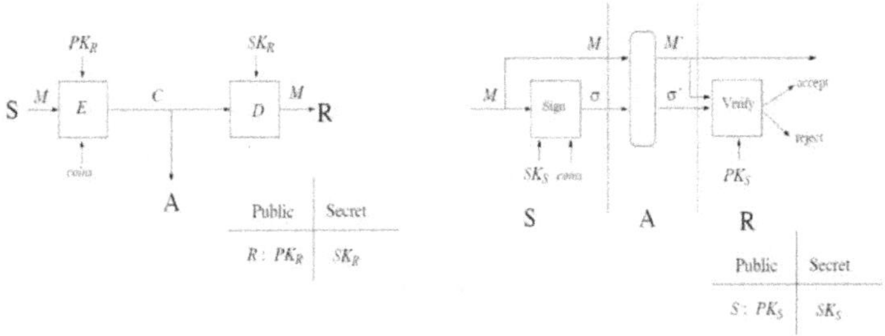


Bellare & Rogaway (2005) distinguished between a public key ($pk$) and a secret key ($sk$). In a asymmetric setting, the sender encrypts a message with his private key ($PK_R$) and sends a ciphertext that to the receiver, who in turn uses his secret key ($SK_R$) to encrypt the message. The sender only has to know about the receiver's private key in order to send an encrypted message that no third party can decrypt. In order to send a message, a sender adds a signature ($\sigma$), by signing it with his private key, to the message, which is verified or rejected by the receiver, based on a signing-verification algorithm. Addresses are derived from the public key.

Figure 20: Elliptic-Curve Public Key to BTC Address Conversion

Source: Bitcoin Wiki. Technical Background of Version 1 Bitcoin Addresses, 29.05.2014

A Bitcoin address is a 160-bit hash that is derived from the 256-bit public part of the key pair. As such, an address is a hashed version of the public key.

$$a = f(pk)$$

It follows that the address is a one-way function of the public key which implies that an address can be derived from the public key but not vice versa. Addresses are 27-34 long alphanumeric characters that are used as identifiers between which BTC can be transferred. Addresses have to be input in a complete and case-sensitive manner in order to avoid being rejected.

Nakamoto (2008) recommended creating a new address for each transaction. In fact, users can create new addresses almost instantaneously and at zero cost. Address reuse is actually considered a bad practice that exposes users to a number of risks.[42] Addresses are stored as a file in user's wallets, will remain active and reusable and require only very limited memory space. Bitcoin's technology allows for the creation of $2^{256}$ private keys and $2^{256}$ public keys, which corresponds to $2^{160}$ possible addresses. To put these numbers into perspective, the total number of possible addresses that could be generated would be about $1.4615 \times 10^{48}$, while the number of private/public keys would be about $1.1579 \times 10^{77}$. As a comparison, the total number of atoms in the universe is currently estimated to amount to about $1.0 \times 10^{80}$ atoms.[43] Dividing the possible number of addresses by the current human population, this results into:

$$Addresses\ per\ Capita_{2014} =$$

$$\frac{1.461.501.637.330.902.918.203.684.832.716.283.019.655.932.542.976}{7.140.000.000} = 2.04691\ x\ 10^{38}$$

It could therefore be stated that there are many orders of magnitude more possible addresses than the human population could ever use over a feasible time horizon. Improper address reuse should therefore not be an issue that would originate from the technology of Bitcoin.

Addresses can also be designed to require multiple private keys in order to enhance security. Multisignature addresses allow securing several private keys at different locations, e.g. partly online and offline or within several wallets. Goldfeder et al. (2014) explained that multi-signature transactions require users involve several private keys in transactions but do not require all of them combined in order to sign transactions. Diversifying private key storage vastly increases the difficulty of stealing bitcoins. They also allow for more than one person to be involved into

42 c.p. Bitcoin Wiki. Address reuse, 26.04.2014

43 Wolfram Research, Inc. (n.d.), https://www.wolframalpha.com/input/?i=2^256 (16.05.2014)

transactions, thus mitigating risks for companies using bitcoin balances and shared funds between groups of people.

Figure 21 illustrates a transaction of 3.80274341 BTC of a customer between two bitcoin exchanges – Bitcoin Deutschland AG to Kraken Payward Inc. – that the author of this thesis has conducted.

Figure 21: Bitcoin Address on Blockchain.com

Source: Blockchain (2014), www.blockchain.info, 09.06.2014

Figure 21 also shows how the block chain offers an easy was to track bitcoins between different Bitcoin addresses. In fact, Meiklejohn et al. (2013) characterized addresses as 'users pseudonyms' that are identified by a public key. Bitcoin transactions can be seen as a chain of transactions from one owner to the next, in which the current owner is identified by the pseudonymous public key.

## 3.6 Public Key

A public key is obtained by applying a set of mathematical operations to a given private key. The method chosen by Nakamoto (2008) to base Bitcoin on was Elliptic Curve Cryptography (ECC). ECC is a concept that originated in the field of public-key cryptography. Its core characteristics are asymmetric keys for encryption purposes that differ in purposes. It allows relatively easy computation of the public key when the private key is known, but makes deriving the private key from a public key infeasible and nearly impossible.[44] In cryptography, ECC offers the benefits of small key sizes, efficient implementation and very high security with lower bit-length than comparable concepts.[45]

Sample public key: 1LisNtnY79JuBamhDxbtSrvHNPv2xSn7xV

The public key is a number that corresponds to the private key. Public keys can be illustrated in a compressed and an uncompressed form. As the name suggests, public keys are publicly accessible, transparent keys that can be known by any other market participants without risking the theft of coins or other malicious behavior.

Bos et al. (2013) explained how Bitcoin addresses are derived from elliptic-curve public keys and transactions are authenticated by using digital signatures. One can verify this signature value with the signers corresponding public key and prove that an intentional, unaltered transaction has been performed. Bitcoin uses a 256-prime order curve that is based on an Elliptic Curve Digital Signature Algorithm (ECDSA) called secp256k1.

$$F_{256} = 2^{256} - 2^{32} - 977$$

Public keys can also be created in a manner that includes a meaningful phrase within the random alphanumeric characters. Vanity addresses allow users to include certain words, phrases, names or patterns into their public Bitcoin address. Vanity addresses are created by Vanitygen, which is a command-ling Bitcoin address generator. Inputs form one or several patterns which the generator searches for and produces a list of addresses and corresponding private keys.

Example: $ ./vanitygen 1Boat

Difficulty: 4476342

Pattern: 1Boat

Address: 1BoatSLRHtKNngkdXEeobR76b53LETtpyT

Privkey: 5J4XJRyLVgzbXEgh8VNi4qovLzxRftzMd8a18KkdXv4EqAwX3tS

The longer the desired phrase to within the Bitcoin address the more difficult the operation gets and requires significant hardware resources to perform. Vanity address generation is free of charge for the first six digits but increases in difficulty

44 c.p. Koblitz (1987), p.206

45 c.p. Bos et al. (2013), p.1

and costs to generate exponentially. However, skilled users can create vanity addresses without relying on third party services.

Vanity addresses can be used to identify certain persons or businesses or to convey messages. As an illustrating event, anonymous Bitcoin users sent thousands of satoshis/bits (0.00000001 BTC) to random addresses conveying the message "Enjoy" and "Sochi" during the Winter Olympics 2014 in Sochi, Russia.

1Enjoy1C4bYBr3tN4sMKxvvJDqG8NkdR4Z

1SochiWwFFySPjQoi2biVftXn8NRPCSQC

These transactions, however, did not meet transaction fee criteria and were mostly disregarded by mining pools and therefore never received. Vanity addresses allow users to create personalized and potentially non-anonymous addresses, which could be utilized by certain businesses or services that intend to be publicly connected to the address.

## 3.7 Private Key

Deriving the private key that corresponds to a given public key is an intractable problem, which means that it would require too much effort or time in order to feasibly pursue solving it. Elliptic Curve Cryptography (ECC) based on the assumption that that finding the discrete logarithm of a random elliptic curve element originating from a publicly known, given base point is infeasible.[46] This problem is known as the elliptic curve discrete logarithm problem and allows the Bitcoin network to create secure transaction inputs and verifiers. As has been explained earlier, private keys are a means to sign transactions. Transaction signatures would vary significantly if anything other than the correct private key was used. The cryptographic signatures of Bitcoin private keys are based on Elliptic Curve Digital Signature Algorithm (ECDSA).

The private key is a randomly generated number that consists of a 256-bit integer.

Sample private key:

5JdjK9YiUDU2ZGfzGgRggQxZ69wfUhpW8BbkmYGdqshg1q8dpmM

---

46 Bommisetty (2014), http://www.securitylearn.net/2014/02/28/elliptic-curve-cryptography-a-case-for-mobileencryption/, 14.06.2014

Private keys are used to decrypt data that is encrypted with public keys. This implies that any individual who possesses the private key can access the data stored within the public key. As asymmetric key-pairs are used to securely store and transact bitcoins, private keys must be stored securely in order to protect the user's funds from being stolen or lost.

ECSDA also specifies the range of valid private keys, however nearly every 256-bit number is a valid private key. What makes them a secure means of signing transactions is the degree of randomness and the aforementioned intractable problem.[47] Private keys therefore require secure storage and significant security, as anyone who possesses a private key can use it to create transactions. Moreover, if a private key is permanently lost, there is no conceivable way to access the funds stored on the related address any longer. Bos et al. (2013) argued that the main threats to ECC based cryptography in practice are implementation issues, software bugs or exploitation of design flaws. However, it is also possible that users may create insecure keys due to insufficient randomness.

## 3.8 Mining

'Mining' is a term within the Bitcoin system which refers to the process of creating and distributing new bitcoins. Bitcoin's SHA-256 algorithm is designed to create new blocks every 10 minutes for which miners are competing against each other in order to solve the block first. *Miners* solve cryptographic puzzles in order to record a set of transactions and in turn be rewarded with a *block reward*, which are newly created bitcoins. In order to mine a block, miners calculate summary information about the next proposed block. This summary is combined with a 32-bit nonce in order to form a block header. A cryptographic nonce is an arbitrary, random or pseudo-random number that is used in cryptographic transmissions of information. Following the generation of the block header, the SHA-256 hash that is contained within the header is calculated by the miner. The obtained result is compared to a 'target', which is a very large 256-bit number that acts as a global target value for all network participants. In order to find a valid block, the SHA-256 hash of the generated block header must be below the target value.[48] Nakamoto (2008) noted that proofof-work (PoW) based mining involves scanning for a value that when hashed, the resulting hash begins with a certain number of zero bits. A block

[47] Bitcoin Wiki. Private key, 16.06.2014

[48] c.p. Bitcoin Wiki. Proof of work, 02.04.2014

is deemed valid by the majority of the network if the incremented nonce results into a value of the block's hash that has the required number of zero bits at the beginning. If the miner finds an invalid block, whose hash is above the target, he generates a new nonce and repeats the process.

Table 7 illustrates how the process of varying inputs until a SHA-256 hash with a certain number of zeros at the beginning is found. The base string of "Hello, world!" receives integer values (nonces) at the end of the string. It required 4251 attempts (hashes) in order to find a hash with the required number of eros at the beginning of the hash. This example is, however, only illustrative, as Bitcoin mining is significantly more complex and additionally depends on the Merkle tree and included transactions of the miner.[49]

Table 7: Proof-Of-Work Example

| **Base String** | **SHA-256 Hash** |
|---|---|
| "Hello, world!0" | 1312af178c253f84028d480a6adc1e25e81caa44c749ec81976192e2ec934c64 |
| "Hello, world!1" | e9afc424b79e4f6ab42d99c81156d3a17228d6e1eef4139be78e948a9332a7d8 |
| "Hello, world!2" | ae37343a357a8297591625e7134cbea22f5928be8ca2a32aa475cf05fd4266b7 |
| (.....) | (.....) |
| "Hello, world!4249" | c004190b822f1669cac8dc37e761cb73652e7832fb814565702245cf26ebb9e6 |
| "Hello, world!4250" | 0000c3af42fc31103f1fdc0151fa747ff87349a4714df7cc52ea464e12dcd4e9 |

Source: Bitcoin Wiki, Proof of Work, 02.04.2014

Due to the nature of cryptographic nonces, the process of generating valid blocks is essentially based on resource input and luck and cannot be dominated by individual miners or mining pools. As it is theoretically inconceivable to predict which nonce will result into the correct hash, the mining process is essentially based on repeatedly calculating various hashes until the correct solution is found. Mining is based on proof-of-work (PoW), as iteration of the correct nonce requires time and resources. PoW is given when the process of calculating a valid result is difficult

[49] c.p. Bitcoin Wiki. Proof of work, 02.04.2014

and costly, so that there are barriers to entry to the miner network and valid blocks cannot be identified without resource contribution. Proof-of-work and difficulty adjustments are required to enforce competition in the network in order to prevent one party to dominate the network. Essentially, miners compete to add the newest block to the block chain. If one party could overpower all other parties in the network, they could add incorrect transactions to the block chain and double-spend bitcoins.

The Bitcoin network is maintained by the miners, who act as transaction verifiers, and nodes that form the network collectively.[50] Miners compete against each other to generate the next canonical block. Following the explanation of Miers et al. (2013), the essential process is as follows: Miners have to solve a proof-of-work in order to generate a valid solution for a block so that a specific solution can be obtained. Once a valid solution is identified, the miner broadcasts the valid solution to all peers in the Bitcoin network. The network will only accept the new block if all transactions in it are valid and the proof-of-work correctly links to previous block in the block chain. The block will then be linked to the block chain and the process repeats itself.

The SHA-256 algorithm defines the formula for solving a block as:

$$SHA256(SHA256(B)) = 0^{l}||\{0,1\}^{256-l}$$

where... $l$ = Difficulty

$B$ = Block

As the Bitcoin protocol is designed to allow one block every 10 minutes, 'difficulty' adapts according to the collective network strength of the miners in order to keep the time per block within limits. In order to calculate the average block generation time at a given difficulty the formula works as follows:

$$Time = \frac{Difficulty * 2^{32}}{(3600 * Hash\ Rate\ per\ Second)}$$

The 'Hash Rate per Second' refers to the hash rate of miner's hardware and the exponent of 32 refers to the nonce, which is a 32-bit integer number. Decker & Wattenhofer (2013) noted that proof-of-work based mining aims towards the correct nonce, which when combined with a block header, results into a hash with a given

50 c.p. Miers et al. (2013), p.1-3

number of leading zero-bits. This zero-bit hash is defined as the *target* that is utilized in finding the correct nonce and adapting mining difficulty.

The Bitcoin network has a build-in incentive for miners to contribute their hardware to the network as miners compete against each other and more mining power increases the chance of solving a new block before other miners do. Moreover, many Bitcoin clients require users to pay a small 'miner fee' to the miners within a pool in order to compensate them for their services (verification and securing of transactions).

Rosenfeld (2011) showed that mining profitability can be calculated as

$$\frac{(1-f)htB}{2^{32}D}$$

where $f$ denotes the fees that are attributed to the pool, $ht\,B$ is the hashrate over time times the mined bitcoins and $2^{32}D$ represents the current difficulty of mining a block. O'Dwyer & Malone (2014) described the trade-off between two time-varying factors that determine mining profitability: energy costs of discovering a block and cash reward of rewarded bitcoins and fees.

Figure 22 depicts a comparison of different mining techniques' energy costs and the value for generating bitcoins. Dashed lines indicate the phases in which the respective mining hardware was not yet active.

Figure 22: Cost of Generating One Bitcoin vs. Resulting Reward

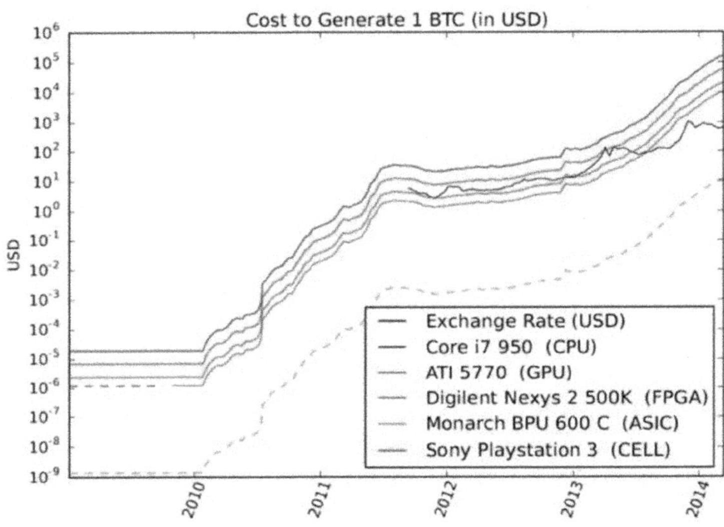


Source: O'Dwyer & Malone (2014) p. 4

Due to the design of block rewards, forming pools increases individual miner's chances to solve blocks and reduces their income variance. Due to the very low probability of successfully finding a valid block, miners can increase their chances for generating a block when they form pools.[51] Blocks are the units of transactions for miners. Each valid block contains the solution to a cryptographic problem, including the hash of the transactions in the current block, the Bitcoin address to which the block reward is credited to and the hash of the previous block.[52] Block rewards are newly mined bitcoins that are allocated to that node that successfully finds the next valid block and links it to the block chain. Miners choose to keep the BTC or sell them immediately in order to compensate their expenses that are related to mining (electricity costs). Miner fees are fees that Bitcoin clients require if transactions meet certain criteria are met or when the client requires them for other reasons. Initially the standard fee was set to 0.01 BTC. However, as Bitcoin experienced tremendous increase in exchange prices, the fee scheme was adapted

51 c.p. Eyal & Sirer (2013a), p.2

52 c.p. Eyal & Sirer (2013a) p.3-4

and the current standard fee is set to 0.0001 BTC. Fees are also set in order to avoid "dust spam" transactions of very small size and in order to compensate miners.

$$Fee = \frac{Standard\ Fee * Transaction\ Size}{(1 - \frac{Block\ Size}{500\ kB})}$$

Transaction fees can be included voluntarily of are imposed if a transaction meets certain criteria. Fees are necessary if the transaction is smaller than 0.01 BTC, smaller than 1000 bytes or have a certain priority value (depending on age, size and number of inputs of the coin).[53]

Eyal & Sirer (2013a) described this threat as: "The Bitcoin protocol requires a majority of the miners to be honest; that is, follow the Bitcoin protocol as prescribed. By construction, if a set of colluding miners comes to command a majority of the mining power in the network, the currency stops being decentralized and becomes controlled by the colluding group."[54]

Courtois et al. (2013) refered to the Bitcoin mining process as Constrained Input Small Output (CISO). The goal of CISO hashing is to produce solutions that satisfy all require conditions and constraints imposed by the protocol. A miner solves the CISO problem if he finds a solution that is below the current target, e.g. $H2 < target$ on a trial-and-error basis. (see chapter 3.9).

The graph below illustrates how the block hashing algorithm transforms a 32-bit random nonce into a 256-bit random number.

---

[53] c.p. Bitcoin Wiki. Transaction Fees, 19.05.2014

[54] Eyal & Sirer (2013a), p.1

Figure 23: Constrained Input Small Output Illustration

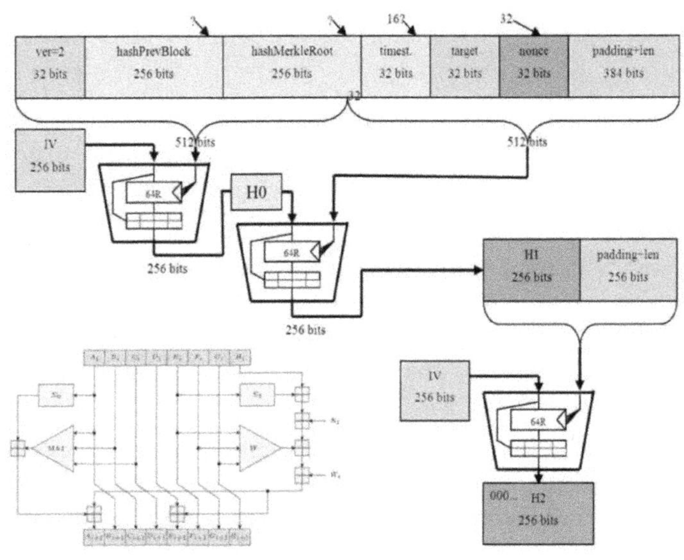


Source: Courtois et al. (2013), p. 13

Inputs are the nonce, the hash of the previous block, the Merkle root, a timestamp, and the current target relating to the difficulty of mining. Padding+len are two constants that are standard inputs of the SHA-256 hash function. This process is done repeatedly at very high iteration rates until a solution is found that satisfies all conditions to be considered valid, broadcasted to the network and verified by other nodes in the global network too. Once a miner broadcasted his solution of the CISO block the remaining network and it has reached a sufficient amount of network nodes the remaining miners will begin working on the next block and begin the process anew.

Courtois et al. (2013) further distinguished four generations of Bitcoin mining. Naturally, the adapting level of mining difficulty that derives from the current hash rate, created a competitive market for miners. Mining is essentially a lottery, in which miners can increase their chances of winning block rewards by increasing their hash rate and forming collaborate mining pools where rewards are also distributed according to contributed hardware power. In the early days of Bitcoin, mining was based on central processing units (CPU), as competition and therefore hardware requirements have been very low. Standard home PC hardware was sufficiently efficient in order to mine significant amounts of bitcoin. The second generation of bitcoin mining was based on computer graphic cards' graphic processing units (GPU). As GPUs outperformed CPUs in both hash rate and energy consumption, the mining network soon was revolutions by the emergence of dedicated GPU "mining rigs". This was followed by field programmable gate array (FPGA) mining that were produced specifically for bitcoin mining operations and represented the start of the market for Bitcoin mining hardware producers. The fourth generation of bitcoin mining was also responsible for the largest shift of mining power. Application specific integrated circuit (ASIC) miner hardware entered the market in 2013. The first retargeting of mining difficulty on January8th 2013 adjusted the current difficulty to 3,249,550.00 and hash rate 23,261.00 GH/s (9.06% increase compared to previous difficulty). Over the year 2013 several specialized ASIC mining firms delivered their newly developed miners to customers, which resulted into tremendous increases in hashing power and difficulty. What added to it was the rise in popularity of Bitcoin during the bubble of 2014. By the end of 2013, the last retargeting o Dec 21st 2013 yielded a difficulty of 1,180,923,195.00 and a hash rate 8,453,378.00 GH/s.[55]

Courtois (2014) noted that there has been an uninterrupted explosion of investment in Bitcoin mining hardware at a pace that has not slowed down significantly since. This has resulted into rapidly decreasing returns for miners and many have been crowded out by peers who added more resources and more sophisticated hardware to the network. Over the period of April 2013 to April 2014 the network has seen a more than 1000 fold increase of hashing power while the total supply of Bitcoin only increased about 1% over the same time.

The chance for a single Bitcoin miner to find a valid block is very low. Raulo (2011) compared mining Bitcoin to a lottery, in which all miners try to find the winning ticket.[56] In order to increase their rewards and reduce income variance, Bitcoin miners formed pools. Pooled mining combines multiple clients and combines the resources in order to generate a block. Block rewards are shared with the pool in proportion to the contributed computational power. Rosenfeld (2011) described

---

55 c.p. Bitcoin Wiki. Difficulty, 19.05.2014

56 c.p. Raulo (2011), p.1

the rationale behind forming a mining pool and analyzed multiple reward distribution schemes. Ceteris paribus, without looking at reward schemes, a single miner earns as much reward as a miner who joins a pool, but the variance of the reward will decrease by joining a pool.

Block rewards that award the miner or mining pool that successfully solves the most recent block are set to decrease by 50% every four years or every 210.000 blocks. Nodes are incentivized to authorize and broadcast transactions by block rewards and mostly voluntary miner fees. Nodes that generate blocks can choose not to include transactions that offer no miner fees, but are discouraged by the protocol to do so.[57] As the block reward of newly created bitcoins is set to decrease over time, it is assumed that miner's incentives will shift towards fees in order to generate returns. This incentive shift is, however, seen critical by some. Babaioff et al. (2012) argued that as a result of this incentive shift, at a certain point in the future, some miner nodes will be incentivized to withhold information about transactions that include fees to other nodes, because nodes compete against each other in authorizing transactions and by eliminating competition the node increases its chance to authorize the transaction first and claim the fee. This could become a devastating issue in the future and will have to be addressed by core developers of the Bitcoin protocol. An incentive shift that makes withholding transactions attractive could potentially harm the entire concept of a trustless, decentralized peer-to-peer network. Barber et al. (2012, p. 10) argued that "since transactors have an incentive to disseminate their data as quickly and widely as possible, not only is retention futile, but economic forces will counter it by fostering circumvention services." Therefore Babaioff et al. (2012) proposed an augmentation of the Bitcoin protocol that eliminates the incentive to withhold transactions and information propagation.

## 3.9 Difficulty

Difficulty is a measure in the bitcoin system that refers to the difficulty of solving a block in a certain time. Nakamoto (2008) stated that in order to compensate for anticipated increasing hardware requirements and varying interest in running a node, proof-of-work difficulty has to be adapted over time. The difficulty changes according to how complicated it was for miners to find a valid block that included

---

[57] c.p. Bitcoin Wiki, Weaknesses, 24.04.2014

a hash below the current target. Difficulty is dependent on a moving average of the average number of blocks per hour.

$$Difficulty = \frac{difficulty\_1\_target}{current\_target}$$

The difficulty is the result of the maximum target divided by the current target. The formula implies that there is a minimum difficulty but no cap on a maximum possible difficulty.

As an example: As each hash results into a random number between zero and a maximum value of a 256-bit number. The resulting equivalent of 256 binary bits is a sting of code consisting of 64 hexadecimal characters that each encode 4 bits of binary data.

Given the maximum target of the SHA-256 is:

$$D = \frac{0x00000000FFFFFFFFFFFFFFFFFFFFFFFFFFFFFFFFFFFFFFFFFFFFFFFFFFFFFFFF}{0x00000000FFFFFFFFFFFFFFFFFFFFFFFFFFFFFFFFFFFFFFFFFFFFFFFFFFFFFFFF}$$

This results into

$$\frac{1}{pow(2{,}32)} = \frac{1}{(2^{32})}$$

, therefore it can be stated that each hash a miner calculates has 1 [58] a probability of

$$\overline{(2^{32})}$$

to find a valid block if the difficulty is equal to 1.

A difficulty of e.g. 16307.669773817162 would be equal to:

$$D = \frac{0x00000000FFFFFFFFFFFFFFFFFFFFFFFFFFFFFFFFFFFFFFFFFFFFFFFFFFFFFFFF}{0x00000000000404CB000000000000000000000000000000000000000000000000}$$

The difficulty is designed to adapt every 2016 blocks. After solving this pre-specified number of blocks the software will analyses the time that was required to solve the previous 2016 blocks and adapt the difficulty accordingly. As each block is meant to be solved in 10 minutes, 2016 blocks would add up to exactly two weeks' time. After that period each Bitcoin client compares how long the mining process

[58] c.p. Bitcoin Wiki. Difficulty, 19.05.2014

actually took and sets a new target according to the percentage difference of estimated time to actual time. This feature prevents future technological advancements to disrupt the intended coin creation pace and allows the miner network to adapt and plan their economic rewards for mining in advance.

Figure 24: Bitcoin Hash Rate vs. Difficulty

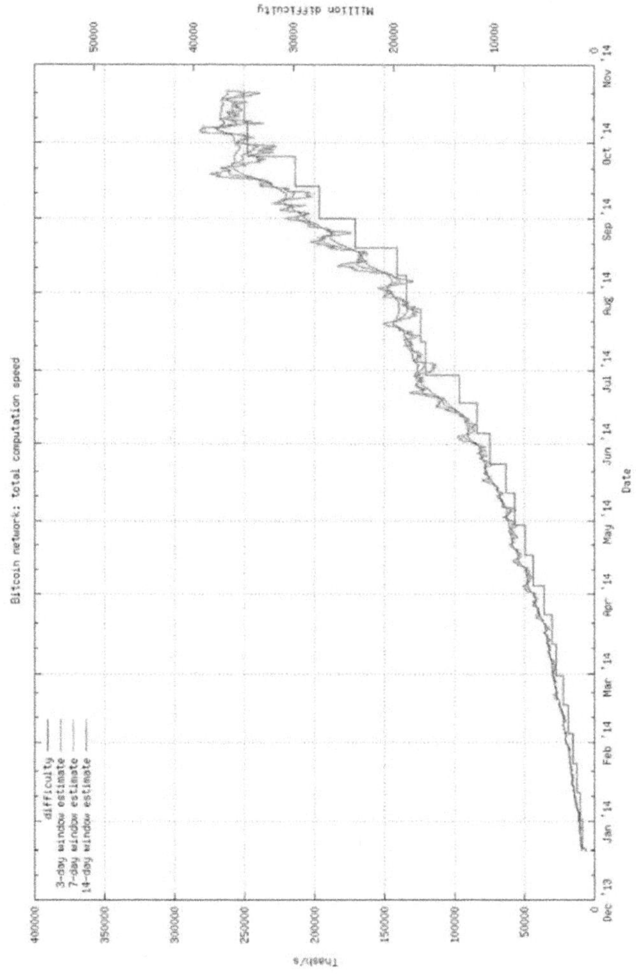


Source: Bitcoin Sipa (2014), Bitcoin Network: Total Computation Speed, 21.10.2014

As miners constantly enter and leave the network, depending on the quality of their mining hardware and mining profitability among other reasons, the difficulty adapts and increases or decreases accordingly. The combined hash rate directly influences the Block Generation time (blue line) as higher hash rates reduce the time for finding a new valid block. As the difficulty is only updated once 2016 blocks have been validated, the hash rate varies constantly, while difficulty only changes periodically. The hash rate fluctuates for a number of reasons. One of the main reasons appears to be the fact that the number of active miners varies constantly and more sophisticated mining hardware is entering the market periodically. Several specialized firms have developed dedicated Bitcoin mining hardware that is shipped to customers at certain intervals. Large jumps in the hash rate and subsequently in the difficulty can be largely explained by this. As a result some miners will cease to mine bitcoins as increased difficulty makes mining unprofitable for them, while others replace them.

Güring & Grigg (2011) noted that hash rate fluctuation is the result of interrelated variations of mining profitability. Mining can become unprofitable for many miners when BTC prices decline and miners fail to pay their electricity costs. In this case, some miners will, however, continue mining at a loss in anticipation of future price increases. Others will cease mining and may sell or dispose of their mining equipment. The network hash rate can also decrease sufficiently enough so that some previously exited miners can join the network again and mine at profitable rates.

Figure 25: Bitcoin Hash Rate Fluctuation

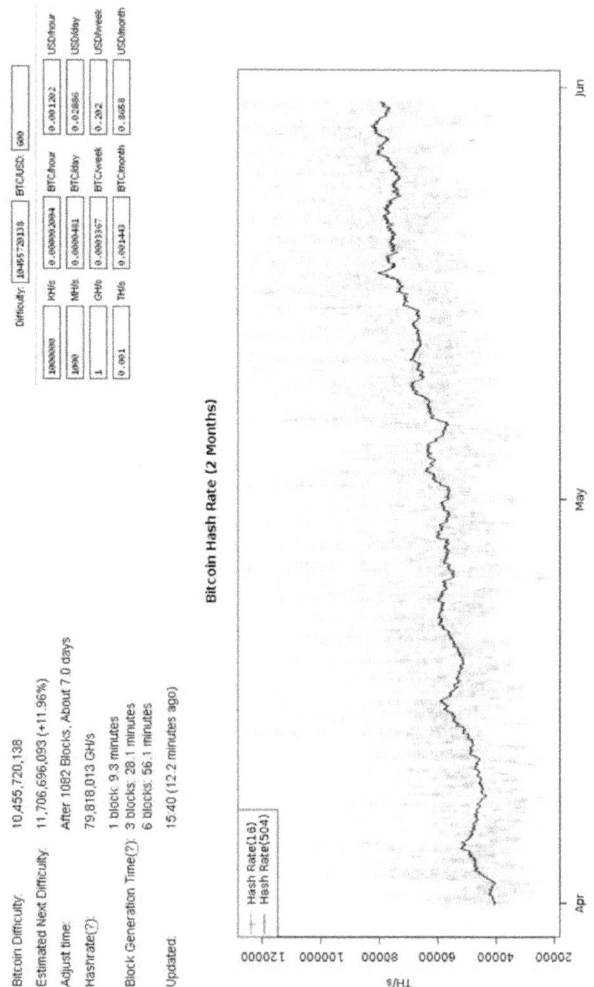


Source: Bitcoinwisdom (2014), Bitcoin Hash Rate (2 Months), 30.05.2014

It can be observed that Network hash rate constantly fluctuates around an upwards trending mean due to aforementioned reasons.

Figure 26: Total Bitcoins in Circulation

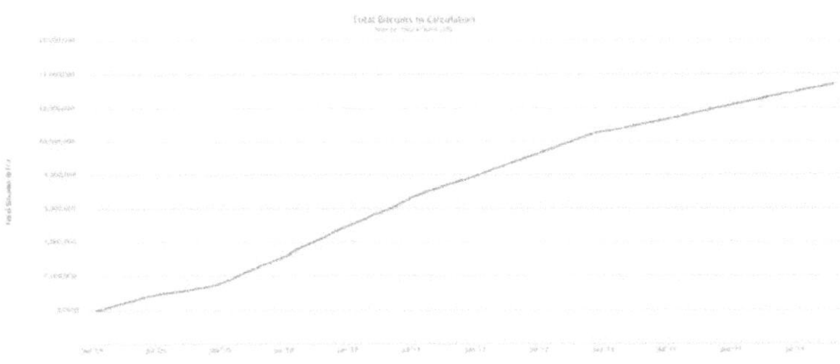

Source: Blockchain (2014), Total Bitcoins in Circulation, 14.10.2014

Figure 26 illustrates the number of total bitcoins in circulation beginning at the genesis block until October 14th 2014. One can observe that the linear growth of mined bitcoins is not perfectly linear, as the difficulty is not adapted directly according to the current network hash rate. As new hashing power is added to the network, blocks can be solved faster than the average 10 minutes intervals, thus causing diversions to the linear money supply model.

The fact that the combined hash rate fluctuates constantly but the according difficulty only changes every 2016 blocks also causes variation in confirmation times. New mining technology is developed constantly, thus the time lag between difficulty adjustments causes blocks to be solved and confirmations to be received at varying time intervals.

Figure 27: Average Transaction Confirmation Time

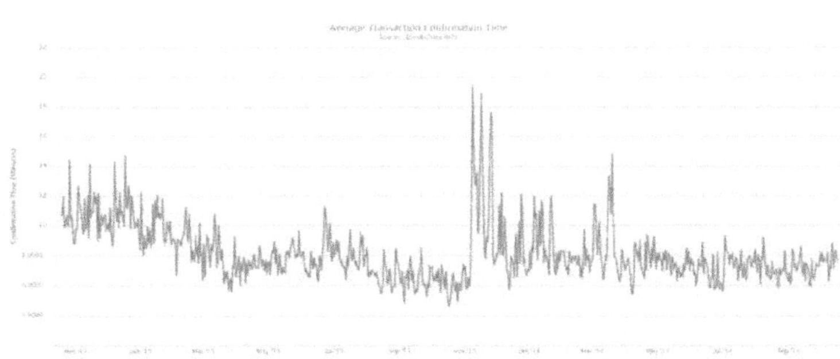

Source: Blockchain (2014), Average Transaction Confirmation Time, 14.10.2014

## 3.10 Anonymity

Nakamoto (2008) argued that privacy in the traditional banking model is achieved by limiting access to information to the parties involved in the transaction. As Bitcoin requires publicly announced transactions that have to be verified by its peers, Nakamoto (2008) emphasized privacy by anonymizing public keys and recommended the creation of new key pairs for each transaction.

Figure 28: Banking Privacy to Bitcoin Privacy Comparison

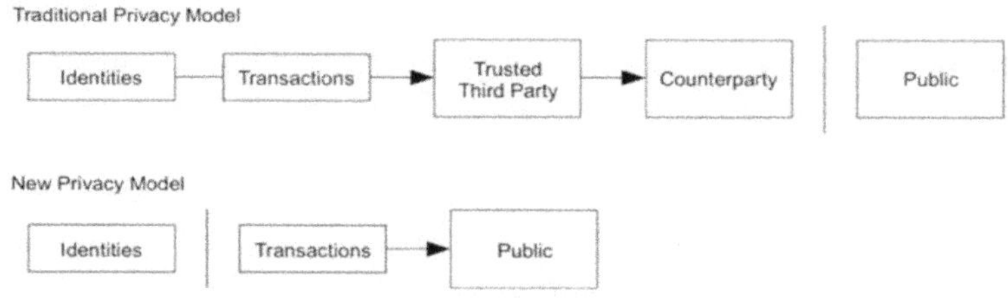


Source: Nakamoto (2008), p. 6

Bitcoin is often incorrectly described as a completely anonymous and untraceable method of transferring monetary funds and conducting payments. It is of high importance to clarify that neither of these characteristics fully apply to Bitcoin. In fact, the concept of Bitcoin would not even be functional if transactions were intractable, as Nakamoto (2008) stressed the need for public transactions that are confirmed by all within the network in order to achieve a trust-less system without the need for intermediaries. The block chain acts as a public ledger that shows and saves all transactions within the peer-to-peer Bitcoin network. Transactions are completely public and each transaction is broadcasted across the entire network and all peers reconcile the transaction. Bitcoin does not offer full privacy or anonymity as it is only the user behind the public key that is not identified but not the public key itself. In theory, if one could identify an individual behind a public key, all transactions that the individual conducted with this key would be known. Every single bitcoin transaction also links to the entire transaction history that it has undergone, as every transfer is becoming part of the code. Signing a hash in order to transfer bitcoins also records the public addresses it has been sent from and received at.[59]

[59] c.p. European Central Bank (2012), p.23-24

Green (2013) noted that Bitcoin is actually between cash and credit cards concerning its anonymity. Bitcoin's biggest asset – the block chain – is also its greatest weakness from a privacy perspective. As already discussed, the block chain records and archives all transactions and makes them public to everyone. The bitcoin duality of being a special kind of currency as well as a transaction system implies that one cannot own and use Bitcoin without one's actions being recorded on the block chain.

Much to the misfortune of people who engaged into illicit activities and exploited Bitcoin due to the misconception of intractability and anonymity, each server within the Bitcoin network contains a complete record of all transactions. Villasenor et al. (2011) argued that information processing methods can easily be implemented in order to detect and trace illicit financial transactions. They conclude that virtual networks offer a vastly expanded set of new avenues for conducting illicit transactions and that it is reasonable to assume future development of technology to trace these transactions. Also, they anticipate according action of sovereign and international regulators that aim to prevent illegal activities within the money transaction sector. Litke & Stewart (2014) argued that transparency of bitcoin transactions could allow third parties to obtain inside information of companies' financial transactions by tracing the flow of transactions related to companies' known addresses. Notably, Spagnuolo et al. (2013) developed a modular framework that parses the data contained within the block chain in order to cluster addresses into groups that likely belong to a number of known individuals. Moreover, they were able to extract and visualize data about the infamous Ross William Ulbricht case by analyzing public information contained within the block chain. Möser et al. (2013) argued that Bitcoin is in fact not at all anonymous, as the block chain archives all addresses and transactions and allows to identify civil identities through Know-YourCustomer (KYC) and other identification requirements. All interactions where bitcoins are exchanged for other currencies, goods, services and the like can be used for customer identification.

Androulaki et al. (2013) were modelling and quantifying privacy through an adversarial model. Privacy is defined here as unlinkability of activities and indistinguishability of user profiles. They analyze multi-input transactions (transactions involving several addresses) and shadow addresses (an automatically generated address that collect the change resulting from transactions) in a heuristic manner and behavior based clustering techniques in order to relate generated clusters to the number of users in an experimental setting. The show that when no one is privacy aware in the Bitcoin network, clustering allows to capture the preferences (25 different options, 3 types of users) of 42% of users in the network with 80% accuracy, while in the case when every user is fully privacy concerned, clustering still allows to identify the preferences of 35% of all users with 80% accuracy. By doing so, Androulaki et al. (2013) managed to unveil the profiles of 40% of the Bitcoin users within their experimental setting. They recommended using new addresses for each transaction in order to increase anonymity, such as Nakamoto (2008) advised in his original white paper. Additionally, users could use the services of reliable third-party entities that enable users to hide the relationship between transactions that users conduct. Holdgaard (2014) also adds that the question of how anonymous Bitcoin users are also depends on how many addresses an individual uses. Chances for identifying an individual behind an address through behavioral analysis diminish if said person would constantly create new addresses at zero cost for each transaction. Reid & Harrigan (2013) provided a detailed analysis of anonymity in the Bitcoin network. They managed to deduce information from transaction flows between public addresses and link those addresses to geolocated IP addresses. This is however only possible in scenarios where knowledge about IP addresses and connected public keys is obtained through informed third parties or voluntary disclosure. Kaminsky (2011) argued that Bitcoin is not totally anonymous due to the TCP/IP operation of the peer-to-peer network. Layer information of TCP/IP allows mapping IP addresses to public keys. Dan Kaminsky explained that if one manages to connect to all nodes within the decentralized network, one could identify the first node that broadcasts a transaction, which can thus also be identified as the source of the transaction.

Another issue that reduces or even eliminates anonymity is the use of Bitcoin addresses as donation addresses or addresses that are for some other reason directly recognizable as belonging to a certain individual. As transactions are publicly accessible, anyone can observe how much BTC the individual received and currently holds on the address and where the user transfers them to. In certain cases, this knowledge could provide linkages to other addresses the individual owns and even allow to obtain knowledge about what the user spends his funds on.

The research provided by the abovementioned authors could also point in the direction what Eric Posner argued in GoldmanSachs (2014). The block chain offers the possibility for technological developments around it that could be utilized to prevent money laundering and fight theft of bitcoins. Available academic work has already illustrated that Bitcoin pseudonymity is vulnerable and more research into this direction is anticipated.

Most businesses in the Bitcoin economy require KYC/AML/CFT-compliant procedures and practices in order to comply with regulations and prevent criminal activity. Furthermore, regulatory requirements, such as the Travel Rule, Suspicious Activity Reporting (SAR) and Currency Transaction Reports (CTR), as well as further regulations by e.g. the Office of Foreign Asset Control (OFAC)[60] or the European Union's anti-money laundering directive (AMLD)[61], will certainly be applied to cryptocurrency transactions in the near future.

In conclusion, Bitcoin transactions cannot be described as perfectly anonymous but rather pseudonymous. This still opens avenues to conduct illicit transactions but will be important at that point when respective regulatory frameworks will begin to include Bitcoin. Another often underestimated issue are over-the-counter (OTC) bitcoin transactions that are conducted by creating wallets holding a certain amount of bitcoins, and merely exchanging the private keys that allow access to them. These types of transactions are akin to cash transactions in which the parties involved remain completely anonymous. In addition, there are several options within the Bitcoin economy to tumble or mix transactions in order to obfuscate transaction flows. Ruffing et al. (2014) emphasized that Bitcoin transactions are linkable and proposed a decentralized mixing protocol that allows to anonymize users by severing the link between input and output transactions without relying on a trusted third party.

---

60 c.p. Protiviti (2012)

61 c.p. Kariņš & Sargentini (2014)

# 4 The Shortcomings of Bitcoin

Bitcoin is not designed to be the perfect model of a decentralized electronic currency. It is important to understand that the technology is still in development and the current version of Bitcoin is still a beta version. At the time of writing this thesis, the Bitcoin core version history stood at version 0.9.3.[62] Nakamoto (2008) stated clearly that he created Bitcoin as an open source project that can be constantly improved upon in a collaborative manner. Acknowledging the speculative nature of Bitcoin's development, he also stated that "I'm sure that in 20 years there will either be very large (bitcoin) transaction volume or no volume."[63] Courtois et al. (2013) argued that Bitcoin is not a state-of-the-art cryptographic system, but rather a practical and successful system, which therefor also suffers from a number of shortcomings. In a later article Courtois (2014) evaluated further on the technological shortcomings of Bitcoin in more detail, in which he very critically accessed the concept. As Bitcoin is not yet a finished technology or product it is within a phase of constant review and adaption. Recently cryptocurrencies have attracted a significant number of academics that analyze the technology in great detail and point out a number of issues. In addition, the increased public and academic level of awareness of Bitcoin did led to the development of a growing number of proposals that may benefit security, features, adoption rate and efficiency of the technology. Some of these proposals resulted into alternative cryptocurrency projects, others aim to provide extensions to the protocol or solutions to certain issues.

With the growth of awareness about Bitcoin and its presence in mainstream media, many prominent people in finance, business and academics emphasized flaws and hurdles that Bitcoin is facing. Krugman (2011) stated that Bitcoin does not actually offer significant innovation over the current electronic payment industry. He criticized that it fails to make society as a whole better off, suffers from significant price fluctuations and incentivizes hording due to Bitcoin's deflationary bias. Krugman compares the fixed-supply based cryptocurrency to the gold standard, concluding that it could lead to money-hoarding, deflation and depression [64] Later, Krugman

[62] c.p. Bitcoin Project (2014), https://bitcoin.org/en/version-history 19.10.2014

[63] c.p. Marion (2014), http://crypt.la/2014/01/06/satoshi-nakamoto-quotes/, 18.04.2014

[64] c.p. Krugman (2011), http://krugman.blogs.nytimes.com/2011/09/07/golden-cyberfetters/?_r=0, 03.03.2014

(2013) prominently criticized Bitcoin for it lacking the characteristic of being a reasonably stable store of value as it does not offer any fundamentals that would give value to it and there is no central entity that stabilizes its exchange rate. When compared to Gold or the U.S. Dollar, it would be clear to see that Bitcoin lacks intrinsic value. [65] Warren Buffet even referred to it as a "mirage" and recommended to do not invest money in it.[66]

GoldmanSachs (2014) also emphasized the argument about lacking intrinsic value, but further stated that gold does also have very little intrinsic value reflected in its price and the most of its valuation is based on gold being perceived as a store of value by a large enough group of people. Eric Posner explains that gold has become medium of exchange and store of value due to its properties of being easily dividable, it is possible to carry and transport it at reasonable cost, it has limited supply and it is difficult to counterfeit gold. These characteristics can also be found within Bitcoin, but Posner states that what makes Bitcoin fail as a good substitute of fiat money is lack of governmental control.[67]

On the other side, The Economist (2014) argued that Bitcoin resembles the early phases of the Internet, where critics repeatedly predicted the coming demise of the Internet because of bugs, shortcomings, technical issues and assumptions about human behavior. Technical fixes and business development, however, dispelled all of these claims repeatedly.[68] Likewise, Bitcoin has never experienced a shortage of critics, many of which failing to understand the basics of the technology behind it. Kaminsky (2011) argued that Bitcoin is an impressive concept that eliminates entire classes of bugs and fixed all flaws that are not due to its own design. He also mentioned that he required several instances until he finally understood it as it is such a novel concept. He can be quoted stating: "The first five times you think you understand it (Bitcoin), you don't."[69]

---

65 c.p. Krugman (2013), http://krugman.blogs.nytimes.com/2013/12/28/bitcoin-is-evil/, 03.03.2014

66 c.p. Crippen (2014), http://www.cnbc.com/id/101494937, 08.10.2014

67 c.p. GoldmanSachs (2014), p.4

68 c.p. The Economist (2014) http://www.economist.com/news/finance-and-economics/21599054-how-cryptocurrency-could-become-internet-money-hidden-flipside, 08.07.2014

69 Kaminsky (2011), p.7

As Bitcoin is the first major cryptocurrency of its kind and may be the origin of a special type of future financial technology, this section focuses extensively at current issues and shortcomings of Bitcoin.

## 4.1 Zero-Sum Game and Investor Problem

Hanley (2013) argued that a Bitcoin financial system must essentially be a zero-sum game. He explained that due to a fixed money supply of a maximum of 21 million BTC and the impossibility to create new money, Bitcoin must evolve into a zero-sum game. For each winner there must be an equally large loser. In such a system wealth is merely redistributed but not created, and utility is not increased. A fixed money supply eliminates interest payments and investment return payouts, thereby causing the outcomes of many transactions and many market participants to become Gaussian.

Figure 29: Gaussian Loss versus Return on Zero-Sum Investment

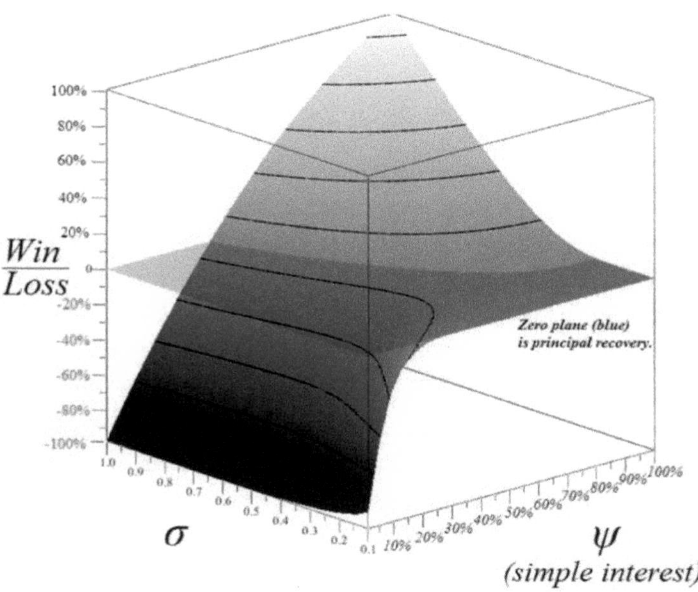


Source: Hanley (2013), p.23

Hanley (2013) described that Bitcoin's nature forces a zero-sum state that equals a loss for every gain. The Gaussian distribution shows how rare large losses or gains are determined by standard deviation and consistent exceptional returns are only possible by rigging the system. The risk-return relationship in a zero-sum game imposes a limit to investors and forces the system to return to a zero-sum even balance. It can therefore be assumed that Bitcoin could be dependent on fiat money supply in order to grow further at a certain point of time, especially as the rate of money creation against permanent loss of bitcoins will become negative over time. It is reasonable to assume that Bitcoin will experience difficulties if being used as a currency, as interest payments and investment returns that would spur economic growth are not present within the Bitcoin economy. This is however only the case if one looks at Bitcoin in isolation. Issues that will arise in a zero-sum game can be mitigated by means of alternative cryptocurrencies or Bitcoin side chains (see chapter 5 & 7). Interest payments could simply be conducted by adding an additional Bitcoin-type cryptocurrency as another protocol layer to Bitcoin itself. This interest payment-specific cryptocurrency could eliminate zerso-sum game properties of Bitcoin, but would be conflicting with Nakamoto (2008), who imposed a fixed cap to the total amount of bitcoins. Andresen (2014b) called the argument that Satoshi Nakamoto's intentions when initially creating Bitcoin should be strictly followed, as this would constitute a "argument from authority" fallacy.

## 4.2 Price Volatility

Perhaps the most crucial impediment to adoption that cryptographic currencies such as Bitcoin are facing is their price volatility. GoldmanSachs (2014)'s Dominic Wilson argues that in order to be classified as a successful currency Bitcoin must be widely accepted as a medium of exchange and a stable store of value. While he is positive that Bitcoin could become more widely accepted and the surrounding infrastructure for connecting Bitcoin with the financial sector and implementing ways to hedge price risk, store of value functionality remains doubtful.

Bitcoin is a new and experimental technology. It follows that market sentiments, rate of adoption, regulatory uncertainty, news and events, etc. are likely to have a more pronounced impact on exchange prices than it would be the case with established currencies and other assets. The current value of the cryptocurrency is determined on a few exchanges with limited infrastructure and almost no opportunities to hedge positions. In fact, only the minority of currently active bitcoin exchanges offer some form of hedging tools or advanced trading methods. This could indicate that bitcoin exchanges represent an inefficient market. In addition, there are widely varying perception on its intrinsic value. Krugman (2013) compared Bitcoin to gold or the U.S. dollar and argued that bitcoins have no underpinning for its value and nothing that could place a floor on it. Barber et al. (2012, p. 6) argued that "Bitcoins much more than any other currency in existence derive their value from the presence of a live, dynamic infrastructure loosely constituted by the network of verifiers participating in block creation." The European Central Bank (2012) referenced Jon Matonis stating that Bitcoin does not satisfy the "Misean Regression Theorem", which holds that monies becomes accepted not because of government or social convention, but rather due to its expression of purchasing power and related commodity value. However, Matonis (2011) also stated that Bitcoin's intrinsic value could originate from its Byzantine-resilient, proof-of-work based, peer-to-peer transaction technology.[70] When compared to other major currencies or CPI inflation over longer time periods, Bitcoin's volatility is significantly more intense than that of other currencies. GoldmanSachs (2014) argued "But bitcoin has no equivalent authority prepared to act to guarantee the stability of its value. And because its supply is ultimately limited, prices will need to vary to accommodate shifts in demand, not the other way round."[71]

Figure 30: Bitcoin Price Volatility Comparison

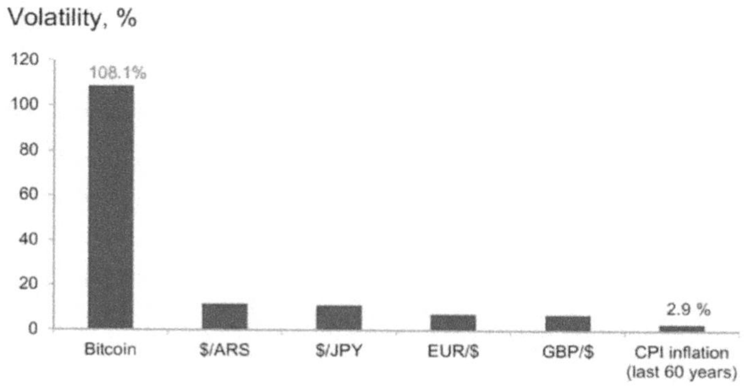


Source: GoldmanSachs (2014), p.6

This intense volatility is found even when compared to very volatile phases of major currencies in the past few decades. In a later report, Citigroup (2014) provided

70 Matonis (2011), http://themonetaryfuture.blogspot.co.at/2011/06/why-are-libertarians-against-bitcoin.html, 18.04.2014

71 GoldmanSachs (2014), p.6

the following comparison of realized volatility over a 250-days period compared to other major asset classes:

Figure 31: Bitcoin Price Volatility Comparison

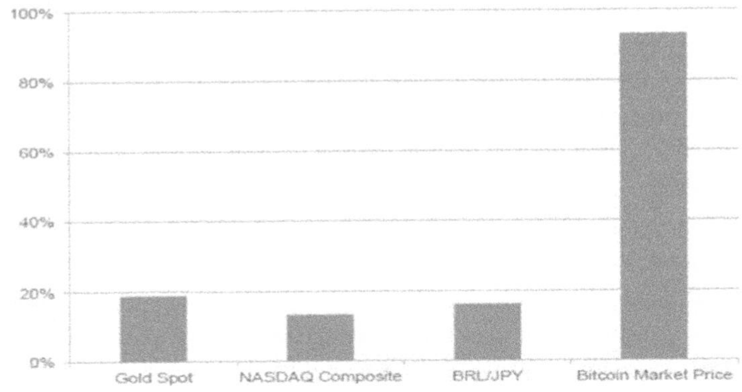

Source: Citigroup (2014), p.20

Certainly, Bitcoin is subject to intense fluctuations in value and significant daily volatility, which is an argument against its use in commercial business. Bitcoin's value appears to be attention-driven and susceptible to speculation and manipulation.[72]

Comparing the volatility of a fundamentally new asset type that still somewhat dwells in its infancy with established, centrally managed currencies will however be of very limited use. Certainly, Bitcoin is a new and experimental technology that grew rapidly and should therefore be perceived as a high risk financial investment. Bitcoin prices across exchanges are heavily sensitive to negative news and speculation. There have been several events in Bitcoin's history that led bitcoin prices decline intensely over a short period of time and across all exchanges. Woo et al. (2013) argued that if Bitcoin should be interpreted as a type of currency, its high volatility compromises its use as a store of value. Its vulnerability to speculative attacks and market manipulation is hindering its acceptance as a store of value or a medium of exchange. Price fluctuations are a result of low circulation and poor

[72] c.p. Srinivas et al. (2014), www.deloitte.com, 15.08.2014

liquidity within the Bitcoin market. Due to these circumstances dollar price fluctuations of Bitcoin amount 10% on a daily basis, with episodes of 190% daily fluctuation.[73] Such volatility can lead to practical issues as well as behavioral finance issues. As an example, should a business be obliged to refund bitcoins that have previously been exchanged for goods or services, high volatility can result into refunding customers at considerably higher prices than have been paid earlier. In ecommerce business, many companies might be very reluctant to accept Bitcoin as a means of payment due to unpredictable exchange rates that complicates liquidity management. It is as such no surprise that one of the largest firms within the Bitcoin economy – BitPay – provides businesses with the opportunity to immediately exchange Bitcoin for fiat money.

Notably, Kroll et al. (2013) noted that a strong price decline due to high volatility could lead to a death spiral for Bitcoin as miners loose incentives to mine at certain prices and reinforce loss of confidence in Bitcoin. As a result, price volatility could be detrimental to Bitcoin was substantial price declines self-reinforce themselves. Courtois et al. (2013) argued that Bitcoin is subject to unreasonable cyclical properties and instability that originate from the ways its mining rewards and incentives are designed. Block reward halving and variable fee income would increase volatility. Courtois (2014) noted that there are strong incentives to hoard bitcoins due to the expectation that their value will appreciate and consequently users will exclude a significant part of the money supply from circulation. Another consideration that must be made is that the money supply is decentralized and conducted by miners. These miners incur electricity costs in order to perform their processes and thus create a constant selling pressure for newly created bitcoins.

One important question is how the price volatility is developing over time. This is especially interesting due to increased mass awareness, growing media coverage and continuing evolution of the surrounding infrastructure. Levin (2014) provided simple linear probability model and finds that expected volatility of any given day over the past four years has decreased from approx. 9% to about 4.5% in the beginning of 2014.

---

[73] c.p. Woo et al. (2013), https://ciphrex.com/archive/bofa-bitcoin.pdf, 19.07.2014

Figure 32: Trend of Bitcoin Volatility

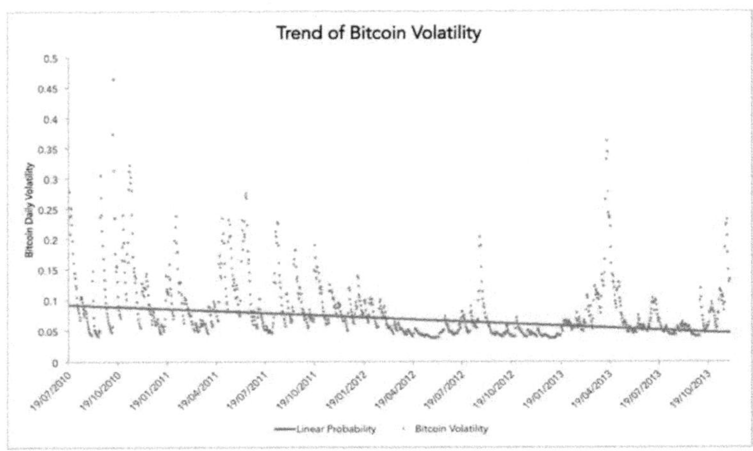


Source: Levin (2014), www.coinometrics.com, 17.05.2014

The dispersion of value changes around the average change tends to decrease over time as the Bitcoin economy is growing and liquidity is improving. Moreover, the frequency of extreme market movements is declining. Figure 32 also captures the ongoing development of the experimental cryptocurrency and its evolving economy to a certain degree. One condition for Bitcoin to succeed is that it achieves a reasonably low exchange rate volatility. While volatility may remain significant for a reasonable amount of time the declining trend is promising.

## 4.3 51% Attack

A 51% attack is the case when a miner or a group of miners in the network acquire a mining hash rate that is so powerful that it would account for more than 51% of that of the network. Bradbury (2013) stated that owning the majority of the network hash rate would allow miners to create a fork in the block chain and verify their own transactions. As the network is consensus based, the majority of the network could agree on its own blocks, allowing the attacker to include fraudulent transactions to the forked chain. Within the forked chain double-spending attacks would no longer be prevented. Nakamoto (2008) emphasized that the block chain is the result of a consensus between the majority of the network hash rate and is only valid as long as the majority consists of honest nodes. Decker & Wattenhofer (2013) noted that attacker with more than 50% network hash rate is able to find proof-of-work solutions to blocks faster than the rest of the network, whereby he creates his own fork. The attacker enters a binominal random walk, in which he essentially a race between honest and dishonest nodes about how many blocks one is ahead of each other.[74] As long as the attacker's resources are sufficient, he will be ahead of the honest peers and will have an effective monopoly on which blocks to include in the block chain. This effectively eliminates Bitcoin's decentralized characteristics.

74 c.p. Nakamoto (2008), p.6

Figure 33: Miner Network Distribution

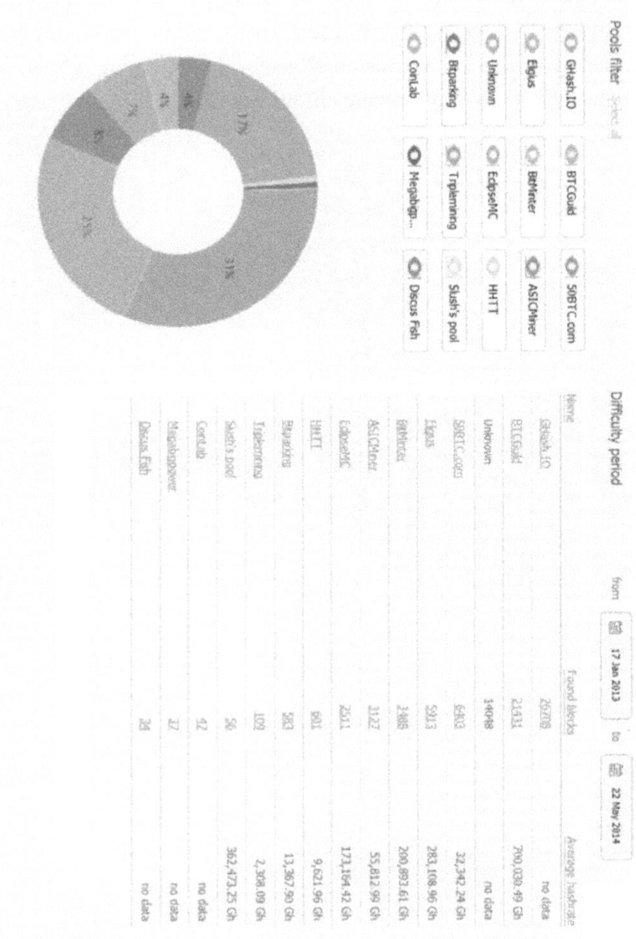


Source: Blockchain (2014), Hashrate Distribution, Accessed: 22.05.2014

Recall that miners tend to form mining pools in order to increase their returns and reduce return variance.[75] Figure 33 illustrates the current distribution of the miner network as of 22.04.2014.

[75] c.p. Rosenfeld (2011), p.1-3

While the distribution of the miner network is akin to a competitive market, there is no guarantee that one or several malicious peers could collude or provide enough new hash power to the network so that they could in fact dominate the distribution. The network is designed to be open and free and thus miners can choose to enter or exit the network at any time. A 51% would require significant resources invested in it as accumulating sufficient computational power is highly hardware-intensive and therefore costly.[76]

Eyal & Sirer (2013a) argued that Bitcoin is not protected against colluding miners and therefore its decentralization is constantly at risk to become centrally controlled by a strong enough mining pool. Profit-maximizing miners would join the selfish miners and form colluding groups. They question the assumption that Bitcoin mining is incentive-compatible by demonstrating that as selfish mining pools can exceed threshold sizes and as such mining is only incentive-compatible as long as 100% of the miners are honest. As revenue oriented miner pools can obtain more than their ratio of the total mining power, poll sizes will increase until one becomes a majority. Sompolinsky & Zohar (2013) showed that larger miners can get more of their fair share of $p_v \geq 0.0$ of $\sum_{v \in V} p_v = 1$ by exploiting network delays and manipulating the network propagation performance. They find that with a short enough block interval and a high enough stale block rate and due to network delay, smaller mining pools have significantly higher chances of producing a stale block, whereas larger blocks benefit from their size. This prevents smaller pools from contributing to the network security and at the same time allows larger pools to potentially exhibit de facto control over the network even if their relative share is below 50%.

Courtois et al. (2013) emphasized that the independent peer-to-peer network is the heart of the security assurance that Bitcoin is built on. Decentralization would make it very difficult and costly to corrupt or overpower enough nodes in the network to threaten the security of the system. Contrary to that, Güring & Grigg (2011) argued that Bitcoin is very vulnerable to a botnet attack. Botnets can infect millions of PCs and laptops and accumulate significant hashing power that could be misused to double-spend bitcoins. Whether botnets could infect ASIC mining hardware and thereby obtain significant network hashing power, is not yet established.

---

[76] c.p. LearnCryptography (2014), http://learncryptography.com/51-attack/ 19.05.2014

While a 51% attack is in theory possible but very costly, it is one of the major threats to the Bitcoin protocol as emphasized by Cortois (2014). A successful attacker would be able to

- Control which transactions will be included in the block chain.
- Negate all mining effort of other miners.
- Reverse any of his transactions that were included in the last block.
- Double-spend bitcoins.

To clarify, a 51% attacker would not be able to reverse other peers' transactions, influence the number of bitcoins per block, prevent other peers from sending bitcoins or create bitcoins out of thin air.[77]

However, the danger of such an attack occurring cannot be disregarded. Illustrating the dangers of highly sophisticated mining hardware entering the network too quickly and crowding-out miners with less hash rate, in May 2014 Litecoin's miner network almost fell victim to a 51% attack. As specialized Scrypt ASIC mining hardware was shipped to customers during May, one mining pool managed to account for 50.4% of total network hash rate within a few days.

Figure 34: Litecoin Hash Rate Distribution

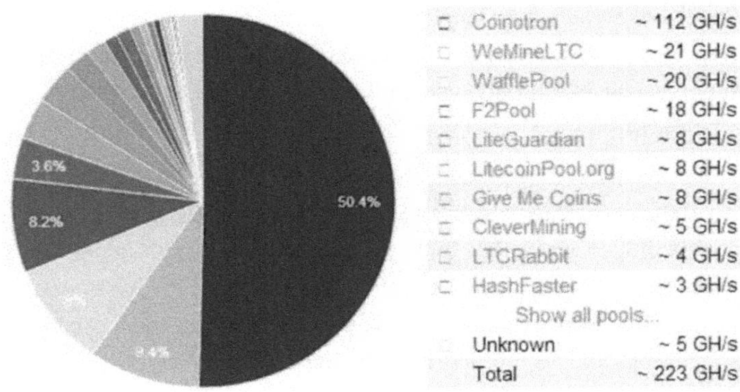


Source: Chen (2014), www.cryptocoinsnews.com, 09.06.2014

77 c.p. Chen (2014), https://www.cryptocoinsnews.com/warning-litecoin-miners-need-leave-coinotron/, 25.05.2014

Chen (2014) reported that users could freely join the Coinotron mining pool, while the managers of the pool did not engage into any countermeasures (increase fees, contact large miners). This episode demonstrated that cryptocurrencies are in fact threatened by 51% attacks. They are essentially free markets that cannot be restricted and are dominated by members with great hash rate.

Soon after Litecoin's almost-51% attack, Bitcoin fell victim to similar situation. The largest mining pool – Ghash.io – began to approach the 50% threshold several times over the course of a few days. GHash offered zero fees and many other benefits to miners that made it a very popular pool. Eventually, despite community wide efforts and encouragements of key people within the Bitcoin community, GHash.io briefly accounted for 51% of network hash rate on Friday, 13.06.2014.

Figure 35: GHash.io Mining Distribution Dominance

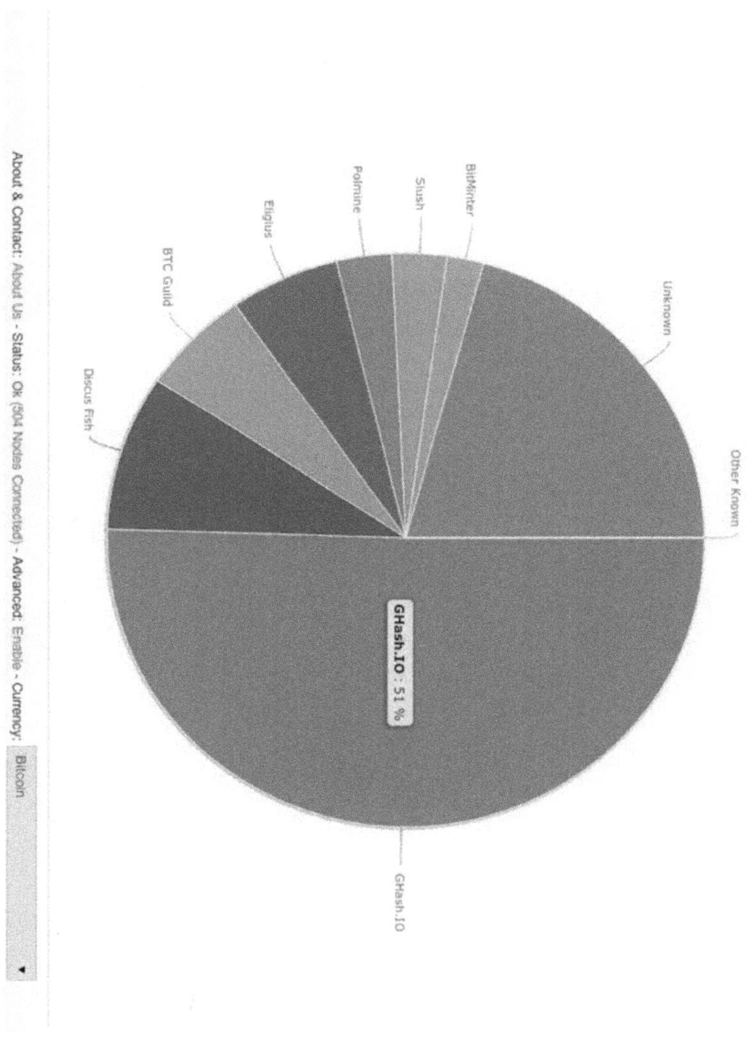


Source: Wile (2014), www.businessinsider.com, 09.06.2014

A self-regulating market, users urged miners to leave GHash.io and strengthen other pools on a voluntary basis. Prior to reaching majority, Bitcoin markets became startled by the impending danger to the network, causing (among other reasons) a significant decline in market price levels from approximately $630 to $550 within one day, eventually leveling at $570 at the time of the 51% majority of the pool. Despite this event, the potential threat of a 51% attack remains unresolved and has yet to be addressed by core developers. There are no built-in mechanisms that can prevent a mining pool from reaching majority. Notably, this event happened several months after GHash.io issued a statement in which it detailed efforts to prevent the pool from growing any further in the future.[78] Chief Scientist of the Bitcoin Foundation Gavin Andresen issued a statement detailing the risk of centralized mining, but does not indicate any intended steps to reduce this risk.[79]

If measures are developed to prevent 51% attacks in the future they must also account for the effects of network delay. Decker & Wattenhofer (2013) showed that due to a current 11.37 second delay each time a block is found, the actual portion of the network hash rate that an attacker who manages to reduce the delay needs to account for is closer to 49.1%. Importantly, as this delay is a function of block size and transaction volumes, it can be assumed that the delay is even more pronounced at current dates. Sompolinsky & Zohar (2013) developed a model for a new policy for selection of the main chain which includes a threshold for a 51% attack at 50% network hash power. As both block sizes and transaction volumes increase delay and result into more forks and less security, they find that as both factors increase, a centralized attacker could successfully conduct a 51% attack at increasingly lower levels of network hash power. At the most pessimistic scenario, double spending would be possible at a network hash rate of 25%. Their solution is a new policy for the selection of the main chain in the block tree that begins at the genesis block and chooses the difficulty-wise heaviest sub-tree at any fork. This implies that orphaned block hashes of discarded forks will also be included in the heaviest chain of blocks, which would eliminate the threat of 51% attacks being possible at lower network hash rates than 50%. This Greedy Heaviest Observed Sub Tree (GHOST) would also result into significant acceleration of Bitcoin payments.

GoldmanSachs (2014)'s Eric Posner stated that Bitcoin is already not completely autonomous but has its own form of a central bank by relying on the Bitcoin network. It is based on a majoritarian process and suffers from the threat of a majority influencing the supply side of Bitcoin. Bitcoin's longest chain rule would imply that

---

78 c.p. Smith (2014), https://ghash.io, 28.05.2014

79 c.p. Andresen (2014a), https://bitcoinfoundation.org/2014/06/13/centralized-mining/, 28.05.2014

the longest chain would become a fork that is controlled by the attacker only. Moreover, once an attacker would in fact account for the majority of the hash rate, as only his blocks would be accepted the network would cease to be decentralized.

Courtois (2014) noted that the Bitcoin miner network has seen intense increases in hash rate and difficulty respectively. This development has been fueled by expensive ASIC mining technology that has entered the market in 2013 and the growth in network hash rate has not significantly slowed down since then. As such, it can be assumed that the longer the Bitcoin network exists, the more costly and therefore less likely a 51% attack will become. Contrary to that assumption, Kaminsky (2011) argued that scalability issues will force more and more nodes to discontinue participating in the network as the larger, and more hardware intensive the network gets, the fewer nodes can preserve it. Eventually, the peer-to-peer characteristic would vanish and be replaced by supernodes. There supernodes essentially represent 'Bitcoin banks' and with larger scale, the network segmentation may diminish and result into supernodes that account for more than 51% of the network hash rate. He emphasized that fewer, more concentrated pools would increase the risk of one pool being subject of a Denial-of-Service attack that could quickly shift network hash rate distributions. Moreover, a decreased number of nodes in the network would increase the risk that some of them form a cartel and abuse their relative power within the network. On top of all, it would no longer be a decentralized network but a centralized system of a few colliding supernodes.

Courtois (2014) moreover argued that if the block reward is halved and the market price remains the same the hash rate will be divided by 2 approximately. He listed such events after alternative cryptocurrencies experienced an about 50% decrease in network hash rate after block halving events. In such an event, the distribution of network hash power among mining pools may shift significantly and could potentially result into a 51% share for one pool due to this shift. In conclusion, the network architecture in its current form is permanently threatened by a 51% attack as there are no measures to prevent any pool from becoming a majority. The GHash.io incident has proven that this is in fact a very likely threat. This consistent risk currently represents a key impediment to the development of Bitcoin.

## 4.4 Mining Incentive Scheme Flaws

As already discussed in chapter 3.8 the incentive scheme for miners involves block rewards and transaction fees in exchange for their service of providing proof-of-work based verifications of transactions and keeping the network secure. The network is based on the assumption that Bitcoin is fundamentally incentive-compatible, meaning that incentives are strong enough to adhere to the protocol as in intended. Nakamoto (2008) repeatedly emphasized that the Bitcoin protocol's functionality requires the majority of miners to be *honest*. Recall that mining a block for a single miner is very unlikely and requires very long time, whereas mining pools have much higher chances to find a block, share revenues and therefore reduce revenue variance considerably. Incentivecompatibility entails that mining pools have no incentives to collude and form a dishonest majority or to withhold blocks or transactions from the network. Therefor the Bitcoin protocol allows for creating a trustless decentralized network for transactions, but the mining network itself involves certain aspects of trust. With the emergence of mining pools the network became significantly more centralized, as has been discussed in the previous chapter. In order for such a network to function, it has to be incentive-compatible in order to discourage exploiting centralized power or exploit properties of the protocol that would benefit them at the expense of others.

Eyal & Sirer (2013a) analyzed the mining network and find that Bitcoin is in fact not incentivecompatible. They explore the ramifications of 'selfish mining'. They show that even a dishonest minority can obtain shares of revenue larger than what their respective share of the network simply by leading honest miners to wasting computations by mining blocks that are destined not to be included in the block chain. To do so, the dishonest miners create a longer fork of the block chain as soon as they find a block (and are therefore one block ahead of the other pools) but withhold information about their blocks and thereby creating a 'private branch' of the chain. Honest miners continue to mine on the shorter public branch for as long as the dishonest minority can keep their chain longer. Eventually, dishonest peers will reveal their blocks to the network, prompting the honest majority to switch to the longer chain, while abandoning the former public branch.

Figure 36: Pool Revenue of Selfish Miners

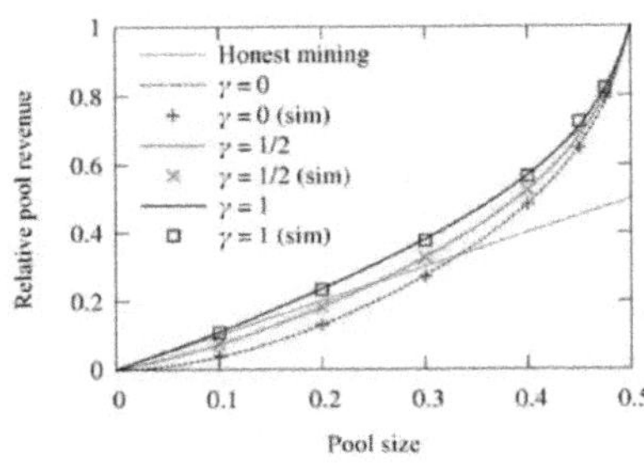


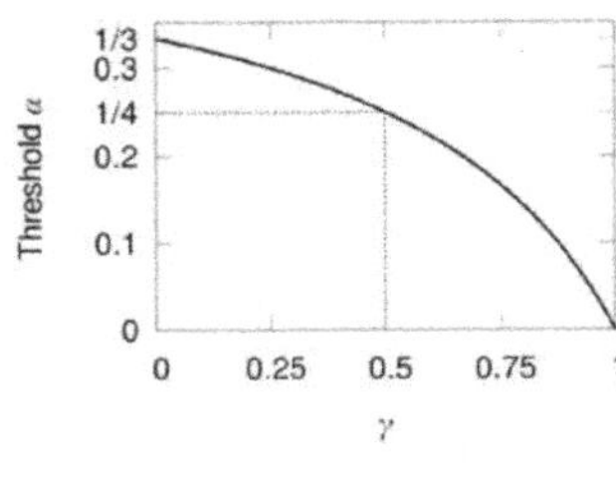


Source: Eyal & Sirer (2013a), p. 11-12

Applying a 'Selfish-Mine algorithm' and simulating the miner network with a Monte Carlo simulation, where γ denotes the ratio of miners that mine in the selfish pool to the miners that mine the other branch, whereas α denotes the pool size. Figure 36 illustrates that selfish mining is more profitable above a certain threshold (α), depending on γ. They identify the range in which selfish mining produces revenue in excess to the relative size of the network hash rate and α at:

$$Selfish\,mining\,range \;=\; \frac{1-\gamma}{3-2\gamma} \;<\; \alpha \;<\; \frac{1}{2}$$

As a result, they show that once the pool is above the threshold, selfish miners earn higher revenue for all increases to the size of their pool (α). Therefore incentive-compatibility in this scenario is no longer given and rational miners will want to join the selfish pool in order to maximize their revenue, while the pool will accept them to increase their own revenue. At the point when the selfish pool reaches more than 50% network hash rate, selfish mining is no longer necessary, as the pool is taking over the network and deciding singularly which blocks to include. As has been argued in the previous chapter, there is no measure in place to prevent pools from exceeding 50% network hash rate. Eyal & Sirer (2013b) argued that due to their detected vulnerability that Bitcoin can be considered 'broken', due to the possibility that a minority group of miners can obtain revenues in excess of their fair share and thereby grow in number until they reach a majority. At this point Bitcoin ceases to be decentralized and loses its core characteristics. Notably, this must not necessarily be the result of malicious peers intentionally attacking the network, but can be the result of miners wanting to increase their profits by resorting to selfish mining. Eyal & Sirer (2013b) do not, however, take into account that by obtaining a size larger than 50% of the network hash rate will cause a significant percentage of the market participants to sell their Bitcoin holdings and drive the market price down markedly. A selfish pool would therefore always have an incentive to remain smaller than 50% (a < ½ ) in order to maximize revenues.

Duffield & Hagan (2014) argued that abrupt reward halving could cause large distortions to the mining network as incentives and profitability would immediately shift. Recall that block rewards are reduced by 50% every four years (or 210.000 blocks). They argue that this abrupt shift adversely affects miners, as revenue streams are shifted, profitability calculations have to be adapted and many miners may be driven out due to suddenly changing conditions that can make it uneconomical for them to continue their mining operations. Courtois et al. (2013) also claimed that this artificial 4 year reward cycle is very questionable and causes a significant portion of the miner network to become abruptly unprofitable. Kroll et al. (2013) argued that increasing specialization in mining hardware continuously increases the barriers to entry for miners and results into a more concentration of the mining network, which is then comprised of peers that are less reliable than a larger, and more decentralized set of miners. The further argued that miners loosing profitability due to substantial bitcoin price declines could lead to a death spiral that reinforces price declines due to lower mining rate and loss of confidence.

Another potential flaw in the incentive scheme for miners is discussed by Babaioff et al. (2012). Block reward half-life is set to reduce Bitcoin supply exponentially and over time to shift mining incentives from block rewards to transaction fees. Currently, 3600 BTC are mined every day and about 50 BTC are transacted in form on transaction fee. [80] Here relies another incentiveincompatible problem, as network nodes have an incentive to withhold information about transactions that include fees from other nodes. Any other node that is made aware of these transactions would compete to verify the transaction first in order to obtain the associated fees. As such, there is an incentive for nodes to not propagate these transactions as this increases the chance to claim the fees themselves. With each income shift from block rewards to transaction fees, the incentive to withhold transactions will become more pronounced. As a result, decentralized verification and consensus finding about a single history of transactions is threatened and the network would be slowed down considerably and lose core characteristics. In addition, Buterin (2014) identified a 'tragedies of the commons' problem with Bitcoin's fee system.

80 c.p. Kroll et al. (2013), p.12

As transaction fees are voluntary and only incurred by the miner that validated the block with transactions that he chose to include, the cost of propagating these transactions through the network is borne almost completely by other nodes. He further stated that miners have an incentive to only include transactions for which their benefit exceeds the cost of including them. Decker & Wattenhofer (2013) emphasized that the current method of network information propagation is subject to delays depending on block size and inconsistency of synchronizing the block chain between peers.

They find that due to network shortcomings, the probability for a Bitcoin fork is about 1.78% and that at each time a block is found, 11.37 seconds of the entire network hash rate is wasted, causing an accordingly long delay. Miners who dedicate their hardware to a fork that will become orphaned after a few blocks will have wasted their resources.

With the substitution of bitcoin rewards by fee rewards, it is doubtful that the current scheme of both no fees and partly voluntary fees for transactions can be sustained. Kaskaloglu (2014) predicted an inevitable end to the near-zero transaction fee regime of Bitcoin as fees will be a necessary component of the protocol in order to sustain a large enough miner network when block rewards are reduced. Andreesen (2013) argued that the dominating cost for a miner to include more transactions in their blocks is an "orphan cost". Larger blocks take longer to be sent to other nodes and being validated by them. Thus, miners risk being outrun by smaller blocks that – if accepted faster – would supersede his block and leave it orphaned. A rational miner should therefore demand a fee of 0.0008 BTC (at the current block reward of 25 BTC) for each transaction to compensate his risk.[81] However, this issue could be solved by imposing e.g. fixed-size headers, which would eliminate speed advantages that result of excluding transactions.

81 c.p. Andresen (2013), https://gist.github.com/gavinandresen/5044482, 21.08.2014

Figure 37: Threats to Mining and Decentralization

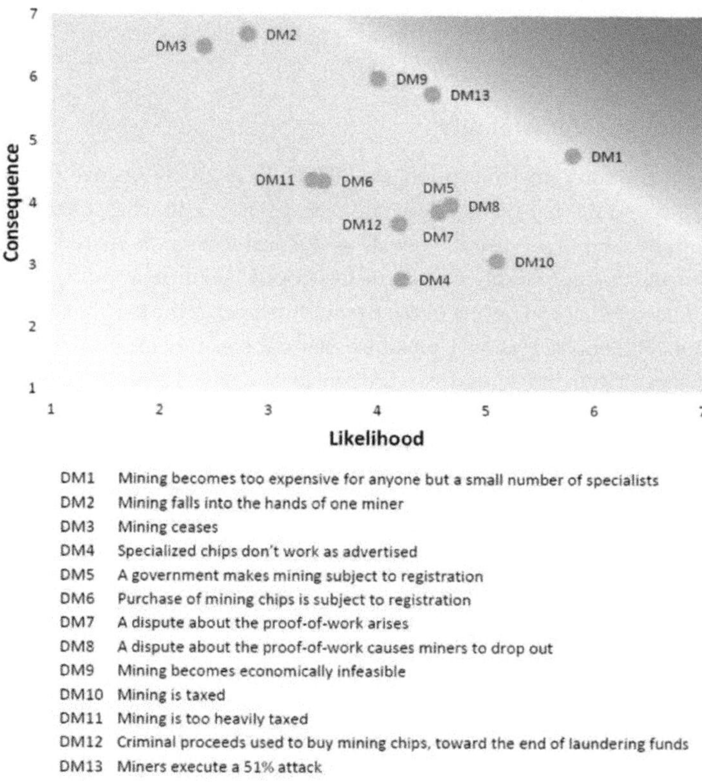


Source: Bitcoin Foundation (2014), www.bitcoinfoundation.org, 29.07.2014.

A functioning mining network is essential for the security of the network. In a risk analysis news brief, the Bitcoin Foundation (2014) provided the following assessment of major risks to the mining network. It can be stated that mining concentration represents the biggest threat to the network, which highlights the importance of efficient mining incentive schemes that discourage centralization.

It can be concluded that the current mining incentive scheme is in fact flawed in several aspects levels and could eventually be changed at a future point in time in order to eliminate current disincentives present in Bitcoin's core system – the mining network. It is very likely that zero-fee or near-zero transactions fees will have to be abolished at some point in the future time. Thus Bitcoin's current low cost characteristic is not likely to prevail. Mining is the core technological basis of the entire decentralized network and thus key to Bitcoin's security and long-term prospects. However, in its current form it is hardware intensive, subject to network propagation delays and flawed incentives.

## 4.5 Private Key Vulnerability

There is a common misconception about Bitcoin as many believe that they are simply files of data that are filed on data storage media. In truth, bitcoins exist on thousands of computers simultaneously as the protocol uses a shared database. As such, bitcoins cannot simply be lost or destroyed when their storage medium is compromised. What can be lost or destroyed, however, is the key that allows access to bitcoins. Bitcoins are 'stored' on addresses and can only be accessed and transferred when an individual possesses the private key, which is required to sign transactions and from which the public key and the Bitcoin address are derived from. Loss of bitcoins must therefore refer to actual loss of the means of accessing them – the private key. Barber et al. (2012) argued that system failures, malware and human errors are among the main reasons for loss of bitcoins. In all evaluated cases either private keys were permanently inaccessible or knowledge of the private keys was obtained third parties, who were subsequently able to access the bitcoins relating to these keys. They proposed several possible solutions that can be introduced to Bitcoin in order increase safety.

Knowledge of the private key is equivalent to possession of the bitcoins that are stored on the related Bitcoin address. Anyone who obtains another person's private key can send the stored bitcoins to any other address to which the original owner does not have access, or exchange them for products and services. Transactions are non-reversible and pseudonymity of addresses protect the identity of the perpetrator. Meiklejohn et al. (2013) argued that many forms of interaction with Bitcoin services involve the necessity that the service provider also knows the users private key. Therefore they argued that control defined solely by knowledge of the private key is not well defined. In fact, security vulnerabilities of Bitcoin applications and services bear the risk of compromising private keys. Instances such as the compromising of Bitcoin transactions through Android wallets[82] or social engineering

[82] c.p. Klyubin (2013), http://android-developers.blogspot.co.il/2013/08/some-securerandom-thoughts.html, 03.06.2014

attacks on wallet service Inputio[83] support this claim. Rogers (2014) listed a number of ways how through botnets, phishing or malware bitcoin exchanges or mining pools are attacked and linked to a list of over 150 different malware types that are dedicated to specifically targeting Bitcoin wallet files containing private keys.

If private keys are lost, forgotten or deleted, users permanently loose access to their funds. As it is infeasible to derive a private key from a public key or a bitcoin address, loss of the private key inevitably implies loss of bitcoins too. Barber et al. (2012) referred to BTC that are subject to unknown or lost private keys as "zombie coins." Bitcoin inventor Satoshi Nakamoto was aware of the problem of non-recoverable bitcoins but did not offer a solution to this apparent issue. In an online conversation from June 21st, 2010 he stated: "Lost coins only make everyone else's coins worth slightly more. Think of it as a donation to everyone."[84]

Due to the fact that securing private keys is such an important issue for Bitcoin users, several specialized services that aim to provide secure wallets or specialized encryption services have emerged. This implies, however, giving access of one's private key to a third party and thus involving an intermediary may or may not be trusted.

Benger et al. (2014) report that they were able to obtain private key recovery for Bitcoin's secp256k1 curve when a sufficient number of signatures were made with the same private key. They recommended to limit the number of times a private key should be used, and periodically switch to a new public/private key pair to reduce the chances of success for such an attack. Another potential vulnerability is described by Neagle (2013). Default wallets are created and stored without proper encryption, causing access to these wallets is significantly easier to achieve for attackers than in the case of encrypted wallets. Moreover, it is possible to access older copies of certain wallets, when users employ password backup facilities. Newer versions of a wallet can be accessed by obtaining an older version of the same wallet with an outdated password, as it still contains the same information about the public-private key pair and corresponding address.[85] Neagle (2013)'s example

83 c.p. Dent (2013), http://www.engadget.com/2013/11/09/bitcoin-hijack-1-2-million/, 03.06.2014

84 c.p. Marion (2014), http://crypt.la/2014/01/06/satoshi-nakamoto-quotes/, 18.04.2014

85 c.p. Neagle (2013), http://www.networkworld.com/article/2167062/software/10-scary-facts-about-bitcoin.html, 21.04.2014

shows that it is of utmost importance to keep information concerning a private key strictly secret and protected against any forms of cyber-attacks or fraud.

Goldfeder et al. (2014) elaborated how wallets that store Bitcoin private keys are subject to different types of risks.

Figure 38: Taxonomy of Wallet Threats

| Adversary | Hot wallet | Cold wallet |
|---|---|---|
| Insider | Vulnerable by default: our methods are necessary | Reduces to physical security by default: our methods can help |
| External (network) | Reduces to network security by default: our methods can help | Safe |

Source: Goldfeder et al. (2014), p. 5

Recall that hot wallets are connected to online devices and cold wallets are a secure means of offline storage for bitcoins. From the perspective of Bitcoin businesses private keys are at risk from both internal and external sources. However, individuals may also face the threat of relatives of acquaintances obtaining private keys in order to steal funds.

It can thus be stated that Bitcoin private keys themselves might very well represent an exceptionally secure form of securing funds, but they are also a key risk to Bitcoin users, as they are only strings of alphanumeric characters that can be lost, stolen or obtained through other types of attacks. As Bitcoin is native to the Internet and requires third party services to be exchanged or stored in secure wallets, private keys are at risk from malicious software, phishing and hacking attacks. It can, however, be expected that technological innovation and development within the Bitcoin economy will over time mitigate these risks accordingly. Nevertheless, properly handling private key security is in most cases the responsibility of users themselves, which in turn requires relevant knowledge about encrypting wallets, securely storing private keys, creating backups or choosing the right third party service providers.

Private key vulnerability is, however, a well-known issue within the Bitcoin community. Multisignature wallets that require more than one but not all private keys in order to sign a transaction are one method for mitigating these risks. They allow storing private keys in several locations and different types of wallets. Goldfeder et al. (2014) argued that current Bitcoin technology is inadequate for both business and individuals, especially due to irreversibility, automation and pseudonymity characteristics. As a solution, they developed threshold signature wallets that split control over wallets, enable two-factor security, delegation and secure bookkeeping. Threshold signatures have been proven to be compatible with ECDSA and the Bitcoin block chain.

## 4.6 Irreversible Transactions

What is advertised by many Bitcoin proponents as a benefit that prevents chargebacks, may also be one of its most fatal flaws. The Bitcoin protocol does not allow reversion or annulation of transactions. Bitcoin transaction are executed once the private key of the elliptic-curve key pair is used to sign the transaction, validated by other nodes and included into a block that has been linked to the block chain, after which it enters the entire history of transactions and is final.

This feature exposes Bitcoin users to additional operational risks:

- Incorrect input size of transactions
- Incorrect receiver address
- Fraudulent payments
- Software errors

Should a user realize that a receiver address was mistyped or the declared transaction size was incorrect, there is no way to undo or reverse the transaction. Addresses and private keys consist of a case-sensitive strings of randomly generated characters, which are therefore vulnerable to typing errors. While the chance to accidentally enter a different address that actually exists is negligible, the risk of software bugs or human errors that result into using an incorrect address that actually does exist (e.g. previously copy-pasted address, accidental use of different address, incorrectly referenced address) has to be taken into account.[86] Moreover, the receiver in many cases could be unknown and his identity protected by Bitcoin's pseudonymity. Nakamoto (2008) designed the Bitcoin protocol as a means of transaction that does not require third-party trust. However, within the range of chargebacks, incorrect transaction inputs or fraud, the lack of reversibility

[86] c.p. Shubber (2014), http://www.coindesk.com/9-biggest-screwups-bitcoin-history/, 09.06.2014

certainly is a question of trust. Whereas legitimate businesses would certainly allow disputes and correction of erroneous transactions, there is little incentive to do so in peer-to-peer transactions between peers with protected identities.

These features add vulnerability and risks to bitcoin transactions that are further amplified by Bitcoin being almost exclusively exchanged over the internet. Weaver (2013) noted that "If bitcoin really is the internet applied to money ... then it, too, should have a "back" button." He further argued that without such a function, users can only prevent fraud but do not have the means to actually detect and mitigate fraud.[87] Goldfeder et al. (2014) stated that the prevent-detect-recover scheme that traditional financial institutions have in place in order to mitigate fraud is not applicable to Bitcoin and therefore more resources must be spent on prevention.

As already discussed, Bitcoin's key vulnerability comes from the private key. Possessing one's private key is equivalent to possession of the bitcoins stored on that address is derived from the according public-private key pair. One can use the private key to send BTC to one's own address or any temporary active address and is protected by Bitcoin's pseudonymity. An attacker could utilize newly generated addresses, tumblers or mixers to hide his tracks and spend or keep the stolen bitcoins with negligible risk of being exposed. Litke & Stewart (2014) described tumblers as a means of obfuscating the flow of bitcoin transactions by mixing bitcoins of one user with bitcoins of a number of others and distributing them to completely new addresses at different times.

There are several examples that exemplify the vulnerability that private keys are subject to. A user of a popular online Bitcoin forum reported that he had accidentally sent 800 BTC to an address that belonged to the bankrupt Mt. Gox bitcoin exchange (address: 113MmkyjjH6zS9VMvbwrhBNoMe6upzdvNC). The transacted amount was worth approx.

$500.000 at the time the transaction was conducted. Notably, the defunct exchange was contacted by the user and refunded the entire amount upon learning about the incident.[88] Another user who participated in the funding of Nascar driver Josh Wise, accidentally added an additional zero to his intended donation amount,

87 Weaver (2013), http://www.wired.com/2013/11/once-you-use-bitcoin-you-cant-go-back-and-that-irreversibilityis-its-fatal-flaw/, 09.06.2014

88 c.p. Gillespie (2014a), http://coinwrite.org/bitcoin-user-accidently-sends-800-btc-old-mt-gox-address/, 01.06.2014

thereby sending 20 million Dogecoin instead of 2 million, thus accidentally donating approximately $15,000 instead of $1500.[89] Examples such as these illustrate that the lack of a refund option can potentially cause considerable financial damage to users and constitute a flaw in the protocol that has to be addressed. Nevertheless, Englander (2014) argued that if fraud and chargebacks can be reduced or eliminated by Bitcoin this is constitutes a significant benefit over other transaction methods because it would make Bitcoin transactions and related services much more economical.

## 4.7 Information Asymmetry

When compared to traditional banking or non-bank payment transaction providers, Bitcoin puts its users at significantly higher risk. As Bitcoin lacks a trusted intermediary that accumulates knowledge and experience and uses its economies of scale to provide an array of secure services, users of Bitcoin have to inform themselves about the risks involved with using it. Banks and nonbanks limit operational risks and specialize in identifying potential threats, avoiding them or actively pursuing them. Once a dishonest market participant is found they do not provide services to these fraudulent or malicious services and thereby customers are protected through the trusted intermediary. If banks or payment providers however provided such services to dishonest market participants, transactions can be reversed or victims of such actions can be compensated by the bank or payment service.

Bitcoin lacks this important feature, as transactions are non-reversible once they have been conducted. Fraudulent peers can create nearly an infinite number of addresses and are largely protected by pseudonymity.The European Central Bank (2012) identified a case for information asymmetry, as users of Bitcoin can relatively easy obtain Bitcoin applications, but are let alone when it comes to informing themselves about the variety of potential risks they are exposing themselves. They have to inform themselves about which services or which peers to trust. The Bitcoin Foundation sponsored website bitcoin.org offers a "What you need to know" section, but emphasized that it is ultimately the user's responsibility to identify trusted market participant and secure their wallet.[90]

---

89 c.p. Gill (2014), http://www.coindesk.com/moolah-founder-accidently-donates-20-million-dogecoin-to-sponsornascar-driver/ 01.06.2014

90 c.p. Bitcoin Project (n.d.), https://bitcoin.org/en/you-need-to-know, 02.06.2014

Litke & Stewart (2014) outlined a number of best practices for cryptocurrency adoption and noted a number of ways to mitigate risks associated with handling cryptocurrencies. The emphasized that e.g. Bitcoin wallets represent a key source of risks, as proper handling and risk mitigation requires some level of technical knowledge from customers. As there is no insurance organization for Bitcoin, users are responsible for their losses. Their analysis of potential risks and best practice recommendations for each type of wallets further illustrates that Bitcoin usage requires some level of education about networks, wallets and encryption.

It is logically to assume that services that reduce this information asymmetry for customers will play a larger role within the Bitcoin ecosystem. Cryptocurrencies are designed to enable trust-less financial transactions that do not require intermediaries. However, these intermediaries play an important role in securing customers wealth. In a trust-based customer-institution relationship information asymmetry is mitigated by means of e.g. signaling, screening and contracts.Until its demise in February 2014, Mt. Gox had been the most popular and well-known exchange for bitcoins, despite many rumors and speculation about its solvency that started months before it eventual bankruptcy. Many more experienced users, who also frequented online forums where these speculations emerged, left Mt. Gox months before the exchange halted withdrawals.

Bitcoin advocated tend to promote Bitcoin with outrageous statements such as "Bitcoin will be bigger than facebook"[91], "One Bitcoin could be worth $1 million."[92], or "Here's how Bitcoin is like the early '90s Internet"[93]. This certainly attracts a lot of unsophisticated people who cannot properly assess the risks involved with an experimental technology that is prone to price bubbles and corrections. The lack of regulation and absence of the necessity for businesses to inform customers about the risks involved with Bitcoin, certainly adds to the information asymmetry.

---

91 Channer (2014), http://www.theguardian.com/technology/2014/may/19/winklevoss-twins-bitcoin-bigger-thanfacebook-investors, 05.06.2014

92 CNBC (2014), http://www.cnbc.com/id/101552753, 05.06.2014

93 Bloomberg TV (2014), http://www.bloomberg.com/video/here-s-how-bitcoin-is-like-early-90-s-internetdU0H7ADwTl6arrq122kHPg.html, 23.06.2014

## 4.8 Fraud and Hacking

Bitcoin operates in the environment of networks like the Internet and remains largely unregulated. Naturally, as it is something that is unregulated and of value, it attracts various individuals and groups of the dishonest kind who want to capitalize on it by defrauding people who own bitcoins. The cryptocurrency's pseudonymity and non-reversibility adds to this attraction.

Bitcoin itself may be decentralized and allow transactions without middle-men, but the economy that developed around it is still highly centralized and often operated by less professional personnel. Moore & Christin (2013) evaluated 40 different bitcoin exchanges and found that 18 have been closed at the time their article was published. Exchanges close for various reasons, some are hacked and robbed of their funds, forcing them to shut down. Others intentionally close down and keep customer funds. In some cases the operators of an exchange and the location of its incorporation remained unknown entirely.

Figure 39: Daily Volatility to Risk of Breach Relationship

| | | coef. | exp(coef.) | Std. Err.) | Significance |
|---|---|---|---|---|---|
| log(Daily vol.)$_i$ | $\beta_1$ | −0.173 | 0.840 | 0.072 | $p = 0.0156$ |
| Breached$_i$ | $\beta_2$ | 0.857 | 2.36 | 0.572 | $p = 0.1338$ |
| AML$_i$ | $\beta_3$ | 0.004 | 1.004 | 0.042 | $p = 0.9221$ |
| log-rank test: $Q$=7.01 ($p = 0.0715$), $R^2 = 0.145$ | | | | | |

Source: Moore & Christin (2013) p. 4

They furthermore find that smaller exchanges and exchanges with low trading volume are more likely to shut down, while the presence of anti-money laundering (AML) practices does not show significant correlation with shut downs.

Transaction volume can be seen as an indicator for popularity and degree of awareness about the exchange and is shown to correlate positively with the chances of being breached by attackers.

The number of months the exchange is operating since inception can give some idea about how well the exchange is managed. One could assume that older exchanges are more experienced with fraudulent behavior and hacking attempts. As such, it can be seen that the age of an exchange is almost significantly negatively correlated with experiencing a breach.

Figure 40: Maturity of Business to Breach Relationship

| | coef. | Odds-ratio | 95% conf. int. | Significance |
|---|---|---|---|---|
| Intercept | −4.304 | 0.014 | (0.0002,0.211) | $p = 0.0131$ |
| log(Daily vol.) | 0.514 | 1.672 | (1.183,2.854) | $p = 0.0176$ |
| Months operational | −0.104 | 0.901 | (0.771,1.025) | $p = 0.1400$ |
| Model fit: $\chi^2 = 10.3$, $p = 0.00579$ | | | | |

Source: Moore & Christin (2013) p. 6

High-volume exchanges are therefore more likely to be breached but also less likely to shut down. However, these values just give an indication about which exchanges customers should choose in order to trade bitcoins against fiat currencies or alternative cryptocurrencies. Operational risk is present to a considerable degree within the Bitcoin market. Moore & Christin (2013, p. 5) stated that "For instance, Mt. Gox and Intersango are less likely to close than other exchanges. Meanwhile, Vircurex (established in December 2011 and breached in January 2013) continues to operate despite low transaction volumes and a survival function that estimates one-year survival at only 20%.". However, as of February 2014, both Mt. Gox and Intersango were shut down, while Vircurex is still operational. Chapman (2011) detailed the events during which the Mt. Gox was successfully hacked and attackers managed to steal millions worth of Bitcoin, while driving the price down to from about $17 to $0.01. Cambell (2014) reported that Mt. Gox allegedly faced 150.000 hacking attempts per second in a massive distributed denial-of-service (DDoS) during the final demise of the exchange. The final attack on Mt. Gox allegedly led to the theft of more than 750,000 bitcoins that customers had stored at the exchange. This represents the biggest loss of BTC during a single event and was worth an estimated $575 million.[94]

This was, however, only one of several major attacks on the formerly largest bitcoin exchange. Mick (2011) listed major attacks on Mt. Gox, including an account compromising attack, which crashed the exchange price from about $17.50 to $0.01 per bitcoin in 2011.

94 c.p. Campbell (2014), http://www.telegraph.co.uk/finance/currency/10686698/Bitcoin-exchange-MtGox-faced150000-hack-attacks-every-second.html, 08.06.2014

Figure 41: Mt. Gox Hacker-Induced Flash Crash during 2011

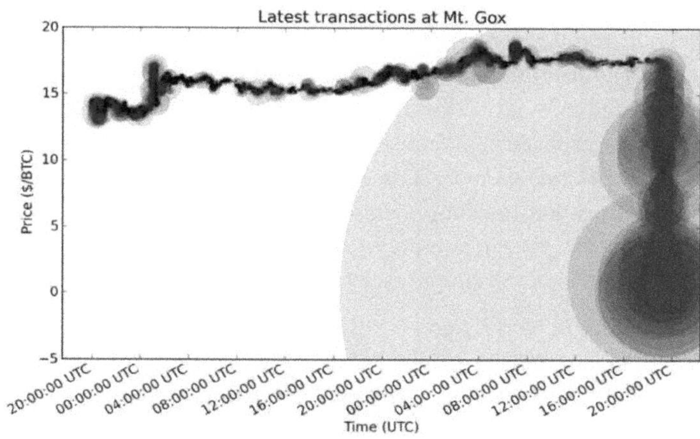


Source: Mick (2011), dailytech.com, 22.08.2014

Bitcoin's history is rich with failed exchanges, theft, fraud and crises. The demise of Mt Gox, Flexcoin and Poloniex caused intense damage to the Bitcoin economy and led many to criticize the validity of the cryptocurrency itself.[95] Hern (2014) provided a list of major Bitcoin-related hacks and shows that during the past years, a significant number of bitcoins owners have lost their funds due to increasingly professional attacks. Hern also reported on a number of cases in which customers were defrauded by exchanges or other Bitcoin services.[96] Another more comprehensive list is maintained on the BitcoinTalk Forum.[97]

The non-reversibility of transactions that is distinctive for Bitcoin facilitates fraudulent attacks. For instance, successful scamming attacks involve exchanging bitcoins for fiat money through PayPal. After receiving the cryptocurrency funds, scammers can dispute the transaction and claim that they have not actually received any funds and thus demand a refund from the payment intermediary. Despite all transactions being public and verifiable through the block chain, scammers are protected by Bitcoin's pseudonymity. As a result it is difficult to prove that the

95 c.p. Biggs (2014), http://techcrunch.com/2014/03/04/fools-and-their-bitcoin/, 28.06.2014

96 c.p. Hern (2014), http://www.theguardian.com/technology/2014/mar/18/history-of-bitcoin-hacks-alternativecurrency, 28.06.2014

97 c.p. dree12 (2012), https://bitcointalk.org/index.php?topic=83794.0, 29.06.2014

transaction has been conducted successfully as identities are not directly verifiable. In practice PayPal has been repeatedly compelled to issue a refund to the scammer.[98] While fraud is generally an important issue at the moment, one can expect that if Bitcoin turns out to become a major means of payment, more sophisticated businesses and new services would develop around it and mitigate the risk that customers are exposed to. Kaminsky (2013) emphasized that Bitcoin offers a profoundly effective system to track thieves as the origins of bitcoins are transparent and the network has to stamp their approval on transactions that involve stolen bitcoins. This offers the possibility to adapt the protocol in order to tag and immobilize stolen bitcoins and simplify the identification of perpetrators.

While examples of hacking and fraud within the Bitcoin ecosystem currently account to a large proportion of losses of bitcoins, those issues are not inherently due to Bitcoin features, but rather a symptom of its still early stage in its developments. Given Bitcoin's transparency and the possibility to easily track stolen funds, it is logical to assume that security will actually be more effective in a more developed Bitcoin market

However, there are persistent issues that are attributable to Bitcoin's technology. Notably, Karame et al. (2012) have attempted thousands of double-spending attacks without any penalty from the network. They were also able to exploit slow transaction confirmation times in an experimental setting in order to successfully double-spend bitcoins for fast payments. In fact, when transactions were conducted fast enough, they found a significant rate of success for double-spending attacks irrespective of network topology. Litke & Stewart (2014) addressed a myriad of risks that are present in the usage of different types of Bitcoin wallets. Accessing bitcoin funds through malware and hacking attacks on wallets is still an issue despite significant improvements of wallet security technology and services. While it is incredibly difficult to attack the network or cryptographically secured aspects of the Bitcoin technology, third party entities such as mining pools, online exchanges and wallet services still represent points of failure that can be attacked by conventional means.

[98] c.p. Jones (2014), http://www.theguardian.com/money/2014/mar/01/paypal-bitcoin-scam-ebay, 28.06.2014

In conclusion, Bitcoin offers very high security for but as it is native to the Internet there are many ways bitcoin funds can still be stolen. This can be mitigated, however, if more sophisticated businesses and services develop within the Bitcoin economy or existing businesses enter this market. Thus, this weakness is not one that is inherit to Bitcoin.

## 4.9 Confirmation Times

Nakamoto (2008) emphasized the importance to prevent attackers from generating alternative chains that include falsified transactions in his conceptualization. Malicious nodes in the network can in fact not do so, as honest nodes will not accept blocks that include invalid transactions, but they can reverse their recent transactions. We have discussed the details of alternative forks and orphaned blocks in the block chain. An attacker with sufficient hash power can create such an alternative chain and start a 'race' between the honest chain and its malicious alternative chain.

Nakamoto described this as a Binominal Random Walk that is akin to a Gambler's Ruin problem[99]. An attacker would create an alternative chain and compete against honest notes that attempt to catch up and let the honest chain prevail in the block chain. This race is described as:

$$q_z = \begin{pmatrix} 1 & if\ p \leq q \\ (q/p)^2 & if\ p > q \end{pmatrix}$$

$p$ = probability of an honest node to find the next block

$q$ = probability of the attacker to find the next block

$qz$ = probability that the attacker will ever catch up from z blocks behind

As long as $p > q$, that is assuming that the honest nodes dominate the dishonest nodes of the network, the probability of q will drop exponentially with each block that the attacker has to catch up with.

Courtois (2014) illustrated the race of two conflicting forks during a double-spending attack. An attacker attempts to produce a forked chain of blocks in order to

[99] c.p. Nakamoto (2008), p.6-7

modify the recipient of one or more some large transactions that he has generated himself.

Figure 42: Bitcoin Fork during Double-Spending Attack

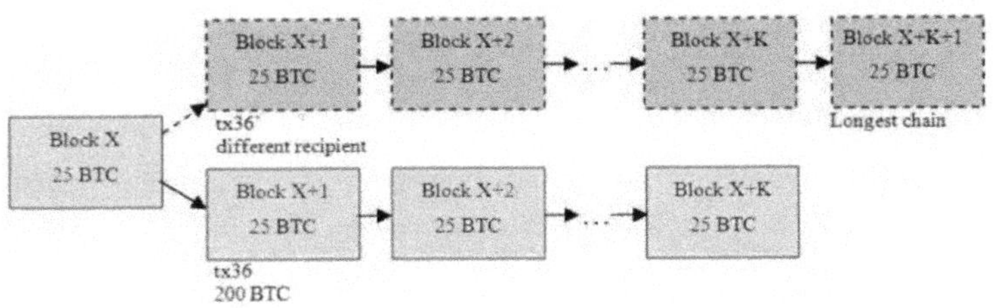


Source: Courtois (2014), p.21

Such an attack, if performed successfully, will open a time window for attackers during which they can also convince a seller of a good or a service in exchange for Bitcoin that they have sent the BTC. As long as the time window is open, a seller that looks at the block chain will see a confirmed transaction that will appear only as long as the attacker is ahead in the abovementioned race.

As a general rule that has been propagated by the Bitcoin community, anyone who exchanges bitcoins against goods or services should wait for six confirmations to be absolutely sure that the transaction was genuine and is included in the longest chain of blocks. This would amount to about one hour of time until parties in of an exchange for goods or services can be assured that the payment in form of bitcoin funds was conducted successfully and will not be reversed due to block chain reorganization. Nakamoto (2008) estimated the probabilities for double-spending attacks based on different numbers of confirmations. If dishonest nodes account for 10% of the hashing network the probabilities per number of confirmations are as follows:

Table 8: Double Spending Probabilities

| Confirmations | Probabilities | | Odds |
|---|---|---|---|
| 1 | z=1 | P=0.2045873 | 1 to 4.89 |
| 2 | z=2 | P=0.0509779 | 1 to 19.62 |
| 3 | z=3 | P=0.0131722 | 1 to 75.92 |
| 4 | z=4 | P=0.0034552 | 1 to 289.42 |
| 5 | z=5 | P=0.0009137 | 1 to 1094.45 |
| 6 | z=6 | P=0.0002428 | 1 to 4118.62 |

Source: Nakamoto (2008), p. 8

What can be seen is that there is a certain risk of being exposed to double-spending fraud when using Bitcoin. While these types of attacks are difficult to conduct and require a lot of resources, market participants cannot ignore this risk. Notably, however, such an attack would only be profitable if the value that is exchanged for bitcoins is above a certain threshold, as obtaining enough collective hashing power and forking and alternative chain is expensive. Nakamoto (2008) provided the aforementioned calculations under the assumption that an attacker obtains 10% of the network hash rate. However, no indication is given about this assumption and why a number of colluding dishonest peers should not be able to amass significantly higher portions of the network hash rate. Clearly, during the time interval between zero confirmations and two or three confirmations, Bitcoin transactions expose users to the highest risk. Recall that for each confirmation one block has to be mined and linked to the block chain and that the risk decreases exponentially with each confirmation.

The lack of instantaneous confirmation of transactions can certainly be a significant impediment to businesses that accept Bitcoin. Karame et al. (2012) analyzed the required time to confirm Bitcoin transactions and found that they can be described with a shifted geometric distribution. The average confirmation times are about 9 minutes and 54 seconds, but its standard deviation lies at 881.24 seconds or about 15 minutes. Only 64% of observed blocks confirm within less than 10 minutes, whereas 36% require between 10 and 40 minutes to actually be confirmed. Because of their analysis they conclude that Bitcoin is not suitable for fast payments, such as vendors, supermarkets, vending machines and the like. Moreover, they showed that fast payments have a considerable success rate in double-spending attacks due.

The fact that transaction confirmation is delayed by a significant time amount and double-spending can theoretically still occur until a certain number of confirmations have been achieved make Bitcoin transactions impractical in certain scenarios. Barber et al. (2012) proposed a short-term bank service or re-parameterizing of confirmation times to shorten times between confirmations. However, the first approach would result into paying fees on otherwise cost-free transactions, while the second approach would potentially slow network communication and increase the risk of forking an alternative chain. Similarly, Sompolinsky & Zohar (2013) reflected on shortening the time between block creation and therefore confirmation generation, but emphasized that this would lead to a sharp increase in forks and orphaned blocks, which causes resilience against double-spending attacks to decrease. As the current 10 minute scheme is hardcoded into to protocol, both block sizes and transaction volumes increase the chances of fork creation. Moreover, Nakamoto's assumption that the time to propagate a block through the network is shorter than the time between two consecutive blocks would no longer hold. Karame et al. (2012) argued that a basic countermeasure could be a simple alert system that would inform the network whenever two or more transactions are received that share similar inputs and outputs.

Sompolinsky & Zohar (2013) developed and alternative to Bitcoin's current longest chain rule, called the Greedy Heaviest Observed Sub Tree (GHOST). This alternative chain rule would allow intense acceleration of block creation and confirmation times. They estimated that this chain rule would result into a rate of 1 block per second at 10,000 transaction hashes per block.

In conclusion, the transaction confirmation scheme currently active within the Bitcoin protocol represents a major impediment to the future prospects of Bitcoin. Confirmation times are slow and suffer from significant standard deviation. Many payment scenarios depend on quick verification of transacted funds and thus the use of Bitcoin in these scenarios would be severely impeded by the need to wait for several confirmations. Furthermore, double-spending is shown to still constitute a major risk for fast payment scenarios. The alternative chain rule developed by Sompolinsky & Zohar (2013) currently represents the most promising solution to these issues.

## 4.10 Deflationary Bias

One of Bitcoin's signature features is its finite money supply. The protocol is designed so that there is a fixed cap to the total supply of bitcoins at about 21 million BTC. Ren (2014, p. 10) argued that Nakamoto created "a modern digital version of the gold standard world in which the money supply is fixed rather than subject to increase via printing press." The Bitcoin protocol is designed to keep the approximate time of block creation at about 10 minutes for each block. If the network hash rate exceeds the current difficulty level, blocks will be solved faster and the difficulty will increase at the next difficulty retargeting. Block rewards that compensate miners with bitcoins (and fee revenue) are not held constant, but decrease geometrically by reducing the amount of bitcoins per solved block approximately every 4 years. It is presumed that this rate was chosen in order to replicate the assumed level of growth of goods that can be exchanged in order to achieve stable prices.[100]

Table 9 illustrates the rate of bitcoin creation until the cap is reached around the year 2141.

[100] c.p. Hajdarbegovic (2014), http://www.coindesk.com/bitcoin-mining-can-longer-ignore-moores-law/, 11.10.2014

Table 9: Projected Bitcoin Money Supply

| Year | Block | Reward Era | BTC/block | Beginning BTC | End BTC | BTC Added | BTC Increase | End BTC % of Limit |
|---|---|---|---|---|---|---|---|---|
| 2009 | - | 1 | 50.000000 | - | 10,500,000.000 | 10,500,000.0000 | - | 50.000000003% |
| 2013 | 210,000 | 2 | 25.000000 | 10,500,000.000 | 15,750,000.000 | 5,250,000.0000 | 50.000000000% | 75.000000004% |
| 2017 | 420,000 | 3 | 12.500000 | 15,750,000.000 | 18,375,000.000 | 2,625,000.0000 | 16.666666667% | 87.500000005% |
| 2021 | 630,000 | 4 | 6.250000 | 18,375,000.000 | 19,687,500.000 | 1,312,500.0000 | 7.142857143% | 93.750000005% |
| 2025 | 840,000 | 5 | 3.125000 | 19,687,500.000 | 20,343,750.000 | 656,250.0000 | 3.333333333% | 96.875000006% |
| 2029 | 1,050,000 | 6 | 1.562500 | 20,343,750.000 | 20,671,875.000 | 328,125.0000 | 1.612903226% | 98.437500006% |
| 2033 | 1,260,000 | 7 | 0.781250 | 20,671,875.000 | 20,835,937.500 | 164,062.5000 | 0.793650794% | 99.218750006% |
| 2037 | 1,470,000 | 8 | 0.390625 | 20,835,937.500 | 20,917,968.750 | 82,031.2500 | 0.393700787% | 99.609375006% |
| 2041 | 1,680,000 | 9 | 0.195313 | 20,917,968.750 | 20,958,984.375 | 41,015.6250 | 0.196078431 % | 99.804687506% |
| 2045 | 1,890,000 | 10 | 0.097656 | 20,958,984.375 | 20,979,492.188 | 20,507.8125 | 0.097847358% | 99.902343756% |

| | | | | | | | |
|---|---|---|---|---|---|---|---|
| 2049 | 2,100,000 | 11 | 0.048828 | 20,979,492.188 | 20,989,746.094 | 10,253.9063 | 0.048875855%<br>99.951171881% |
| 2053 | 2,310,000 | 12 | 0.024414 | 20,989,746.094 | 20,994,873.047 | 5,126.9531 | 0.024425989%<br>99.975585943% |
| 2057 | 2,520,000 | 13 | 0.012207 | 20,994,873.047 | 20,997,436.523 | 2,563.4766 | 0.012210012%<br>99.987792975% |
| 2061 | 2,730,000 | 14 | 0.006104 | 20,997,436.523 | 20,998,718.262 | 1,281.7383 | 0.006104261%<br>99.993896490% |
| 2065 | 2,940,000 | 15 | 0.003052 | 20,998,718.262 | 20,999,359.131 | 640.8691 | 0.003051944%<br>99.996948248% |
| 2069 | 3,150,000 | 16 | 0.001526 | 20,999,359.131 | 20,999,679.565 | 320.4346 | 0.001525925%<br>99.998474127% |
| 2073 | 3,360,000 | 17 | 0.000763 | 20,999,679.565 | 20,999,839.783 | 160.2173 | 0.000762951%<br>99.999237066% |
| 2077 | 3,570,000 | 18 | 0.000381 | 20,999,839.783 | 20,999,919.891 | 80.1086 | 0.000381473%<br>99.999618536% |
| 2081 | 3,780,000 | 19 | 0.000191 | 20,999,919.891 | 20,999,959.946 | 40.0543 | 0.000190736%<br>99.999809271% |
| 2085 | 3,990,000 | 20 | 0.000095 | 20,999,959.946 | 20,999,979.973 | 20.0272 | 0.000095368%<br>99.999904638% |
| 2089 | 4,200,000 | 21 | 0.000048 | 20,999,979.973 | 20,999,989.986 | 10.0136 | 0.000047684%<br>99.999952322% |
| 2093 | 4,410,000 | 22 | 0.000024 | 20,999,989.986 | 20,999,994.993 | 5.0068 | 0.000023842%<br>99.999976164% |
| 2097 | 4,620,000 | 23 | 0.000012 | 20,999,994.993 | 20,999,997.497 | 2.5034 | 0.000011921%<br>99.999988085% |

| 2101 | 4,830,000 | 24 | 0.000006 | 20,999,997.497 | 20,999,998.748 | 1.2517 | 0.000005960%<br>99.999994045% |
|---|---|---|---|---|---|---|---|
| 2105 | 5,040,000 | 25 | 0.000003 | 20,999,998.748 | 20,999,999.374 | 0.6258 | 0.000002980%<br>99.999997026% |
| 2109 | 5,250,000 | 26 | 0.000001 | 20,999,999.374 | 20,999,999.687 | 0.3129 | 0.000001490%<br>99.999998516% |
| 2113 | 5,460,000 | 27 | 0.000001 | 20,999,999.687 | 20,999,999.844 | 0.1565 | 0.000000745%<br>99.999999261% |
| 2117 | 5,670,000 | 28 | 0.000000 | 20,999,999.844 | 20,999,999.922 | 0.0782 | 0.000000373%<br>99.999999633% |
| 2121 | 5,880,000 | 29 | 0.000000 | 20,999,999.922 | 20,999,999.961 | 0.0391 | 0.000000186%<br>99.999999820% |
| 2125 | 6,090,000 | 30 | 0.000000 | 20,999,999.961 | 20,999,999.980 | 0.0196 | 0.000000093%<br>99.999999913% |
| 2129 | 6,300,000 | 31 | 0.000000 | 20,999,999.980 | 20,999,999.990 | 0.0098 | 0.000000047%<br>99.999999959% |
| 2133 | 6,510,000 | 32 | 0.000000 | 20,999,999.990 | 20<br>,999,999.995 | 0.0049 | 0.000000023%<br>99.999999983% |
| 2137 | 6,720,000 | 33 | 0.000000 | 20,999,999.995 | 20,999,999.998 | 0.0024 | 0.000000012%<br>99.999999994% |
| 2141 | 6,930,000 | 34 | 0.000000 | 20,999,999.998 | 20,999,999.999 | 0.0012 | 0.000000006%<br>100.000000000% |

Source: Bitcoin Wiki, Controlled Supply, 26.04.2014

Thus it can be stated that Bitcoin's monetary base is equal to the current level of mined bitcoins. It can also be observed that the amount of existing bitcoins is set to increase very strongly at the beginning of the timeline and that money supply will decrease very rapidly after the 5th reward era.

Figure 43: Bitcoin Monetary Base and Growth

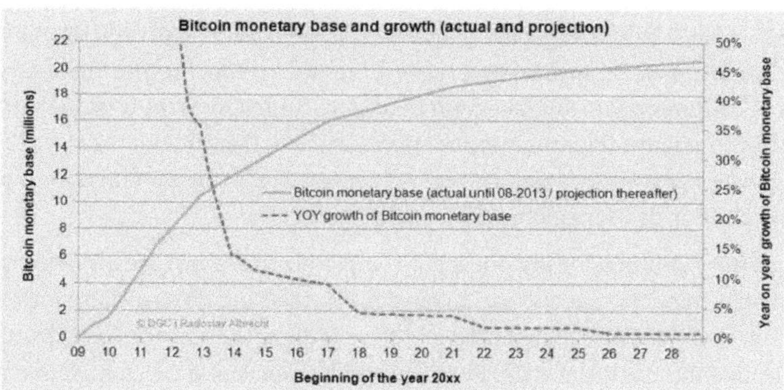


Source: Albrecht (2013), www.dgcmagazine.com, 22.07.2014.

One can assume that a deflationary pressure is present as long as demand for bitcoins is larger than the rate of bitcoin generation. In simple terms, as more market participants would buy bitcoins than bitcoins being sold on average, including newly generated BTC, prices would necessarily increase. However, as this finite supply will only be reached many decades in the future, the more pressing question is how the rate of bitcoin creation will influence the price of a single Bitcoin. How deflationary the cryptocurrency really is, will depend on complex interrelationship of the rate of adoption and whether miners, who crate new bitcoins sell them immediately in order to pay for their mining expenses or to incur profits, or hoard the coins in anticipation of higher prices in the future. Moreover, as deflation encourages hoarding of BTC, the number of bitcoins that are actually in circulation may add to the deflationary pressure of the currency. It is also important to understand how the price of bitcoins would affect this deflationary pressure. If deflation would increase the price for newly created bitcoins, how would the fixed supply of 50 new bitcoins every 10 minutes affect deflation? After all, the price of bitcoins reflects the value of fiat money that is exchanged for them.

What adds to the deflationary bias is hoarding behavior that artificially removes a significant proportion of Bitcoin's money supply from circulation. Ron & Shamir (2012) found that 78% of all existing bitcoins remain in addresses that have never moved or spent them. Meiklejohn et al. (2013) later find that 64% of existing BTC is held in such addresses and only a mere 4 million of the approximately 11 million existing bitcoins at that time were actively in circulation.

Furthermore, as bitcoins can be irretrievably lost due to hardware-, software- or human error, it can be expected that a considerable fraction of total bitcoins will in fact become lost or inaccessible over time, thus reducing the monetary base. Bitcoin's inventor Satoshi Nakamoto noted "Instead of the supply changing to keep the value the same, the supply is predetermined and the value changes. As the number of users grows, the value per coin increases. It has the potential for a positive feedback loop; as users increase, the value goes up"[101]

Deflation or inflation for Bitcoin is not completely the same case for bitcoins as for most other modern currencies. Currencies like the Dollar, Yen or Euro have a finite minimum unit and are distributed in different dimensions, whereas Bitcoin is theoretically infinitively divisible. Even a single bitcoin would be enough to make the entire Bitcoin transaction system possible.

Bergstra & de Leeuw (2013) argue that a successful establishing of Bitcoin would enable it to have a deflationary bias. Deflation would be the result of a growing customer base in relation to rate of Bitcoin creation with respect to the then large inequality between of Bitcoin ownership between early adopters and subsequent adopters. They go on to presume that if the 'expectation paradox' of Bitcoin holds true, meaning that if Bitcoin for instance survives until 2040 it must do so in a strong manner, causing price deflation to value bitcoins at very high prices and encourage hording them. This would make them impractical as a barter system. Deflation is seen as a non-desirable state for a currency by many. Barber et al. (2012) propose a possible long-term solution to the thread of deflation. Their approach would be a decentralized inflationary feedback built-in that would manage the global coin creation rate based on certain factors. Their proposal remains theoretical with the precise factors not fully defined yet. Nevertheless, an adaption of the Bitcoin protocol in order to fight overly strong deflationary characteristics, while

[101] Liu (2014), http://motherboard.vice.com/blog/quotes-from-satoshi-understanding-bitcoin-through-the-lens-ofits-enigmatic-creator, 21.07.2014

keeping the system decentralized, could be a possible solution at some point in the future. They also illustrate how deflationary expectations threaten the long-term security of the Bitcoin network, as Courtois (2014) stated that Bitcoin's restricted monetary supply is a self-defeating property. He argued that Bitcoin may suffer from excessive deflation that would be circumvented by switching to alternative cryptocurrencies. Moreover, deflationary pressure of Bitcoin will encourage hoarding behavior, which in turn will increase the deflationary pressure as less BTC are actively traded and exchanged.

As with fiat currencies, it is possible to extent the monetary base of Bitcoin by lending. Certain types of Bitcoin lending are already in existence in form of private fractional reserve banking and peer-to-peer lending. [102] However, Bitcoin's persistently high volatility exposes lenders and borrowers to significant risk, and deflationary pressure may incentivize saving over borrowing. Counterparty risk is significant at this point of Bitcoin's development. Hanley (2013) argued that fractional reserve banking with bitcoins is impossible, as they are not duplicable and Bitcoin represents a zero-sum game as new money for interest payment and investment returns cannot be created. Despite all these current drawbacks, it can be assumed that a Bitcoin fractional reserve system based on Bitcoin extensions that will be discussed later in this thesis, could alleviate deflationary pressures given a more mainstream and developed Bitcoin economy.

As discussed earlier, it is feasible that Bitcoin could be extended by an additional cryptocurrency layer that functions as an addition to Bitcoin. This extra layer could be a Bitcoin 2.0-type cryptocurrency that extends the money supply and could have its own protocol that bases its mining properties and supply und its underlying Bitcoin base. Another possible solution to deflationary pressures could be achieved by the side chain proposal of Back (2014), which will be discussed in chapter 7.

## 4.11 Bitcoin Wealth Distribution

When Bitcoin began during January 2009 large numbers of bitcoins could be mined with standard home PC equipment. As the network was small and only a few individuals actively mined bitcoins. Therefore it was simple to accumulate large amounts of bitcoins quickly and very low cost. Over time, as more and more miners

102 c.p. Albrecht (2013), http://www.dgcmagazine.com/bitcoin-money-supply-and-money-creation/, 22.07.2014

entered the network, increasingly powerful mining hardware was necessary in order to profitably generate BTC. With each additional miner adding to the combined hashing power, the difficulty of finding a valid block and creating mining rewards would increase. Miners would form mining pools in order to increase their chance of solving blocks and mining new BTC. Eventually, those pools had to divide their rewards among an increasing number of peers that had to provide more and more efficient mining hardware over time in order to keep their mining operations profitable. Over time, bitcoin exchanges have been established, in which individuals could exchange fiat money for bitcoins. Rising prices over time had a similar effect to Bitcoin inequality, as earlier adopters could obtain larger holdings of bitcoins at much lower prices. Moreover, Kroll et al. (2013) argue that due to increasing sophistication and price of mining hardware, barriers to entry to the mining network rise and result into more concentration. Also, miners who entered the network earlier can reinvest their profits in order to keep their hash rate share of the total network, while new entrants face significant initial investment requirements in order to establish a profitable mining operation.

As a result, a few individuals could very easily accumulate large quantities of bitcoins during its earlier days while subsequent adopters faced already higher mining difficulty and exchange prices. Thus, the current distribution of bitcoin holders is very unequal. Moreover, Ron & Shamir (2013) showed that many early adopters could keep their relative share of the bitcoin market largely the same over the analyzed time horizon. Barber et al. (2012) argued that Bitcoin's predictable money supply in combination with increasing difficulty of mining new bitcoins favors early adopters. Should Bitcoin be successful, the fixed monetary supply could lead to excessive deflation and encourage hoarding of BTC, which in turn would further amplify deflation as less BTC would actively circulate in the economy. Heiko (2014) added that due to the invention of ASIC mining hardware for cryptocurrencies, which are vastly more efficient than initial CPU/GPU mining hardware, barriers to entry of the mining network are too high for ordinary users.

As it is not possible to know exactly who is behind the Bitcoin addresses with huge amounts of bitcoins on them and if they keep the BTC on one or several addresses, there is no precise way to estimate Bitcoin wealth distribution. Sardesai (2014) estimated that the top 1% of bitcoin holders own 78% of the currently existing bitcoins. This is compared to the Credit Suisse Global Wealth Report, in which is described that 1% of the global population own 46% of global assets.[103] Importantly however, Sardesai (2014) also emphasized the difficulties in estimating wealth distribution of individuals, as it is not known whether several addresses belong to the same individual or if some users share addresses.[104]

Figure 44: Inequality Distribution

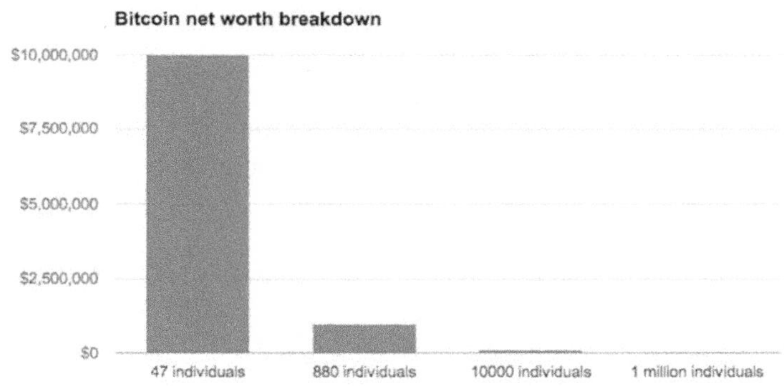


Source: Wile (2013), www.businessinsider.com, 27.06.2014

Wile (2013) gave an approximation of the distribution of bitcoin holders. He finds that 47 individuals hold approximately 28.9% of all existing bitcoins at that this date and overall, 927 individuals own more than 50% of the entire supply of BTC.

Table 10 lists the current distribution of known Bitcoin addresses and their respective funds. These numbers illustrate the intensely skewed distribution of bitcoin addresses that resulted from the preferential conditions that early adopters faced. Again, only the distribution among addresses is shown, as no assumptions about the ownership of these addresses can be made.

---

103 c.p. Credit Suisse (2013), https://publications.credit-suisse.com/tasks/render/file, 18.08.2014

104 c.p. Sardesai (2014), http://www.cryptocoinsnews.com/news/owns-bitcoins-infographic-wealthdistribution/2014/03/21, 22.07.2014

Table 10: Bitcoin Distribution by Address at Block 300,000

| Bitcoin Balance Ragne | Number of Addresses | Percentage of Addresses | Number of Bitcoins Owned | Percentage of all Bitcoins |
|---|---|---|---|---|
| 0 - 0.001 | 34,074,124 | 95.90% | 227.185 | 0.00% |
| 0.001 - 0.01 | 373,719 | 1.05% | 1,423.925 | 0.01% |
| 0.01 - 0.1 | 494,246 | 1.39% | 15,159.122 | 0.12% |
| 0.1 - 1 | 279,107 | 0.79% | 96,874.994 | 0.76% |
| 1 - 10 | 198,379 | 0.56% | 558,520.363 | 4.38% |
| 10 - 100 | 96,774 | 0.27% | 3,484,914.008 | 27.34% |
| 100 - 1,000 | 13,115 | 0.04% | 2,995,546.517 | 23.50% |
| 1,000 - 10,000 | 1,426 | 0.00% | 3,165,366.311 | 24.83% |
| 10,000 - 100,000 | 98 | 0.00% | 2,284,998.798 | 17.93% |
| 100,000 - 21,000,000 | 1 | 0.00% | 144,341.534 | 1.13% |
| Total | 35,530,989 | 100% | 12,747,372.757 | 100% |

Source: Bitcoin Rich List (2013) www.bitcoinrichlist.com, 21.06.2014

Ron & Shamir (2013) found that 76% of existing bitcoins at their point of observing the distribution of addresses are received but never spent. Even by excluding 'old coins' until a certin cutoff point, 73% of bitcoins within their period of observation remained dormant and were never spent or moved between addresses. They also speculate that a significant portion of 'old coins' are lost and cannot be retrieved, as many early adopters might have seen Bitcoin as an experiment and did not preserve the means to access these funds. They also found evidence that many of the larger (e.g. >50.000 BTC) addresses appear to belong to the same owner, and a number of smaller addresses (e.g. 1000 BTC) actually are diversified 'saving accounts' that initially belonged to the same single address. These findings show that it is very difficult to analyze the actual distribution of bitcoin ownership.

Courtois (2014) emphasized that inequality of the distribution of bitcoins could become a larger issue, as it can be assumed that later adopters will not be happy with the unequal distribution and are likely to promote a different cryptocurrency at some point in the future, which will offer a more equal distribution. While this must not necessarily be the case, excessive inequality still remains an issue for Bitcoin, as wealth concentration as well as mining power concentration go against the premise of a decentralized currency. In the presence of deflationary bitcoin prices, late-adopters will own increasingly smaller fractions of the total money supply, which might deter future adoption, as the perceived value of small fractions of the money base might make buying bitcoins less attractive. High exchange prices and very costly barriers to entry to the mining network aggravate the obstacles new adopters face in an increasingly larger fashion. In any case, it must be assumed that if Bitcoin becomes part of the financial sector, it will suffer from extreme wealth concentration due to a bias of strongly favoring early adopters.

## 4.12 Scalability

Scalability issues refer to the problems that arise over time as the block chain continually grows larger and requires more hardware or network resources to store. Both block size and transaction volumes require storage nodes to provide data storage capacity. Barber et al. (2012) pointed out several issues concerning Bitcoin scalability.

Data Retention and Communication Failures: Babaioff et al. (2012) argued that in the long term, incentives for miners to act as nodes and provide their resources to the network will shift from block rewards to transactions that contain fees. Block rewards are set to decrease exponentially at a time interval of four years between each decrease. As a result, at some point miner will begin to withhold information about transactions that pay miner fees, as withholding information from other nodes increases the miners chance to verify it first and collect the fees. This could result into devastating outcomes for the Bitcoin network as competition and communication diminishes.

Linear Transaction History: Nodes are required to store the entire transaction history that that has been agreed upon by all other nodes. In the long term, this will result into scalability problems for devices with lower memory storage, such as smartphones. Mobile devices will not be able to cope with computational overhead and bandwidth requirements, which will potentially make them impractical as a mobile payment method. Barber et al. (2012) proposed a 'Bitcoin filtering service' that acts as a third-party could service which only sends relevant transactions to the nodes that use this filter.

Delayed Transaction Confirmation: As has been discussed earlier in this thesis, Bitcoin suffers from extensively long confirmation delays for transactions and expose users to double-spending risk until a certain number of confirmations is achieved.

Dynamically Growing Private Key Storage: Nakamoto (2008) recommended creating a new address – with corresponding private key and public key – for each transaction. This results into a scalability issue as each individual private key has to be stored.

Kaminsky (2011) argued that scalability issues will eventually result into a segmentation of normal nodes and supernodes, whereby supernodes would essentially represent a banking model without peer-to-peer characteristics. Over time, as Bitcoin would become larger and more broadly adopted, scalability would result into a loss of its peer-to-peer system as standard nodes will no longer be able to support the network. As a result the network would become more centralized over time. Nakamoto (2008) explained that a block header without transactions is about 80 bytes large. This would result into 4.2 MB per year. He refers to Moore's law that predicts a 1.2 GB increase of computer RAM resources and concludes that storage should not be a problem even if all block headers are stored in memory.

Another aspect of the scalability issue is emphasized by Sompolinsky & Zohar (2013). As each block is currently restricted to a maximum size of 1 MB, a long term scenario would imply that at some point the network can no longer scale the number of transactions per second, which is was limited to 3.3 transactions per second. This issue has been addressed by Andresen (2014b), in which he proposed several plans to enhance scalability over time and allow larger block sizes. Currently the network can sustain a rate of 7 transactions per second.[105]

As each transaction is stored within the block chain and each peer in the network has to download the full block chain in order to operate as a full node, scalability could become an issue over time as less and less peers will have the means to store such an amount of data. Moreover, if Bitcoin manages to become a major payment transaction system, the average number of transactions in a given block will increase accordingly. The transactions per second (TPS) are a primary measure for

[105] c.p. Bitcoin Wiki. Scalability, 20.10.2014

Bitcoins scalability, as they represent the rate of growth of the main chain of the block chain.

Figure 45: Block Chain Size over Time

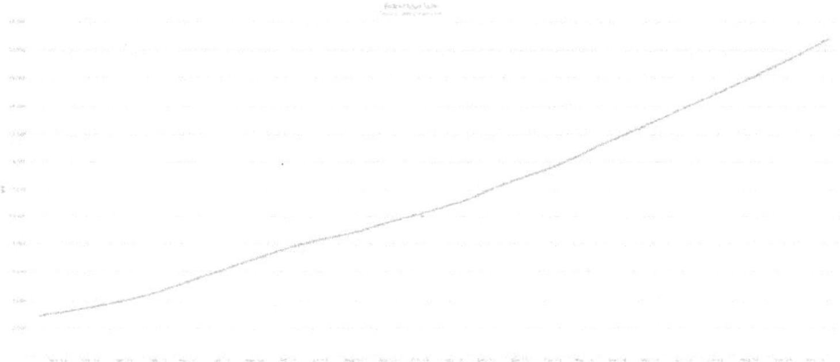

Source: Blockchain (2014), Blockchain Size, 11.10.2014

It can be observed that the current size of the block chain amounts roughly to 22.815 GB of data that all peers have to store. As transaction volume increases and Bitcoin experiences more adaption and wider spread across the globe, transactions per block increase and so do the block sizes.

Figure 46: Average Block Size over Time

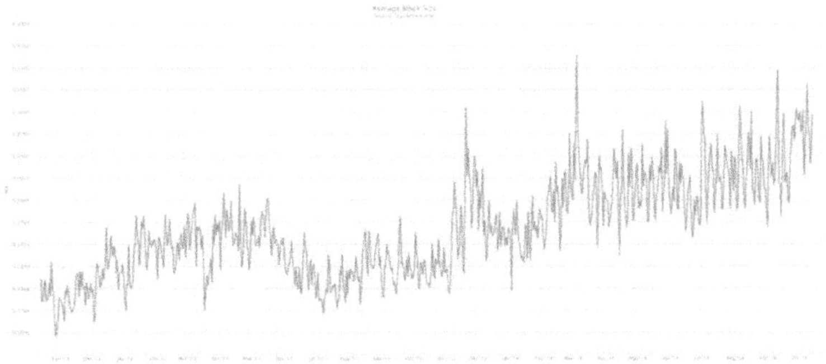

Source: Blockchain (2014), Average Block Size, 11.10.2014

Buterin (2014) noted that the block chain is currently growing by about 1 MB per hour. Should Bitcoin reach a comparable level of transactions per second of Visa (2000 transactions per second), Bitcoin's block chain would grow by about 1 GB per hour and as such would require significant data storage capacities. This supports the case made by Kaminsky (2011), in which he expects super-nodes to evolve over time, while smaller nodes will be driven out, essentially leading to centralization of the network.

Decker & Wattenhofer (2013) and Sompolinsky & Zohar (2013) analyzed Bitcoin's current network propagation characteristics and showed that it faces severe scalability issues in the future as transaction volumes increase. They find a strong correlation between network propagation delays and block size, which work in a linear fashion.

Figure 47: Network Propagation Delays and Block Sizes

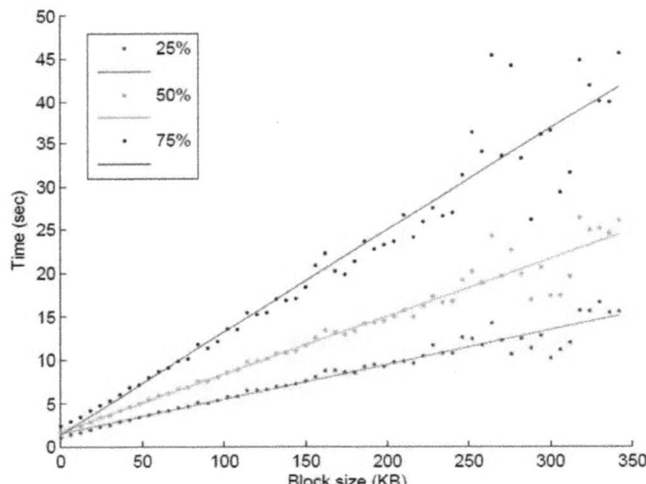


Source: Sompolinsky & Zohar (2013), p.13

It can be observed, they find a roughly linear relationship between block size and delay, which they attribute to bandwidth restrictions and block verification times. Delay costs are shown for the times to reach 25%, 50% and 75% of the monitored nodes. Decker & Wattenhofer (2013) find that, for all transactions that are larger than 20 kb, each kilobyte in size adds additional 80ms delay until the majority of the network knows about the transaction. Once a miner finds a block it takes 6.5 seconds for the block to reach 50% of the other nodes within the network and about 40 seconds in order to reach 95% of the network nodes. This delay cost includes transaction time as well as confirmation time. As a result, long delays between nodes and until blocks have reached all nodes within the decentralized network are common.

Former core Bitcoin developer and now chief scientist of the Bitcoin Foundation Gavin Andresen argued that this delay results in so-called "orphan costs".[106] With the additional 80ms for each transaction above 20kb, different block sizes are not transmitted at the same pace through the network. As a result, miners with smaller blocks have an advantage over miners with larger blocks, as the latter have a higher chance for their blocks to be orphaned. Assuming a current average of 250-byte per transaction, a block generation time of 10 minutes, a 25 BTC block reward and a 80ms delay for each kilo-bite, Andresen estimates a worst-case orphan fee of 0.0008 BTC.

$$1 - e^{\left(-\left(\frac{1}{600}\right)*0.080\right)} = 0.00013$$

which implies

$$25 * 0.00013 * \left(\frac{250}{1000}\right) = 0.0008\ BTC$$

In order to outweigh the risk of finding larger blocks with higher risk of becoming orphaned blocks, Andresen (2013) argued that rational miners would demand a 0.0008 BTC fee for each transaction. This is certainly a threat to Bitcoin's current "no-fee"-transactions scheme.

Andresen (2014b) addressed the current issues concerning scalability of Bitcoin and pointed out several ways to achieve higher scalability over time. Among those are larger block sizes (>1 MB) and improvements the peer-to-peer network, in order to achieve adequate scalability over time. Another option is to require less than the full block chain to be stored within nodes, but keep a reasonably long chain to be unaffected by block chain reorganizations. Moreover it is possible to use a Simplified Payment Verification (SPV) mode that only requires clients to connect to a full node and download only the block headers. Of these blocks, the client can request specific transactions for which the full node will send copies with the Merkle branch linking them to the specific block. This approach is less secure and requires trusting the chosen full node.[107]

Sompolinsky & Zohar (2013) proposed Greedy Heaviest Observed Sub Tree (GHOST) represents a possible alternative to Bitcoin's current longest chain rule

---

[106] c.p. Andresen (2013), https://gist.github.com/gavinandresen/5044482, 21.08.2014

[107] Bitcoin Wiki. Scalability, 20.10.2014

that would significantly increase scalability to 214 transactions per second, including 10,000 transactions per block.

Whether scalability will become an issue for the Bitcoin network depends on how the technology can be adapted to future needs. Network delays will, however, presumably remain a constant issue that cannot be resolved by technological means but through creating the right incentive schemes to the mining network or by adapting the longest chain rule in order to mitigate the causes of network delay.

## 4.13 Energy Consumption

The process of mining new bitcoins can be seen essentially as converting electrical energy into virtual bitcoins. This process also guarantees that transactions are recorded correctly and the system is secured. Mining hardware requires only electricity to perform the computations that solve blocks and produce mining rewards. A miner calculates the profitability of his mining operation based mainly on hash rate, difficulty and energy consumption. Gimein (2013) calculated that April 2013, bitcoin miners produced profits at about $680,000 per day, for which the network required approximately $150,000 of electricity. Ren (2014) emphasized that proof-of-work based mining is highly energy intensive. He estimates the daily revenue of the mining network to about 1.8 million USD, with daily energy costs amounting between 200.000 and 500.000 USD (April 2014). As mining bitcoins will become increasingly hardware-dependent and the miner network grows, energy consumption of the Bitcoin network will increase with it. Miners are incentivized to upgrade their mining operation constantly in order to keep in pace with the network hash rate and avoid operating at a loss. O'Dwyer & Malone (2014) argued that Bitcoin mining is essentially a hardware arms race, and that newer hardware with better hash rates and lower energy consumption has to be included to the network consistently in order for miners to continue mining profitably. Heiko (2014) argued that ASIC mining hardware does not fulfil any legitimate purpose outside cryptocurrency mining and vastly outperform other mining options. Energy consumption is a major factor for mining as it places a floor for mining rewards at which costs disincentive miners from continuing to contribute to the network.

Figure 48: Estimated Power Consumption of the Miner Network

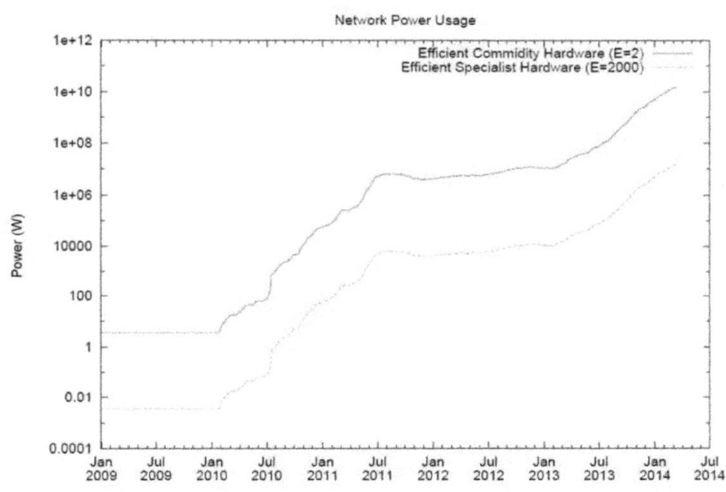


Source: O'Dwyer & Malone (2014) p. 4

O'Dwyer & Malone (2014) compared several alternative mining hardware options and concluded that mining competition causes miners to prefer more energy efficient hardware. Overall they estimate the total power consumption of the Bitcoin Miner Network to amount between 0.1 – 10 GW, depending on the assumptions about the distribution of mining hardware types active within the network. This is compared to the Irish national energy consumption of 3 GW. Clearly, the amount of energy that is currently needed for sustaining the Bitcoin network is significant.

There are several alternatives to mining bitcoins based on proof-of-work which require considerably less energy and which are used for a number of alternative cryptocurrencies (global consensus, proof-of-stake, proof-of-burn, proof-of-excellence, etc.[108]). However, PoW is the core concept that imposes a form of transaction costs and provides a solution to the Byzantine Generals problem, while most alternative concepts are still in experimental phases at this point.

King & Nadal (2012) argued that proof-of-work energy consumption will result into Bitcoin being forced to introduce mandatory transaction fees in order to compensate energy costs of miners. Moreover, as energy consumption needs increase,

[108] c.p. Bentov et al. (2014), p.2

a higher fraction of miners will be forced to discontinue mining at a loss, leading to increased network concentration and higher risk of a 51% attack.

Figure 49: Bitcoin Hash Rate vs. Difficulty

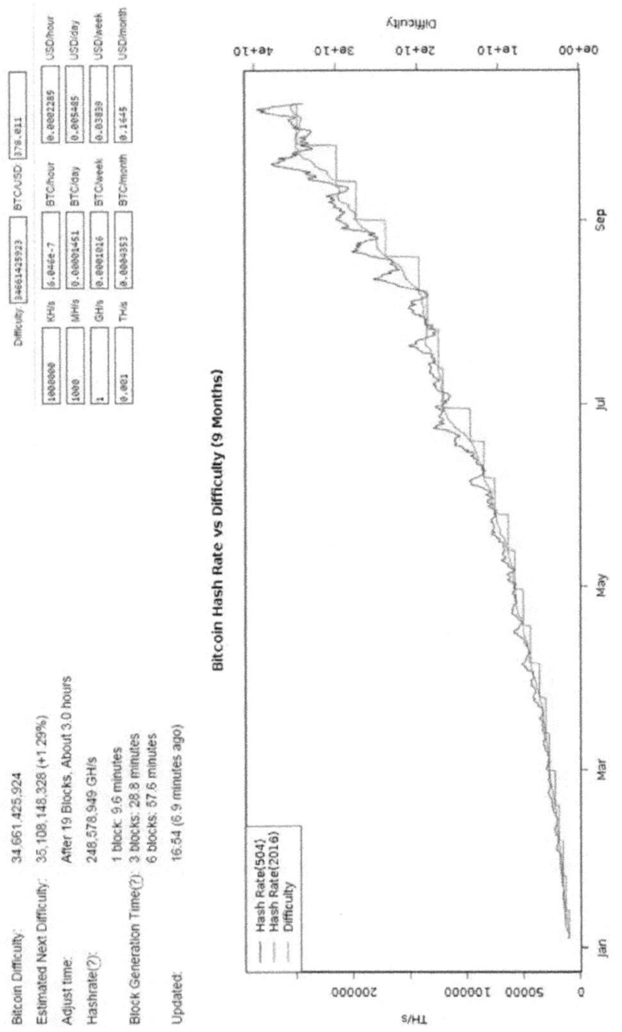


Source: Bitcoinwisdom (2014), Bitcoin Hash Rate vs Difficulty (9 Months), 29.09.2014

The problem at hand with energy consumption is a significant one. These issues threaten both the long term viability of Bitcoin as a technology as the sustainability of the network itself. Gimein (2013) argued that Bitcoin mining is a real-world economic disaster as the mining network is using about 982 megawatt hours a day, which is equivalent to the consumption of 31,000 U.S. home and about half the energy consumption of the Large Hadron Collider near Geneva, Switzerland. Courtois et al. (2013) argued that the emergence of a new generation of mining hardware is inevitable and base their argument on Moore's law. Even a 1% reduction in energy consumption would result into considerable cost savings.

It can be expected that if Bitcoin experiences further success and develops into a mainstream means of payment and other financial applications, the power consumption of the network will increase accordingly. Running a network and securing it with such a degree of energy dependence is, however, very inefficient and may be value-destroying. The Bitcoin network is already by far exceeds the processing strength of the fastest supercomputers worldwide. [109] High energy consumption will, however, only persist as long as technological progress does not provide the means to reduce energy needs or as long as the network continues to grow and will not become more centralized due to diminishing mining profitability, scalability and other factors. Barriers to entry of the mining network consistently grow more significant and mining bitcoins is subject to an arms race in mining hardware that crowds out miners with less efficient hardware resources. It can thus be assumed that the network will experience diminishing returns until equilibrium is found. It is, however, unclear what level of energy dependence will be reached at equilibrium. Nevertheless, the network will always loose a significant percentage of its value generation to the energy consumption needs originating from proof-of-work mining.

---

[109] c.p. Cowley (2013), http://money.cnn.com/2013/05/23/technology/enterprise/bitcoin-supercomputers/, 29.08.2014

## 4.14 Illicit Transactions and Money Laundering

Traditional payment processing businesses within the banking and non-bank sectors are required to provide anti-money laundering (AML), know-your-customer (KYC) and combating of financing of terrorism (CFT) [110] schemes. Bitcoin is still largely unregulated as no dedicated regulation frameworks are present yet. Moreover, many popular exchanges and mining pools are incorporated in countries with low or no regulatory requirements for AML/KYC/CFT frameworks. Effective anti-money laundering and combating terrorism finance is an essential requirement for the integrity of markets and financial systems. The Bitcoin-based financial transaction system provides a global conduit for instantaneous financial transactions that offer limited anonymity. Due to being a relatively new concept of a peer-to-peer decentralized payment system, it remains largely unregulated and is not actively monitored by any institution. As such, it is logically to assume that Bitcoin could very easily be exploited for illegal transactions, tax evasion and money laundering, as its current form facilitates anonymized transactions that. In fact, Bitcoin has been proven to have played a major role in both money laundering and facilitation of purchasing illegal goods in recent history.[111][112]

Möser et al. (2013) provide a comprehensive overview over the possibilities of money laundering within the Bitcoin system. As a relatively unfamiliar method of payment transmission to many and the aspect of supposedly anonymous and untraceable transactions, Bitcoin certainly attracted illicit activity. Perhaps the most significant event that connected Bitcoin to illegal activities, while also accounting for much of its initial growth as a payment system, was the implementation of bitcoin payments at the deep web marketplace Silk Road. The Silk Road was an online marketplace that operated as a hidden service within the TOR (The Onion Router) network. TOR is a decentralized network that directs Internet traffic in an anonymous manner that prevents identification or surveillance of its users.[113]

---

110 c.p. IMF (n.d.), http://www.imf.org/external/np/leg/amlcft/eng/, 29.08.2014

111 c.p. Ax (2014), http://www.reuters.com/article/2014/04/14/us-usa-crime-bitcoin-idUSBREA3D1RU20140414,

112 .06.2014

113 Dingledine et al. (2004), p.3-4

Figure 50: Historical Influence of Silk Road on Bitcoin

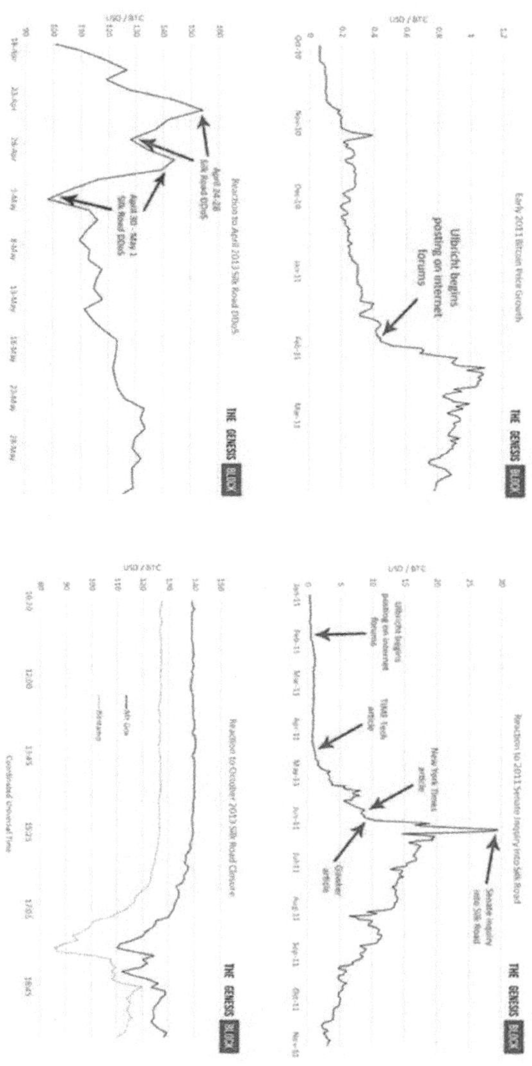


Source: Techfact (2013), www.technews.techfact.org, 25.06.2014

The Silk Road was labeled an "anonymous marketplace", the "eBay for drugs" or "the Amazon for illegal products"[114]. The marketplace was opened in February 2011 and shut down by the FBI in October 2013, when several operators of the Silk Road had been arrested. By analyzing the correlation between the Silk Road activity and bitcoin prices, there is an obvious relationship between both during the period of when bitcoin was the only medium of exchange within the Silk Road market place.

Christin (2013) provides a detailed analysis of bitcoin purchases and corresponding exchange rate developments. The shutdown of the Silk Road initially had a strong impact on its market price but had also been followed by a quick recovery and subsequent breakout to new highs.

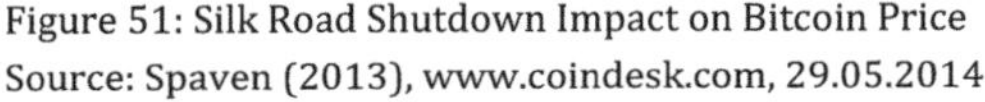

Figure 51: Silk Road Shutdown Impact on Bitcoin Price
Source: Spaven (2013), www.coindesk.com, 29.05.2014

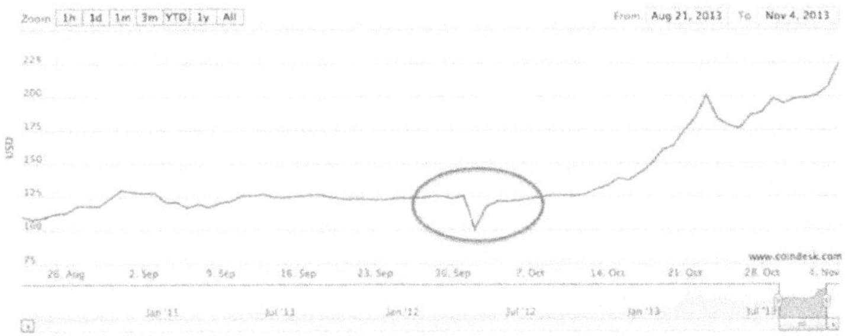


The Silk Road is an example for illicit goods purchases facilitated by cryptocurrencies. Ax (2014) reported the case of Bitcoin entrepreneur and promoter Charlie Shrem, who was indicted on money laundering charges. Shrem is suspected to have sold more than $1 million in bitcoin through his business in order to enable another person to purchase illicit goods on the Silk Road. Cohen (2014) reported that the U.S. federal government expects that Bitcoin is likely to emerge as a major money laundering tool for drug related proceeds.

Stokes (2012) argued that it is fundamentally difficult to apply current regulatory systems to Bitcoin due to its decentralized nature. There is no centralized organi-

[114] c.p. Neal (2013), http://www.ibtimes.com/what-silk-road-4-things-you-need-know-about-underground-blackmarket-shut-down-fbi-1414042, 23.10.2014

zation that money laundering regulations could be imposed on and that could enforce them. Specifically, both value generation and value transfer are based on peer-to-peer technology, whereas current regulatory frameworks depend on a centralized systems. It is, however, not inconceivable that regulatory frameworks will adopt to new technology.

The lack of regulatory coverage, as well as the supposed anonymity and lack of traceability of Bitcoin, appeared to attract illicit activity and as such emphasizes the need to address these features. As already discussed, Bitcoin's anonymity characteristics have been strongly overestimated during this time. Möser et al (2013, p. 1) stated that "Although the relation between Bitcoin accounts and civil identities of their owners is a priori unknown, Bitcoin transactions are not anonymous. A simple abstraction for Bitcoin is to think of it as a public distributed ledger which records all transactions between valid Bitcoin accounts."[115]

Litke & Stewart (2014) argued that private information about the financial position of companies could be obtained through the block chain in case addresses can be connected to them and emphasized the importance of tumbler services that obfuscate the flow of transactions. Möser et al (2013) also provided a detailed analysis of several means to re-anonymize Bitcoin transactions that help users to obfuscate the links between transaction histories and Bitcoin addresses. They noted the possibility of making identities behind Bitcoin's addresses harder to detect by creating multiple addresses or using the services of Bitcoin mixers and tumblers. Bitcoin mixers can swap bitcoins between different individuals, which can make the connection between addresses, transactions and identities very hard to establish. One of their conclusions is that Bitcoin's perfect knowledge about all transactions could be the key to making it compliant with AML/KYC/CFT frameworks. In addition, Kaminsky (2013) noted that Bitcoin offers a profoundly effective system to track bitcoin through the network and also to exude them from circulation. Moreover, it is possible to attach a tag to Bitcoin transactions or mark them by sending very small transactions to the same addresses in order to mix the BTC. Figure 52 illustrates the display of tagged bitcoins on blockchain.info that allegedly belonged to the defunct Mt. Gox exchange.

115 Möser et al. (2013) p.1

Figure 52: Tagged Transactions: Stolen Mt.Gox Bitcoins

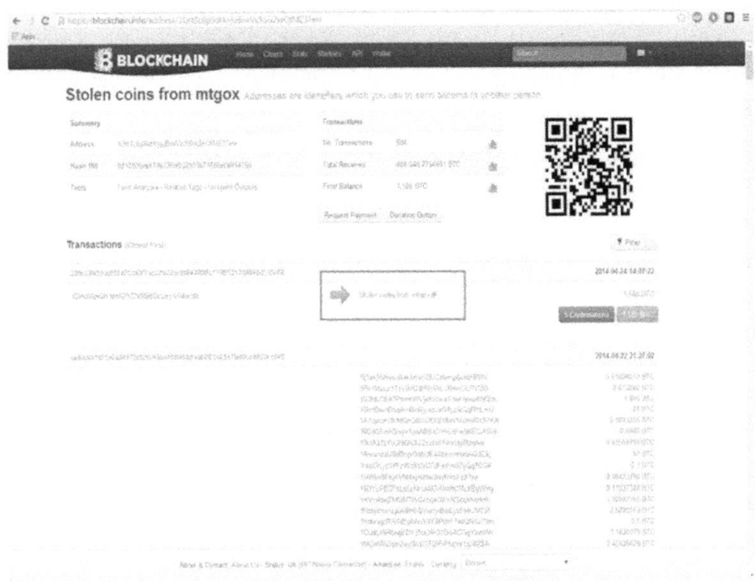


Source: Blockchain (2014), www.blockchain.info, 24.04.2014

The fact that Bitcoin transactions are publicly visible and traceable implies that anonymity is only given as long as identities cannot be connected to individual Bitcoin addresses or transactions. Once an address can successfully be associated to an individual, all past transactions that this individual has conducted with the funds on that address can be also be analyzed and potentially connected to the individual. Know-your-customer frameworks are in fact already applied at almost all major bitcoin exchanges, as well as companies that accept Bitcoin as a means of payment, or Bitcoin ATMs. Moreover, many exchanges between bitcoins and fiat currencies work through banks and other financial institutions and payment providers and are thus covered by necessary regulatory frameworks. The risk that Bitcoin is used for illicit transactions, money laundering, drug purchases, and terrorism finance all are due to the fact that the network is decentralized and protects identities to a certain degree. In chapter 3.10 we discussed Bitcoin's limited anonymity in detail.

Despite being a clear obstacle for Bitcoin adoption and potentially attracting regulatory scrutiny, the pseudonymity of the cryptocurrency must not necessarily be a disadvantage. Stokes (2012) argued that one possible solution to this issue can be found through the core developers of bitcoin that are responsible for the development of the protocol. Thus they could introduce measures into Bitcoin that would make compliance with regulation concerning anonymous transactions and monitoring of transactions possible. Likewise, Bryans (2014) argued that the Bitcoin development team could be identified as a central point within the decentralized network. Regulatory efforts should focus on cooperation the core developers. The Economist (2014) reported that the block chain could become a tool that provides improved visibility, transparency and traceability of fund flows between parties and thus could become an effective tool for regulatory oversight. Ateniese et al. (2014) proposed an optional Bitcoin address certification mechanism, including certified addresses, signature verification and certified transactions, could incorporates trustworthiness from real-world entities into the system without eliminating Bitcoin's key technological advantages.

It can therefore be assumed that the benefits that the block chain offers in form of transparency and traceability of transactions, while rendering fraudulent transactions or non-traceable fund flows theoretically impossible, may outweigh the downsides of pseudonymity. In order to obtain these benefits, however, pseudonymity must be reduced and at the same time protection of private information enhanced.

## 4.15 Conclusions

The Bitcoin protocol does in fact provide users with a number of notable benefits over the traditional banking and payment transaction system. However, it also suffers from a number of noteworthy shortcomings. Some of them are due to the design of the technology and can thus be adapted and improved. Others are specific to Bitcoin and may prove to be impediments to the further development of this technology.

Many of these shortcomings can be also mitigated by third party service providers. As an example, BitPay offers business clients the service of locking exchange prices and immediately converting received bitcoin transactions into fiat currencies. It thus hedges the price volatility for businesses and in turn receives a fee for assuming the risk of price fluctuations.[116] Bitpay is an example for how a flaw in the technology gets resolved by the services of an intermediary.

However, the emergence of third party intermediaries that provide services to Bitcoin users, to a certain degree contradicts Nakamoto's (2008) intention to create a financial transaction protocol does not require trusted intermediaries.

The question whether Bitcoin's code can be redesigned and adapted in order to eliminate current shortcomings in future updates remains open. Some of the aforementioned weaknesses are more serious than others and not all of them can be resolved by simply changing the protocol. Andresen (2014b) called the argument that Bitcoin should strictly remain what Satoshi Nakamoto's envisioned a "argument from authority" logical fallacy. It can be assumed that the core development team will be open to adjustments and improvements in order to support Bitcoin's success.

Bitcoin is the first cryptocurrency of its kind and is developed on an open-source basis. This allows anyone to access, view or copy the programming code of the protocol. An open source process has been chosen for its development in order to create an environment of collaboration. Anyone can suggest updated or changes to the code and with increasing frequency, academics, businesses and independent IT specialists do so.

Its open-source nature and current shortcomings have, however, also resulted in the growth of alternative cryptocurrency projects.

[116] c.p. Zeiler (2014), http://moneymorning.com/2014/09/12/first-u-s-bitcoin-derivative-reduces-risk-forbusinesses/, 22.10.2014

# 5 Analysis: Alternative Cryptocurrencies

One of the most important questions about Bitcoin is whether it will be – if at all – Bitcoin itself that will succeed or the underlying technology. Central within the ongoing discussion about Bitcoin is the persistent question about whether Bitcoin is the 'Napster' or 'MySpace' of cryptocurrencies. Probable case are that either a better competitor arises or regulation will inhibit its development due to some of its features and alternative cryptocurrencies with more sophisticated technology, more applications or better compatibility to financial regulatory frameworks will take its place.

Despite a growing market for Altcoins the vast majority of services, entrepreneurship and public attention still almost exclusively revolves around Bitcoin. Accordingly, Bitcoin profits from a strong and increasing 'network effect' that developed around it and continues to grow at an increasing pace. The network effect (alternatively called: 'network externality' or 'demand-side economics of scale'[117]) describes the effect that a growing number of uses has on the value of the product itself.

Arguably, Bitcoin established itself dominant enough before any of the subsequent generations of alternative cryptocurrencies managed to achieve widespread acceptance and distribution. Thus it can be expected to become very resilient towards competition. While the network itself is purely peer-to-peer, Bitcoin's core development is in fact centralized. Its ongoing development is based on the collaborative work of several core developers that develop the code and allow collaboration of outside people through on an open source process.[118] As such, it is reasonable to assume, that if any Altcoin manages to offer a significant benefit to the field of cryptocurrencies, Bitcoin's code could theoretically be adapted in order to incorporate many of the competing features into it as long as the competing technology is applicable. Comparable strategies against market entry of competitors could be observed when Facebook chose to include hash-tags into its social network or when Red Bull introduced Red Bull Cola presumably to deter competition in the energy drink market.

---

[117] c.p. McGee & Sammut-Bonnici (2002), p.1-4

[118] c.p. Liu (2013a), http://motherboard.vice.com/blog/whos-building-bitcoin-an-inside-look-at-bitcoins-opensource-development, 08.06.2014

Another open question is whether Bitcoin itself will become dominant or only its underlying technology. The solution to the Byzantine Generals problem and the potential of decentralized, cryptographically secure financial services could become a standalone technology that does not depend on Bitcoin in the future.

However, being able to adapt and extend the Bitcoin technology, whilst benefiting from the network effect could put Bitcoin into a strong competitive position that could protect it against potential market entries of current or future competitors. Due to its extensive media coverage, both positive and negative, it has established brand recognition but will always retain the stigma of being used for illegal activity. As Bitcoin is the first successful cryptocurrency of its kind, it suffers relatively more pronounced from the initial difficulties and obstacles that such a new technology can be expected to experience. The fact that it was strongly related to illicit transactions during its initial growth and is only slowly transforming towards mainstream uses nevertheless retains the stigma of being related to drug use, buying illegal goods, money laundering and the like.

It is easy to imagine that at some point a suitable competing cryptocurrency could emerge, which could leverage Bitcoin's success. However, there is also solid ground to believe that Bitcoin is here to stay in some way or the other. The public perspective has already transformed as Bitcoin received major mainstream news coverage and backing from prominent financial experts.

Recall that we have discussed in detail a number of shortcomings that could be identified about the Bitcoin protocol. In what follows we will evaluate a number of competitors that are either based on Bitcoin's technology or are very closely related. We will discuss if there are worthwhile competitors identifiable at this point of time and whether there are features that could or should be integrated into Bitcoin.

## 5.1 Alternative Cryptocurrencies

Cryptocurrencies are a medium of exchange that uses cryptography for verification, executing and securing transactions. Within this market, cryptocurrencies that are based on or related to Bitcoin are referred to as 'alternative cryptocurrencies' or 'Altcoins'. Ahamad & Varghese (2013) noted that 'Altcoin' is a slang term that evolved within the cryptocurrency development community. It is a catch-all term for the growing number of new cryptocurrencies as these are based on or very similar to Bitcoin's technology. They define cryptocurrencies as "physical precomputed files utilizing a public key/private key pairs generated around a specific encryption algorithm. The key assigns ownership of each key pair, or 'coin,' to the person who is in possession of the private key."[119] In fact, the majority of Altcoins currently in existence at this time are forks of either Bitcoin or the second most prevalent cryptocurrency - Litecoin. Bitcoin and Litecoin are very similar in their features but differ in certain aspects, especially in the algorithm that they employ. Bitcoin uses a SHA256 algorithm whereas Litecoin uses a Scrypt algorithm. As both cryptocurrencies are opensource technologies, the concept can be copied and adapted easily and new features or applications are introduced in order to distinguish Altcoins from its original[120] Bornholdt & Sneppen (2014) question if Bitcoin's advantage of a finite maximum total number of 21 million BTC is neutralized by the hypothetically unlimited number of alternative cryptocurrencies. Owners of bitcoins can freely exchange them for Altcoins and miners can switch from mining Bitcoin to alternative cryptos. Some cryptocurrency projects specifically aim to become an extra protocol layer on top of Bitcoin and thus extend it. In fact, however, most of the currently existing Altcoins are merely clones with minor modifications that do not offer any technological innovation and still share the same weaknesses as Bitcoin. The utility of an increasing number of technologically unaltered copies of the same concept is doubtful. Nevertheless, the cryptocurrency market is flooded with new Altcoins constantly.

The growth of the Altcoin market can widely be attributed to the following intentions:

- Genuine attempts to create better alternatives to Bitcoin.
- Genuine attempts to create a 'silver standard' to Bitcoin.
- Attempts to create cryptocurrencies for niche markets or specific purposes only.
- "Jumping on the bandwagon", plagiarism, etc.
- Fraud, deception or misleading of buyers for financial gain.

Due to the fact that Altcoins is a catch-all term for all Bitcoin-based cryptocurrencies other than Bitcoin itself, the term refers to legitimate as well as illegitimate

[119] Ahamad & Varghese (2013), p.43

[120] c.p. Bitcoin Wiki. Creating forks, 10.07.2014

cryptocurrencies. A certain fraction of alternative cryptocurrencies are undoubtedly created with fraudulent intent. Almost all of them are susceptible to pump-and-dump scams, pre-mining schemes or benefit inventors and early adopters on the expense of later adopters (greater fool theory). Many were advertised heavily across the Internet and questionable explanations were given why this Altcoin is "the next big thing" or "about to increase strongly in value". Accordingly, some became essentially worthless very quickly.[121]

Due to this situation of the cryptocurrency market, only a few specific alternative cryptocurrencies will be discussed in this chapter. Within the market of cryptocurrencies a few very sophisticated alternatives are being developed. Most of these genuine new cryptocurrency projects do not confirm to the view of Ahamad & Varghese (2013) on alternative cryptocurrencies, as they offer a wide array of alternatives to the key weaknesses that the Bitcoin protocol and technology is subject too. (see chapter 4)

Alternative cryptocurrencies can largely be distinguished by two categories: Cryptocurrencies that are designed as an independent currency and cryptocurrencies that are developed around the Bitcoin network and are defined as extensions to its protocol.

Table 11 gives an overview over the discussed cryptocurrencies:

Table 11: Altcoin Comparison

| **Crypto-currency** | **Algo-rithm** | **Block time** | **Begin-ning block reward** | **Block reward half-life** | **Total number of coins** |
|---|---|---|---|---|---|
| Bitcoin | SHA256d | 10 minutes | 50 BTC | 210,000 blocks | 21,000,000 |
| Litecoin | Scrypt | 2.5 minutes | 50 LTC | 840,000 blocks | 84,000,000 |
| Dogecoin | Scrypt | 1 minute | 0 – 1.000.000 DOGE | | 100,000,000,000 |
| Darkcoin | X11 | 2.5 minutes | variable | Variable moving averages | ~ 22,000,000 |

121 c.p. N.N. (2013), http://www.cryptobadger.com/2013/05/altcoin-explosion-profit/, 05.09.2014

| Crypto-currency | Algo-rithm | Block time | Begin-ning block reward | Block reward half-life | Total number of coins |
|---|---|---|---|---|---|
| Peercoin | SHA256 /PoS hybrid | 10 mi-nutes | depen-ding on coin age | not ap-plicable | not limited infla-tionary |
| Ethereum | PoW/PoS hy-brid. Varying algo-rithm | 12 se-conds (expec-ted) | not appli-cable | not ap-plicable | not limited di-sinflationary |
| Primecoin | Prime chain detec-tion | 1 - 1.25 minutes | 999 di-vided by thee square of the cur-rent diffi-culty | Adjust-ment af-ter each block | Depending on the natural oc-currence of prime chains Theoretically disinflationary, linked to Moore's law |
| Mastercoin | Scrypt | 35 se-conds | 100 MSC | 2,703,085 blocks | 619,478.5 |
| Ripple | Path fin-ding al-gorithm | 2-20 se-conds | not appli-cable | not ap-plicable | 100,000,000,000 |

Among these cryptocurrencies, Bitcoin's market capitalization and prominence still vastly outperforms that of major alternatives. Figure 53 illustrates the distribution of major cryptocurrencies, while also listing some Altcoins that will not be discussed in detail. For a list of currently existing Altcoins, see Appendix A2.

Figure 53: Bitcoin vs. Altcoin Market Capitalization

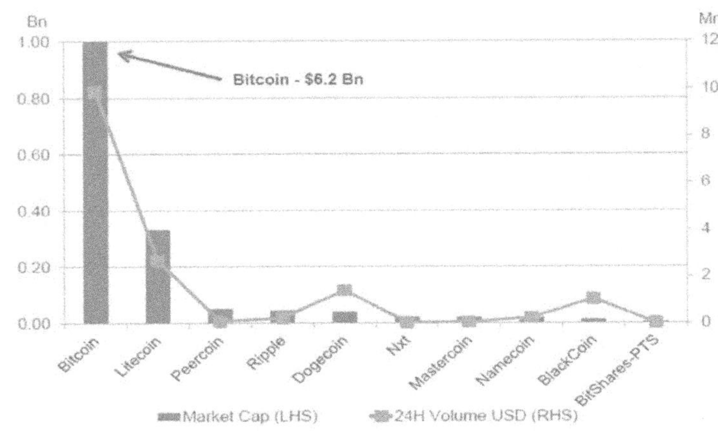


Source: Citigroup (2014), p.20

## 5.2 Litecoin

Litecoin (LTC) is currently the second most successful cryptocurrency. It has been created in 2011 by Charles Lee, a former Google employee and brother of Bobby Lee, who founded the bitcoin exchange 'BTC China'.[122] Litecoin is the second-largest cryptocurrency by market capitalization and trade volume. It was developed in order to offer several perceived advantages over Bitcoin to the growing cryptocurrency market.

Its main features are faster block confirmation intervals that are meant to benefit transactions and the use of an alternative proof-of-work algorithm with the intent of benefitting miners with less sophisticated hardware. The scrypt algorithm was chosen with the intention to alleviate the advantages of CPU over GPU mining and to inhibit ASIC mining. Scrypt is a password-based key derivation function that is not very resource intense, allowing less sophisticated hardware to perform scrypt calculations. It is however computationally intensive if one was to attempt a brute force attack, thus making such attacks very costly. As such, mining Litecoin with its scrypt proofof-work was significantly more equitable and less hardware intensive

122 c.p. Del Castillo (2014), http://upstart.bizjournals.com/news/technology/2014/02/03/bobby-and-charles-leebitcoin-brothers.html?page=all, 09.06.2014

than Bitcoin mining, and network hash rate resided on relatively low levels over much of Litecoin's history. However, over time specialized Litecoin ASIC mining hardware was developed, resulting in a sharp increase in difficulty and a corresponding exodus of GPU and CPU miners. Despite being advertised as "ASIC resistant", Litecoins developers did not prevent the influx of specialized ASIC mining hardware, which resulted into Litecoin eventually becoming essentially Bitcoin with faster transaction confirmations and lower exchange value.[123]

Figure 54: Litecoin Hash Rate vs. Difficulty

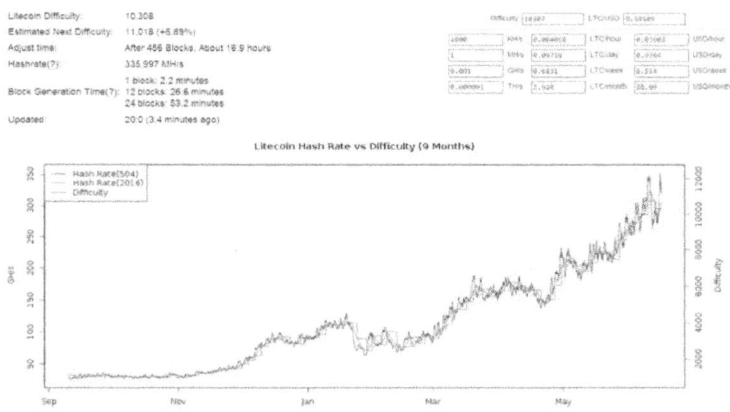


Source: Bitcoinwisdom (2014), Litecoin Hash Rate vs Difficulty (9 Months), 15.06.2014

Litecoin can currently be seen as the 'silver standard' to Bitcoin, based on market capitalization, adoption, popularity, etc. Its confirmation times are four times faster than Bitcoin's (2.5 minutes) and it offers a four times larger money supply (84 million LTC). Historically, its price has been very strongly correlated to Bitcoin's price, with a correlation coefficient of 0.906.[124] The scrypt proof-of-work algorithm was chosen in order to prevent Bitcoin miners to quickly switch from mining Bitcoin to Litecoin, thus increasing the difficulty strongly and leaving the network again. Also, Litecoin developers wanted to avoid competing for miners of the Bitcoin network.[125]

---

123 c.p. Fargo (2014), https://www.cryptocoinsnews.com/litecoin-will-hard-fork-fend-asics/, 08.09.2014

124 c.p. Kimonolabs (2014), https://www.kimonolabs.com/bitcoin/correlator, 18.10.2014

125 c.p. Coblee (2011), https://bitcointalk.org/index.php?topic=47417.0 08.09.2014

Litecoin represents one of the earliest alternatives to Bitcoin that followed the notion of creating cryptocurrency with improved features. Initially, it offered faster confirmation times, more equitable mining and less wealth concentration, as Bitcoin was already somewhat developed and more users had access to relatively larger holdings of the Litecoin money supply. Faster transaction times, however resulted in a higher frequency of orphaned blocks and overall larger block chain size. Moreover, mining quickly became significantly less equitable due to the development of scrypt-based ASIC mining hardware. Nevertheless, Litecoin represent one of the most important and widespread cryptocurrencies that inspired a great number of subsequently developed Altcoins.

## 5.3 Dogecoin

Starting initially as a fun project, Dogecoin managed to become one of the most widely known and used cryptocurrencies. It was introduced in December 2013 by programmer Billy Markus. [126] Despite its farcical nature, it received international attention after being reported in mainstream news media such as Bloomberg, Business Insider, or the Washington Business Journal.[127] The conceptualization of Dogecoin (DOGE) is based on a popular 'Internet meme' featuring the image of a Shiba Inu dog, usually accompanied by text written in comic sans style. Already a few weeks after its launch a vibrant and active community began to build around it that actively promotes Dogecoin by tipping and donating DOGE to other users over the Internet. From a technical perspective, Dogecoin is simply a fork of the open-source code of Litecoin. Notably, Dogecoin was not designed to have a fixed cap on the total number of minable dogecoins. The total number of dogecoins is set to 100.000.000.000 DOGE, which will already be mined and fully in circulation by 2015. After this, Dogecoin will add 5.200.000.000 DOGE per year to its currency supply, thus becoming an inflationary cryptocurreny. [128] In relation to almost all existing cryptocurrenies currently in existence, Dogecoin has an extremely large number of total minable coins, which results into very low exchange prices for DOGE and also considerably high volatility.

---

[126] c.p. Dogecoin (2013), https://bitcointalk.org/index.php?topic=361813.0, 10.06.2014

[127] c.p. McGuire (2013), http://motherboard.vice.com/blog/dogecoins-founders-believe-in-the-power-of-memecurrencies, 10.06.2014

[128] c.p. De la Rouviere (2013), https://github.com/dogecoin/dogecoin/issues/23, 10.06.2014

One of the most significant events in Dogecoin's history was when the community behind it successfully managed to collect enough donations for funding a Jamaican bobsledders team to participate in the 2014 Winter Olympics in Sochi.[129]Later, the community successfully collected Dogecoin denominated funds in order to sponsor NASCAR driver Josh Wise's participation in the

NASCAR Sprint Cup Series in May 2014.[130]

Dogecoin's primary application is social media tipping and donating, e.g. to what the community considers a good cause, valuable insight or funny comment.

Figure 55: Online Tipping

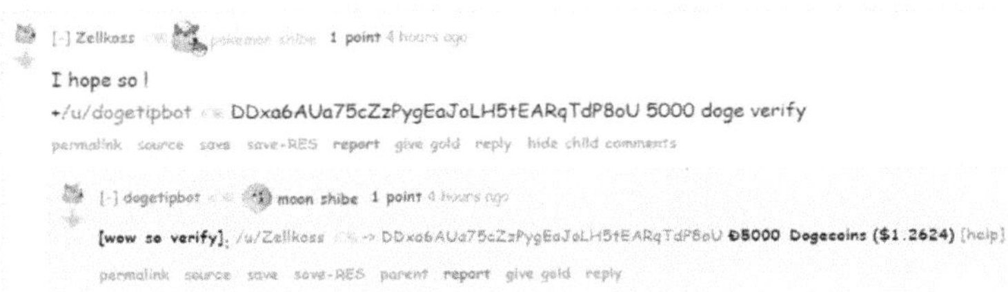


Source: Zellkoss (2014), www.reddit.com, 26.10.2014

Online tipping represents a novelty concept within the Internet and is also conducted with bitcoins and other cryptocurrency. This feature enables simple micro-transactions conducted with cryptocurrencies through social media platforms, such as Facebook [131], Twitter, or Reddit. [132] Notably, receivers of donations and tips do not have to be cryptocurrency users and their received funds will be stored for them until requested.

Courtois (2014) used Dogecoin as an example of the implications that follow the concentration of mining power. He described how the network hash rate was affected by a block reward halving that resulted in an almost equally strong decline

129 c.p. Davidson (2014), http://www.bloombergview.com/articles/2014-02-04/jamaican-bobsledders-ridedogecoin-into-olympics, 06.09.2014

130 c.p. DeCola (2014), http://www.nascar.com/en_us/news-media/blogs/Off-Track/doge-reddit-josh-wisetalladega-superspeedway-aarons-499.html, 12.06.204

131 c.p. Gillespie (2014b), https://www.cryptocoinsnews.com/facebook-approves-dogecoin-tipping-app/, 24.10.2014

132 c.p. Cawrey (2014a), http://www.coindesk.com/dogetipbot-turned-spoof-altcoin-tipping-phenomenon/, 24.10.2014

of hash rate presumably due to miners leaving the network as it became unprofitable for them to continue mining when faced with 50% less profit. As a result, one single miner was able to obtain more than 50% of the network hash rate for a certain amount of time, which would make him a supernode controlling the network.

## 5.4 Darkcoin

Darkcoin (DRK) is a more recently developed alternative cryptocurrency that focuses on what the developers perceive as being a key weakness of Bitcoin: lack of anonymity. Duffield & Hagan (2014) argued that Bitcoin is inherently not private and allows to track all transactions and trace them back to users. We have already discussed that Bitcoin is often incorrectly referred to as an anonymous means of conducting payments, but should actually be described as pseudonymously, as all transactions are publicly and indefinitely accessible through the block chain (chapter 3.10).

Figure 56: Anonymizing of Darkcoin Transactions

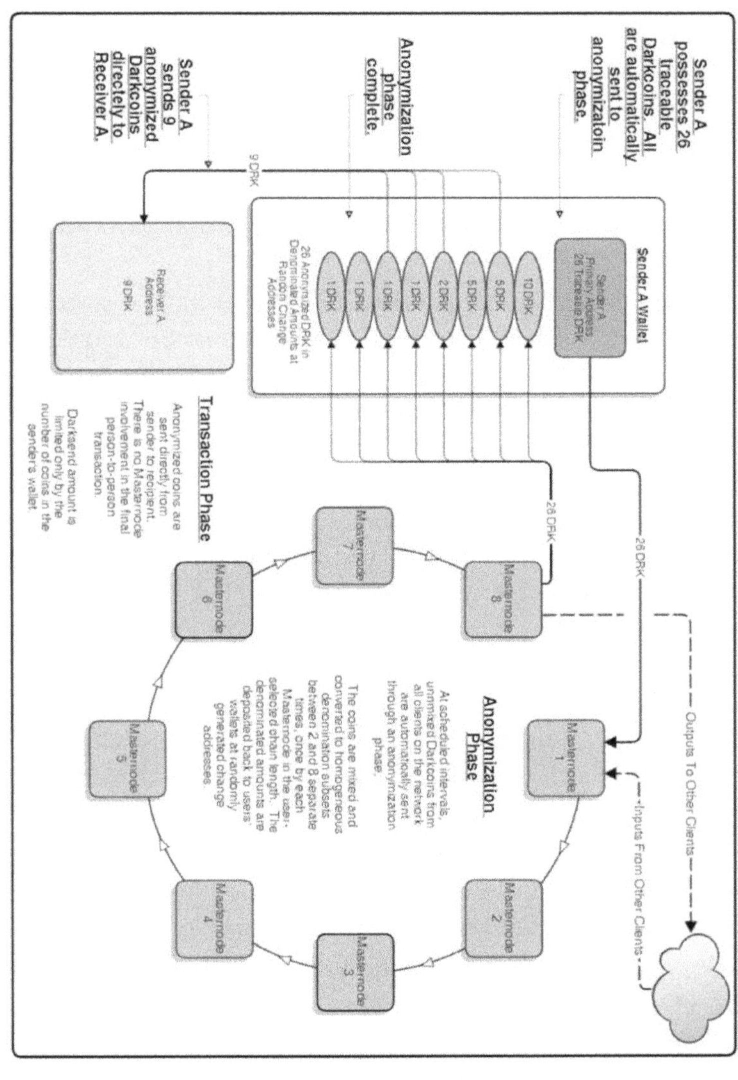


Source: Duffield (2014), www.darkcointalk.org, 23.10.2014

Transactions are anonymized via DarkSend technology that disassociates inputs and outputs via pools that hide user identities. Inputs are of fixed sizes in power of ten and pools have similar sizes to each other in order to eliminate information about transaction sizes that could be connected to a user, whereas outputs can be of any size. As outputs will mostly differ from inputs, the difference of an outgoing transaction to the original input will be 'refunded' to a new random pool address that is not connected to the user's identity. To further obfuscate user information, network nodes brake up and reroute the flow of money, and nodes have a random chance to become a 'Master node' for a limited time, which allows the node to decide which transactions to include in the pool.

Despite its key purpose of protecting user privacy, Darkcoin offers a number of additional optimizations of the Bitcoin protocol:

Chained Hashing Algorithm: Darccoin's algorithm is X11, which consists of 11 rounds of scientific hashing functions (blake, bmw, groestl, jh, keccak, skein, luffa, cubehash, shavite, simd, echo). This is employed in order to discourage or prevent ASIC mining, and reduce energy requirements for GPU miners. Discouraging ASIC mining is an effective way of inhibiting concentrated mining and potentially prevents 51% attacks.[133]

Steady Money Supply: Darkcoin replaces abrupt reward halving by a formula that provides a steady coin generation rate that smoothly decreases approximately 7% per year.

$$Reward\ Curve = \frac{2.222.222}{\left(\frac{(Difficulty+2600)}{9}\right)^2}$$

Darkcoin is not designed to have a fixed schedule for coin generation, but rather begins with an inflationary model that gradually tapers off towards an approximate supply of 1 million coins per year.

Variable Block Rewards: Difficulty retargeting by Dark Gravity Wave (DGW) is based on three exponential moving averages that smoothly adjust the mining difficulty that adhere to certain limits for difficulty retargeting.

Master Nodes: Master nodes are chosen by a pseudo random deterministic algorithm and are then responsible for deciding which transactions to include into the pool. The role of being a master node is assigned anew each round and all nodes are informed what peer currently is the master node. Moreover, the protocol appoints a second node to replace the master node in case it fails or is compromised.

[133] c.p. Duffield & Hagan (2014), p.6-7

Master nodes provide enhanced anonymity by mixing all transactions of a user with those of two other users. In an effort to keep the network decentralized, each node has to prove ownership of 1000 DRK, which is expected to discourage malicious peers in the network. Moreover, master nodes gain 10% of the mined block rewards in exchange for their service.[134]

Darkcoin addresses several major shortcomings of Bitcoin, especially those of anonymity, misaligned mining incentives and diminishing decentralization. Bitcoin proponents have taken admiration in the concept, resulting in Darkcoin being one of the fastest growing Altcoins, which ranked among the top five cryptocurrencies after just a few weeks in circulation and has remained one of the most significant cryptocurrencies since.[135] Darkcoin is akin to Zerocoin, which is another cryptocurrency project that attempts to provide completely anonymous fund transactions. Zerocoin would represent an extension to the Bitcoin block chain that would augment the protocol in order to achieve true anonymity of payments, and as such does not represent an alternative cryptocurrency. [135] However, complete anonymity must not per se be an advantage for cryptocurrencies as it can reasonably be expected that such a transaction system will face tremendous aversion by regulatory supervision and governments. It is therefore doubtful whether cryptocurrencies that specifically aim to enable anonymous transactions will survive.

## 5.5 Peercoin

Peercoin (PPC) is a second-generation cryptocurrency that was developed in 2012 in order to address Bitcoin's energy consumption issue. Bitcoin's proof-of-work algorithm is highly energy intensive and grew very strongly with the invention of Bitcoin ASIC mining hardware.[136] While Peercoin is mostly based on Bitcoin's SHA-256 algorithm and proof-of-work, Peercoin also utilizes a hybrid system with an additional proof-of-stake (PoS) system. PoS is based on coin age and can provide similar features as PoW in terms of security and mining new PPC. Block are separated into two different types, proof-of-work and proof-of-stake blocks. Sprankel (2013) explained that with Peercoin both types of blocks are mined, but PoS blocks do not have a nonce for its data hashing operations. Proof-of-stake requires a

[134] c.p. Duffield & Hagan (2014), p.4-6

[135] c.p. Cipher (2014). http://www.deepdotweb.com/2014/05/20/the-rise-of-darkcoin/, 06.06.2014 [135] c.p. Miers et al. (2013), p.397-398

[136] c.p. King & Nadal (2012), p.2-5

timestamp for each hashing operation, which is calculated for each transaction. The key difference is that PoW produces millions of nonce-based hashes per second, whereas PoS is based on timestamps which only update once for each second.

$$Coin\ Age = Currency\ Amount * Holding\ Period$$

This one-hash-per-second rule is mostly on par with Bitcoin's mining process, yet significantly reduces energy consumption. Moreover, as the Peercoin block chain is dependent on coin age, nodes can easily identify the longest chain among possible chains in the network by basing their decision on total accumulated coin age.

King & Nadal (2012) further address an issue identified by Babaioff et al. (2011) about transaction fee incentives for miners that leads to non-cooperative behavior between miners. Transaction fees for Peercoin are therefore not allocated at the block level but on a protocol level, and are fixed and mandatory. However, these transaction fees are not distributed to the miners but destroyed instead. This scheme is not an ideal choice, as it does not account for changes in value of PPC, and thus has to be adapted in certain uneven intervals. Contrary to Bitcoin's fix-cap money supply model, Peercoin is inflationary as it does not impose a final number of coins and its money supply can grow theoretically indefinitely. Mining new PPC was initially based on proof-of-work, but is to be substituted with the proof-of-stake process over time.[137] Miners generating PoS blocks involves sending some PPC to themselves, thereby consuming their currency coin age level and is rewarded 0.01 PPC for each coin year.

$$Mining\ Reward = Coin\ Days * \frac{1}{36500}\ PPC$$

This causes Peercoin to have a theoretically infinite money supply that is directly connected to accumulated coin age, and moreover results into continuous difficulty adjustments, as opposed to Bitcoin's two-week interval adjustments. Basing the mining network on coin age also considerably reduces the risk of a 51% attack. Individuals holding 1% of PoS peercoins will only be able to create 1% of the PoS blocks. Thus, conducting a 51% attack is extremely costly and inefficient. Peercoin's alternative mining process is therefore extremely energy efficient when compared to that of Bitcoin, and the network is less vulnerable to 51% attacks.

---

137 c.p. King & Nadal (2012), p.3

## 5.6 Ethereum

Ethereum is a special type of cryptocurrency that is one of the few projects within the cryptocurrency ecosystem that aims specifically for developing a 'cryptocurrency 2.0'. Ethereum is a decentralized publishing platform that aims to provide the means to design smart contracts. It uses a base monetary unit called 'ether' in order to facilitate contracts. Buterin (2014a) explained that Ethereum provides a block chain with a built-in Turing complete programming language that allows to design arbitrary functions for a wide array of smart contracts. Possible examples include voting systems, financial exchanges, crowdfunding, gambling, identity- and reputation systems, decentralized file storage, domain name registries, self-enforcing contracts and the like. In fact, the full array of potential applications is not yet fully defined. Ether is the base unit that is e.g. used to pay transaction fees or impose costs as a regulatory system to prevent abuses. It represents the cryptocurrency equivalent within Ethereum and is described as the "fuel for running the contract processing engine".[138]

Ethereum addresses a number of key weaknesses of Bitcoin. Ethereum accounts hold a balance, a contact code, a data store and a unique nonce, whereas Bitcoin can currently only have two states – spent and unspent.[139] Additionally, Ethereum integrates a proposal made by Sompolinsky & Zohar (2013) that addresses a key weakness of Bitcoin. Ethererum uses the Greedy Heaviest Observed Sub Tree (GHOST) protocol, in order to avoid network propagation delays that can cause large mining pools to de facto control the mining process. (See chapter 4.3). Thus the stale block problem discussed earlier will be eliminated by the GHOST protocol and additional measures integrated into the Ethereum mining process.[139] In order to avoid excessive wealth concentration like that of Bitcoin, the developers chose a permanent linear growth model for its money supply in order to achieve a disinflationary monetary base. High initial inflation of 22.4% is steadily decreased towards 1.0%. The remaining 1.0% inflation was chosen in order to match the estimated rate of ether loss over time due to loss or destruction of private keys.

[138] Lubin (2014), https://blog.ethereum.org/2014/04/10/the-issuance-model-in-ethereum/, 18.09.2014 [139] c.p. Goodman (2014), p.4

[139] c.p. Buterin (2014a), p.26

Figure 57: Ethereum Disinflationary Issuance Model

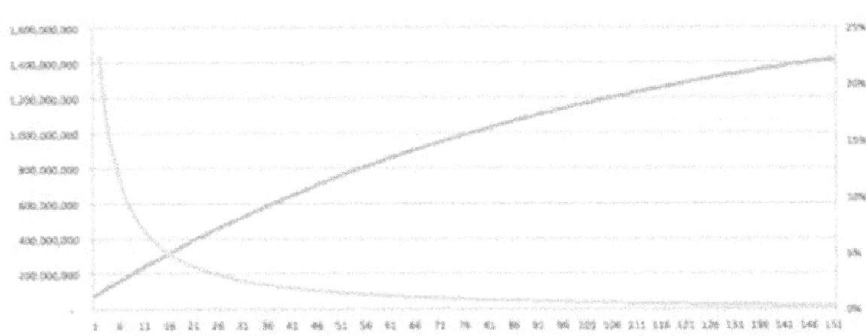

Source: Lubin (2014), www.blog.ethereum.org, 18.09.2014

Furthermore, in order to avoid scalability issues, only the state of the Ethereum block chain must be stored in order to run a full node, and developers plan further strategies to avoid scalability issues and node concentration risk.

Thus, Ethereum can be seen as one of the key innovation projects within the cryptocurrency ecosystem that specifically aims towards improving upon Bitcoin's technology and avoiding errors or shortcomings made with the development of Bitcoin. Moreover, it plans to enhance and broad then fields of applications of the block chain and cryptocurrency technology that goes beyond a mere payment system and can be considered a fountainhead of the decentralization of financial services.

## 5.7 Primecoin

Primecoin (XPM) is an innovative cryptocurrency that was developed in 2013 in order to address Bitcoin's intense computational and electrical resource requirements. Its key innovation is that it is not based on Hashcash proof-of-work, but achieves the same goal by finding prime chains composed of prime number chains, so called 'Cunningham chains' or 'bi-twin chains'. In order to function as a proof-of-work for Primecoin, all nodes must verify an identified prime chain and the proof-of-work must not be re-usable. Non-reusability is achieved by linking the block header hash and requiring that it be divisible by the block header hash ('proof-of-work certificate'), which is then used to compute the block hash.[140]

[140] c.p. King (2013), p.3

Finding prime chains is increasing in difficulty at an exponential rate. This would result in a nonlinear evolution of mining difficulty that would be detrimental to Primecoin's use as a means of conducing financial transactions. King (2013) solves this by utilizing the Fermat test[141] in order provide a relatively linear continuous difficulty curve for any given prime coin length.

$$d = k + (p_k - r)/p_k$$

In this equation, *k* denotes the prime chain length. *r* be the Fermat test remainder of the next number in chain *pk*. The difficulty of the chain is measured by

$$\frac{p_k}{r}.$$

Primecoin's alternative proof-of-work function requires a miner to take multiples of the block header hash and find a solution that results into a Cunningham chain, or first/second order bitwin chains. Based on origin and length of the resulting chain, a miner computes the difficulty of said chain and compares it to the current network difficulty. In case of a greater computed difficulty, the miner has successfully found a valid block, which will then be broadcasted to the network.[142] This alternative PoW process is said to offer value to scientific research by supporting the search for prime numbers and prime number chains.

King (2013) further explained that reliance on prime chains as an alternative method for mining XPM prohibits the use of sophisticated mining hardware. It is thus possible to mine Primecoin with CPUs only which vastly reduces the barriers to entry to the mining network and results in a relatively more equitable distribution within the network. Primecoin thus represents another alternative mining process to the energy dependent and inefficient proof-of-work method.

## 5.8 Mastercoin

Mastercoin (MSC) is an alternative cryptocurrency that also functions as a communications protocol that is built as an extension to the Bitcoin block chain. The intent of its developers is to enable complex financial functions that were not possible based the current bitcoin technology. Willett (2012) explained that Mastercoin is

141 c.p. King (2013), p.3-4

142 c.p. Sprankel (2013), p.15

an additional protocol layer with new currency protocols and different rules built on top of Bitcoin without interfering with it. This was a unique approach for creating an alternative cryptocurrency as creating an alternative block chain is the norm within the Altcoin ecosystem. The name was chosen as a reference to "Metadata Archival by Standard Transaction Embedding". Buterin (2013b) stated that Mastercoin is an alternative way of making sense of Bitcoin transactions that uses the underlying bitcoin transactions and parses them to extract relevant data for the Mastercoin protocol. Mastercoin can thus leverage the very high security of the more established Bitcoin network and offers an attractive way of create protocols that interact with Bitcoin and other block chain protocols in the future.

Figure 58: Mastercoin Protocol Layers

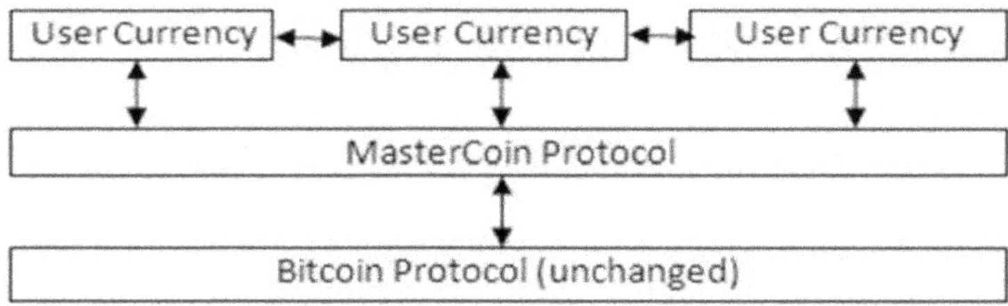


Source: Willett (2014), www.github.com, 12.10.2014

Willett (2012) recognized that building an alternative block chain and standalone cryptocurrencies would dilute their efforts and be detrimental to the cryptocurrency ecosystem. They would compete against Bitcoin financially, create barriers, and hinder adoption of cryptocurrencies in general. As such, he argued that connecting Mastercoin with Bitcoin as an additional protocol layer would increase utility and value of both.

The list of potential applications possible through Mastercoin is largely congruent with those of Ethereum. It enables decentralized exchanges, smart contracts, distributed gambling, distributed sales, contracts for difference, escrow services and the like.[143]

The protocol also addresses a number of aforementioned weaknesses of Bitcoin. Mastercoin enables the creation of savings addresses that allow user to reverse

[143] c.p. Willett (2014), https://github.com/mastercoin-MSC/spec, 12.10.2014

transactions within a predefined time horizon, thus mitigating the risk related to non-reversible transactions.[144] Mastercoin also allows user to create user-defined currencies through the Mastercoin network. Perhaps its most ambitious feature, however, is the plan to develop self-stabilizing currencies. Decentralized bets and contracts-for-difference can already be used in order to hedge a position held in MSC against another asset or currency. Self-stabilizing currencies can be created through the Mastercoin protocol and can be designed to track the price of an underlying index, currency or asset. In order to accomplish this, the protocol enters the role of a central bank that creates and issues units of said currency. This process is based solely on the protocol and the referenced factors price fluctuations and does not involve human interaction after its initial creation. Such a self-stabilizing currency, however, needs some other form of funds in order to exchange them for price stabilization measures and can thus run out of funds and go bankrupt. Also, this concept can potentially be exploited through speculative attacks that deprive the currency of its backing. This obvious flaw is currently a major impediment for this concept. Nevertheless, the idea of a selfstabilizing mechanism without human interaction that allows secure storage of value and a predictable range for price fluctuations holds potential for future developments of the cryptocurrency technology.[145] Overall, the Mastercoin concept is much more centralized than other cryptocurrencies. The network is based on the Bitcoin block chain and thus depends on its data. Furthermore, Mastercoins cannot be mined by a decentralized network of miners but have been issued through a "fundraiser" phase, which makes them centrally issued.

## 5.9 Network Effect of Bitcoin

Bitcoin proponents often emphasize that Bitcoin's intrinsic value and competitive position mostly originates from its network effect. This reasoning is closely related to Metcalfe's law, which was formulated by George Gilder in 1993 and attributed by him to the inventor of the Ethernet Bob Metcalfe.[146] It implies that the value of a

144 c.p. Buterin (2013b), http://bitcoinmagazine.com/7961/mastercoin-a-second-generation-protocol-on-thebitcoin-blockchain/, 18.09.2014

145 c.p. Buterin (2013b), http://bitcoinmagazine.com/7961/mastercoin-a-second-generation-protocol-on-thebitcoin-blockchain/, 18.09.2014

146 c.p. Varian & Shapiro (1999), p.184

telecommunication network is proportional to the square of the number of connected users in the system.

$$V_{Bitcoin} \sim n2 - n$$

Intuitively, one could relate this notion to Bitcoin. Hendler & Goldbeck (2008) note that Metcalfe's law applies best to communication technology, Web 2.0 applications, such as social networks, and the Semantic Web. Relating this concept to Bitcoin, the value of the digital currency would be somewhat directly related to the number of users and the number of places where people can buy and spend BTC. Certainly, its value would tend towards zero if less users or services accept Bitcoin for trading or payment services and its market would decline. As Bitcoin is seen by some as 'the currency of the Internet' and is in fact strongly connected to the web network on which it operates, it is conceivable that Metcalfe's law could be applied to Bitcoin. Varian & Shapiro (1999) noted that Metcalfe's law should actually be interpreted as a rule of thumb and not as a law. It simply implies that there is a direct relationship between the number of users in a network and the networks value, in which a tenfold increase in users results into a hundredfold increase in the networks value. Briscoe et al (2006) argued that Metcalfe's law is flawed and attributed many notable company failures during the Dotcom bubble to an incorrect understanding of it. [147] Odlyzko & Tilly (2005) argued that Metcalfe's law significantly overstates the implied relationship between number of connections and value of the network because of a fundamental flaw in the assumption that each connection is of equal value. They hold that the relationship is closer to a logarithmic value of n.

$$V_{Bitcoin} \sim n \log n$$

Notably, Briscoe et al. (2006) cite to Marc Andreessen, who attributed the growth of the Web and services such as AOL to Metcalfe's law, and who is a prominent Bitcoin investor at this moment. Varian & Shapiro (1999) explained that network externalities make it virtually impossible for a small network to overcome the larger one as long as the network that aims toward introducing a new technology does not overcome collective switching costs of the existing network. Moreover, there are significant complementary assets that develop around a broadly used

[147] c.p. Briscoe et al. (2006), http://spectrum.ieee.org/computing/networks/metcalfes-law-is-wrong, 04.07.2014

network as well as psychological switching costs. Similarly, Luther (2013) applied a model developed by Dowd & Greenaway (1993) on Bitcoin and argued that it is unlikely that Bitcoin will become an alternative currency due to network effects and switching costs. He stressed that this holds true even if all agents agree that the prevailing currency is inferior to the alternative currency. Luther (2013) compared traditional currencies to Bitcoin, whereas his reasoning could also be applied when comparing Bitcoin to alternative cryptocurrencies. Odlyzko (1997) described how social changes, even if the changes do not involve any major social transformations, tend to be very low and do not catch up with the pace of technological development. Later, Odlyzko (2003) argued that changes in payment systems follow a similar slow path and can be subject to cultural and institutional factors. He asserts that debit card penetration of the United States happened significantly faster than would normally be expected due to the role of 'forcing agents' such as banks that wanted to profit from this new market segment. Lack of forcing agents would result into very slow penetration of new payment systems. GoldmanSachs (2014, p.20) stated that "Bitcoin transactions have potential cost advantages over conventional payments and reduce the need for intermediation. The gap between conventional transactions cost and any bitcoin fees for convenience and increased security will allow bitcoin to make incursions into this market."

If Metcalfe's law (or its logarithmic equivalent) does in fact apply to Bitcoin, it could be assumed that the already strong position, compared to any Altcoin currently available, may be a significant entry barrier to competing cryptocurrencies. Switching costs from one service or product to a different one are nonlinear and therefore require considerable efforts or development of a vastly superior competing service or product.

# 6 Analysis: Ripple

Ripple (XRP) is a decentralized payment protocol that enables instantaneous transactions of funds through a global value web. It allows conversion of all currencies or units of value at the same speed as information is propagated through global channels. It is developed by Ripple Labs, a technology company founded by Chris Larsen and Jed McCaleb in 2012, which has attracted significant venture capitalist investment.[148]

Ripple is akin to cryptocurrencies in many aspects, but is usually not subsumed under the umbrella term 'cryptocurrency'. Ripple is an Internet protocol for conducting financial transactions, which focuses on routing payments and settling funds. The most significant difference between Ripple and Bitcoin is that the Ripple payment protocol infrastructure allows direct unit-of-account exchange, and is designed to be "currency-agnostic."[149] Ripple can act as a bridge currency that is exchanged for any fiat currency, commodity, cryptocurrency or any other unit of value. As such, Ripple is functioning as a decentralized exchange for any good that holds value, including gold, mobile points, frequent flier miles, etc.

---

[148] c.p. Ripple Labs (n.d.), https://www.ripplelabs.com/investors/, 16.10.2014

[149] c.p. Ripple Labs (2013), p.3

Figure 59: Ripple Function Schematic

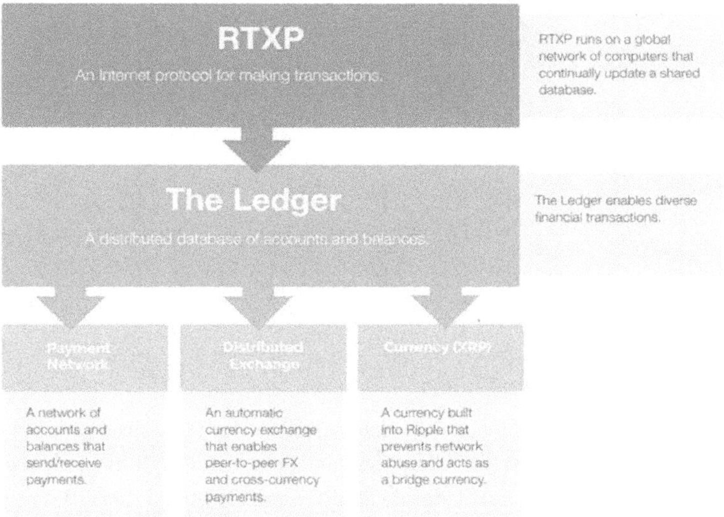

Source: Ripple Labs (2014a), p. 3

Similar to cryptocurrencies, Ripple employs both a transaction protocol and a special type of currency. XRP or "ripples" are units of account that are defined as natively digital assets that only exist within the Ripple network.[150] There was a fixed amount of 100 billion XRP created at inception of the protocol. Units of account that are exchanged against XRP are gateway liabilities that are freely interchangeable in form of balances. As such, there is no requirement to own or hold XRP in order to exchange other units of account. Ripple transactions require *gateways* as entry and exit points in the network, within which XRP is the only asset. Gateways are businesses, banks, marketplaces or any other financial institutions that facilitates Ripple transactions. Ripple employs gateway balances, which would theoretically result into a large and potentially unmanageable number of currency pairs. As such, XRP was designed to obtain the role of a "bridge currency" or "vehicle currency" that eliminates counterparty risk and related fees.

[150] c.p. Ripple Labs (2013), p.7

Figure 60: Multiple Currency Pairs vs. Vehicle Currency

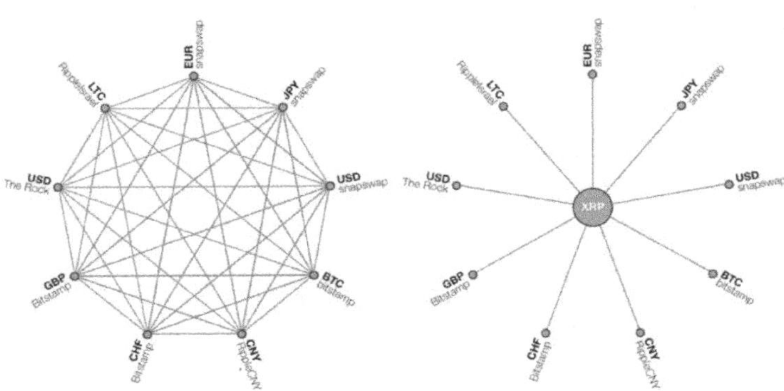


Source: Ripple Labs (2013), p.11

XRP is native to the Internet and on that basis enables frictionless, global transactions without intermediaries. As an Internet protocol, Ripple is compared to the invention of the Email protocol Simple Mail Transfer Protocol (SMTP). The protocol is open-source, distributed and not owned by a central operator. It is envisioned to provide similar benefits to disconnected "walled garden" networks within the realm of financial services. Ripple's creators compare its transaction protocol to that of Email. Electronic mail services are conducted by different mail services (AOL, Gmail, Yahoo, etc.) but all of them use the same Simple Mail Transfer Protocol (SMTP). In the same way, Ripple's protocol is designed to send money to others no matter what financial service company is conducting the transaction. The rationale behind Ripple is that banks and other institutions impede the transfer of funds with transaction fees and processing delays.[151] Liu (2013b) referred to Ripple as a form of social network in which everyone is their own bank and relationships between people are defined by their respective lines of credit.

[151] c.p. Ripple Labs (2014b), p.5

Figure 61: Ripple Protocol to Email Protocol Comparison

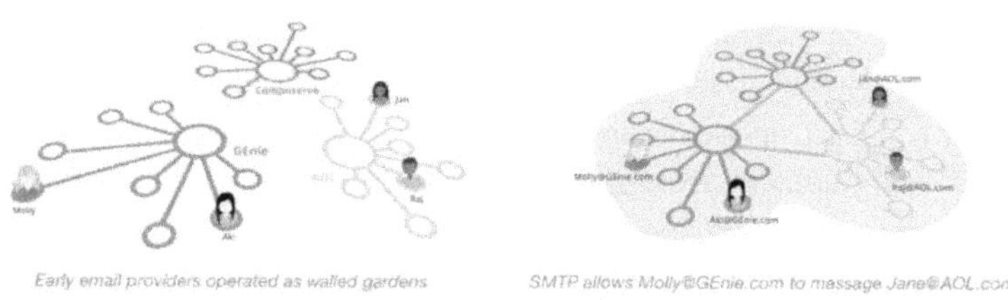


Source: Ripple Labs (2014b), p. 3

Thomas & Schwartz (2013) argued that parties that wish to transact have to use explicit settlement agreements on centralized clearinghouses. These processes that result into high transaction costs, reduced liquidity, poor user experiences and barriers to economic growth.

Ripple is based on a distributed networked database that executes and settles transactions every 220 seconds at the rate a new ledger closes. The shared database contains information about user accounts, balances, trades and respective changes to these items in the ledger. It functions on a globally distributed level-playing-field that eliminates physical location benefits due to absence of centralized exchanges. Network delay or physical latency are a non-issue as speed advantages of different locations are eliminated due to the distributed servers that form the network update the order book simultaneously.[152]

Figure 62: Ripple Ledger

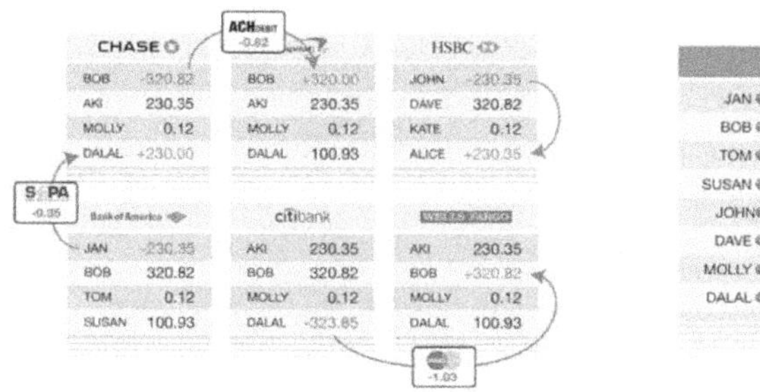


Source: Ripple Labs (2013), p.3

[152] c.p. Ripple Labs (2013), p.14

Similar to Bitcoin and other cryptocurrencies, Ripple uses a shared, public database, where each server keeps a copy of the current ledger including all transactions. However, transactions are conducted as the network mutually agrees on a consensus, and simultaneously offsets accounts and balances. Transactions are verified by consensus of the entire network about which transactions are genuine and which are fraudulent. As Ripple is a distributed network, it is not trustless and therefore faces the double-spending problem and the Byzantine generals problem. Schwartz et al. (2014) explained how Ripple provides a solution to these problems through its Ripple protocol consensus algorithm (RPCA). This algorithm functions by servers broadcasting a set of 'candidate transactions', whose genuineness will be verified by other servers in form of a yes-no vote. Each server within the network maintains a unique node list (UNL) set of other servers in the network, which are queried in order to reach consensus with. After several rounds of votes ($t$), all transactions that reach a minimum of 80% consensus within all unique node lists are applied to the current ledger. The network maintains correctness of all transactions and prevents fraudulent transactions as long 80% of UNLs are honest or $f \leq (n - 1)/5$, where $n$ stands for number of nodes in the distributed network and $f$ denotes the number of Byzantine failures. Thus the system remains intact as consensus requires all nodes in the network to apply deterministic rules to a mutually shared and agreed upon set of transactions. All nodes reach the same consensus regardless of their UNLs, thereby eliminating the double-spending threat by reaching one set of globally recognized transactions. Notably, this system is not trustless, as validators within the network can be cryptographically pseudonymously identified and as such can build up reputation. Dishonest parts of the distributed network which fail to sign the consensus ledger are easily detectable and can be disregarded by honest actors. Liu (2013b) noted that users are obliged to choose their own peers to form their network within the distributed Ripple network. In addition, Ripple Labs will maintain a list of trusted peers and ensure that their will not collude in order to defraud users.

Another difference to Bitcoin is that due to the distributed architecture of the network and the consensus system, there is no requirement for mining XRP. All 100 billion XRP were created at a specific point in time and are since in circulation. Ripple Labs reserved a significant fraction (23,543,355,034 XRP) and plans to distribute the remaining XRP to users, merchants, gateways, market makers, and developers over time.[153] Ripples are, moreover, used as countermeasure against attacks in the network. Each ledger is required to maintain a small reserve of 50 XRP in order to impede the creation of excess ledgers. In addition, each processed transaction destroys 0.00001 XRP and fees are designed to increase when under attacks are registered in order to increase the attackers costs.

The system does not depend on a central network operator due to the self-clearing capability of the network. Servers in the network find consensus about the changes to the ledger and simultaneously update their copies of the ledger. Because of the network is distributed, the threat of single points of failure (SPOF) is said to be eliminated.[154]

Table 12: Proposed Applications of the Ripple Payment System

| **Remittance** | **Prepaid** |
|---|---|
| Expand geographic footprint at no cost • Offer new currencies without capital requirements<br>Pay wholesale forex spreads<br>Earn 100% margin on transaction fees | Expand participating merchant base<br>Acquire a turnkey digital prepaid wallet<br>Enable peer-to-peer payments<br>Allow cross-border payments<br>Create a new revenue channel from balance transfers within Ripple |
| **Bank** | **Merchants & Marketplaces** |
| Charge fees for faster clearing<br>Free, automated clearing house for money movement<br>Create a new revenue channel from balance transfers within Ripple<br>Expand geographic footprint without regional/country risk<br>Facilitate B2B cross-border transactions without currency risk | Own and operate a branded payment rail<br>Acquire a turnkey digital wallet<br>Eliminate interchange fees and fraud • Accept international payments without currency risk<br>Settle funds instantly |

153 c.p. Ripple Labs (n.d.), https://www.ripplelabs.com/xrp-distribution, 16.10.2014

154 c.p. Ripple Labs (2014b), p.6

| Currency Exchanges | Merchant Acquirers |
|---|---|
| Free, global clearing house and prime broker for market makers<br>Create a new revenue channel from balance transfers within Ripple<br>Earn 100% margin on spreads and service fees<br>Expand currency coverage without new capital requirements<br>Expand portfolio of brokered assets | Free payment rail<br>Earn 100% margin on all processing fees • Create a new revenue channel from balance transfers across Ripple • Process cross-border payments at no cost<br>Eliminate buyer fraud from chargebacks • Seamless integration with existing settlement platforms |

Source: Ripple Labs (2014a), p.4

Clearly, Ripple should not be seen as a variation of Bitcoin or other cryptocurrencies. It is a standalone protocol that shares a lot of features with Bitcoin, but offers various additional characteristics.

Figure 63: Fund Flow: Current vs. Ripple

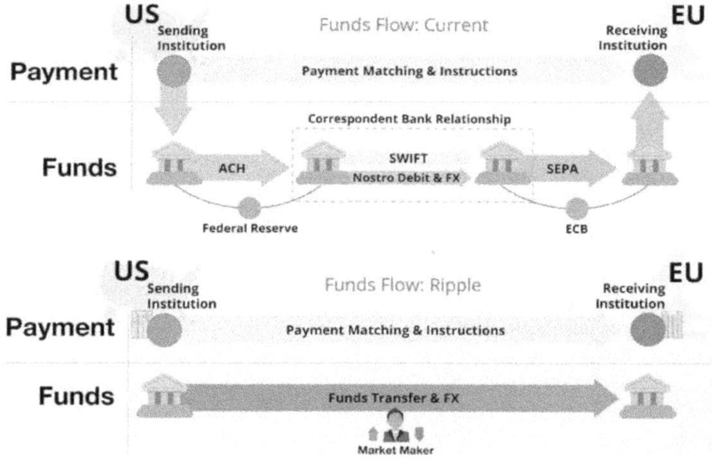


Source: Ripple Labs (2014c), p.3

The technology of Ripple is intended specifically to act as a secure framework for financial institutions and market makers.[155] Ripple promises to offer intra-group

[155] c.p. Ripple Labs (2014), p.3

and inter-bank payment flows between FIs, within FIs and with businesses. At the same time, the technology could reduce or eliminate settlement risk, transaction costs and improve information dissemination. Moreover, due to the pre-funded model, in which clients and market makers provide liquidity, reserve requirements for funding interbank and correspondent liquidity would potentially be eliminated.[156] Therefore Ripple appears to represent a potential alternative to current systems that are subject to increased costs due to recent and developing regulatory frameworks, such as Basel III.

Ripple is certainly an intriguing concept at this point, but it is still in development. It open source nature allowed consistent improvements to security and applicability in the code base. One major achievement has already been reached as German direct bank Fidor Bank AG became the first FI that implemented Ripple as a global settlement system in May 2014.[157] In September 2014, the first local U.S. banks announced plans for implementing Ripple.[158] It can be expected that more banks and financial institutions will follow to integrate Ripple in the near future.

[156] c.p. Ripple Labs (2014c), p.6

[157] c.p. Azzano (2014), http://finance.yahoo.com/news/ripple-labs-announces-fidor-bank-120200943.html, 19.06.2014

[158] c.p. Higgins (2014), http://www.coindesk.com/us-banks-announce-ripple-protocol-integration/, 06.10.2014

## 7 Analysis: Bitcoin Side Chains

We have discussed in detail the various shortcomings and potential issues that Bitcoin is likely to face in the future. Moreover, we have analyzed a number of promising alternative cryptocurrencies that intend to address their perceived flaws of Bitcoin. One additionally possible application that could mitigate these issues and allow incorporation of the features of alternative cryptocurrencies into Bitcoin itself would be adapting Bitcoin's core programming. However, changing the Bitcoin core code is not without risk. For example, Buterin (2013a) reported a major conflict within the network as the most widely utilized mining implementation bitcoind updated from version 0.7 to version 0.8, which resulted in a fork that lasted for 6 hours and forced several major Bitcoin services and mining pools to shut down parts of their systems.

In April 2014, Adam Back and Austin Hill began advocating the idea of creating co-called 'side chains'.[159] Side chains are effectively alternative block chains that would be backed by bitcoins of the original block chain. Side chains would allow additional features or transaction types to be added to Bitcoin, while acting as a separate protocol. Adam Back is a famous British cryptologist, who created Hashcash – a proof-of-work system designed to prevent Denial-of-Service (DoS) attacks and certain types of Email spam.[160] Hashcash technology is arguably one of the core concepts which Bitcoin is based on. In fact, Bitcoin can be seen as a direct offspring of Hashcash.[161]

Contrary to the many attempts of alternative cryptocurrencies to create a Bitcoin 2.0 version, the side chain proposal could actually incorporate features of Altcoins into the Bitcoin system by means of creating specialized side chains. At first glance, this approach is certainly preferable to mutli-cryptocrrency transfers among exchanges in order to use different alternative coins specifically for their offered features. Most Bitcoin-Altcoin trades are currently conducted on niche market exchanges that charge considerable transaction fees. Moreover, multi-cryptocurrency transfers expose users to additional price fluctuations and therefore to increased risk. Thus side chains appear like a promising concept that could foster Bitcoin's

[159] c.p. Buterin (2014b), http://bitcoinmagazine.com/12349/side-chains-challenges-potential/, 28.07.2014

[160] c.p. Back (2002), p.3

[161] Bitcoin Wiki. Hashcash, 09.07.2014

dominant position and potentially drastically reduce or even vastly eliminate competition of alternative cryptocurrencies.

Back stated that side chains could be created for specific markets of tasks, such as micropayment side chains or smart contract side chains. [162] Hopkins et al. (2014) hold that side chains would provide an avenue for developers to add features to Bitcoin while keeping the BTC linked to the main block chain.[163] Side chains would thus allow incorporation of specific features that certain Altcoins provide (faster confirmation times, improved privacy, microtransactions, smart contracts etc.) by using a two-way peg system.[164][165] This option would enable users to 'move' their bitcoins from the original block chain to a side chain that adds alternative features to the pegged bitcoins. Back's initial idea was based on 'one-way pegging', by which a Bitcoin could be moved from one block chain to another by marking the transferred coin and creating a new Bitcoin on the side chain as a representation of the original Bitcoin. Bitcoin developer Greg Maxwell improved upon the initial proposal and proposed 'two-way pegging', through which bitcoins could be moved between the block chain and side chains. This concept would require development that would make bitcoins interoperable between chains but still ensure security of the bitcoins on the main block chain.[166] By doing so, the monetary base of 21 million bitcoins would be preserved, as would be the value of the bitcoins.

Side chains would give bitcoins specific characteristics, while leaving the original bitcoins intact. If a side chain is subject to security mishaps, the bitcoins from the main block chain would not be affected, as only the pegged versions within that side chain would be affected ('firewalled'). Thus, users would not be at risk for using additional side chains.[167] Side chains would eliminate the need to adapt Bitcoin itself, as changing the protocol of the decentralized technology is complicated and

---

[162] c.p. Bradbury (2014), http://www.coindesk.com/bitcoin-core-developers-bitcoin-side-chains/, 28.07.2014

[163] c.p. Hopkins et al. (2014), http://siliconangle.com/blog/2014/04/21/bitcoin-sidechains/, 01.08.2014

[164] c.p. Torpey (2014), http://www.cryptocoinsnews.com/news/adam-back-sidechains-can-replace-altcoins-bitcoin-

[165] -0-platforms/2014/04/10, 01.08.2014

[166] c.p. Hopkins et al. (2014), http://siliconangle.com/blog/2014/04/21/bitcoin-sidechains/, 01.08.2014

[167] c.p. Hopkins et al. (2014), http://siliconangle.com/blog/2014/04/21/bitcoin-sidechains/, 01.08.2014

puts the entire system at risk.[168] Most notably, side chains can be developed by individuals other than the core Bitcoin developers, thus increasing innovation potential. The possibility of adding innovative concepts to the Bitcoin protocol, without interfering with its core development and whilst bitcoins cannot be lost or mishandled due to two-way pegging, arguably bears vast potential for the cryptocurrency's future.

With side chains incorporating characteristics of Altcoins, the current market of cryptocurrencies could be transformed significantly. Standalone alternative cryptocurrencies could potentially lose their raison d'être. Full scale opening of the Bitcoin network to developers and entrepreneurs through side chain implementation could divert intellectual, financial and hardware resources currently tied to alternative cryptocurrencies towards Bitcoin and thus increase its utility. Altcoins could be substituted by Bitcoin-based side chains, which would amplify Bitcoin's network effect in turn. Torpey (2014) emphasized that Altcoins damage the network effect of Bitcoin, which he perceives as its main value proposition. Moreover, side chains would be the first genuine project within the cryptocurrency ecosystem that deserved the title of "Bitcoin 2.0". In fact, it appears much more likely that innovation will concentrate on side chains instead of alternative cryptocurrencies, as contributors would benefit from the already established popularity of Bitcoin. The costs of establishing a new cryptocurrency, market it, convince exchanges to allow trading of their Altcoin and reach new users is arguably larger for independent Altcoins than they would be for contributors to the already existing Bitcoin ecosystem. Notably, many of the most promising cryptocurrency projects currently work towards extending Bitcoin or build applications around it, e.g. Colored Coins, Ethereum, Counterparty, BitShares and Mastercoin.[169]

Buterin (2014b) stated that side chains would complete the quadrant of cryptocurrency choices. Within the current cryptocurrency market, he distinguishes four major categories of which users can choose. This quadrant summarizes the directions that the aforementioned Altcoin and Bitcoin 2.0 projects currently aim for.

[168] c.p. Torpey (2014), http://www.cryptocoinsnews.com/news/adam-back-sidechains-can-replace-altcoins-bitcoin2-0-platforms/2014/04/10, 01.08.2014

[169] c.p. Kharif (2014), http://www.bloomberg.com/news/2014-03-28/bitcoin-2-0-shows-technology-evolvingbeyond-use-as-money.html, 03.09.2014

Table 13: Cryptocurrency Quadrant

| | Use of Bitcoin | Alternative Cryptocurrency |
|---|---|---|
| **Independent Network** | Use a separate blockchain and the Bitcoin currency (Side-chain) | Use a separate blockchain and a separate currency (Ethereum) |
| **Bitcoin Network** | Use the Bitcoin blockchain and Bitcoin currency (Bitcoin) | Use the Bitcoin blockchain and other currencies (Mastercoin, Counterparty) |

Source: Buterin (2014b), www.bitcoinmagazine.com, 29.09.2014

Combining these currently dispersed financial innovation capacities into a combined Bitcoin platform could result in a considerable network effect and boost cryptocurrency utility.[170] It would constitute a significant further step in decentralization, as an even larger and more diverse network would emerge from this transformation. One possible outcome could be a programmable digital money platform that functions globally and without a single point of failure (SPOF) that would threaten the network. Sharma (2014) argued that the block chain technology being the first practical solution to the Byzantine Generals problem would allow to build a number of decentralized features on top of it. Among those are decentralized voting systems, decentralized exchange o storage and bandwidth, smart self-validating contracts, decentralized document verification (proof of existence).

Thus it is reasonable to conclude that Bitcoin will evolve into a decentralized platform for financial services that do not require central intermediaries such as banks and financial institutions. The cryptocurrency part of the Bitcoin protocol may well become just one aspect of the greater block chain technology with integrated side chains. Hill suggests: "We could have US and Canadian dollars, smart derivatives, option shares, and future contracts. A whole series of programmable trust instruments. A lot of people had talked about these things, and how the block chain could be adapted for this, but I hadn't seen anyone lay out how it would come to pass."[171]

The side chain proposal, however, will not result into mitigating certain shortcomings of the Bitcoin protocol. As it only functions as an extension to the existing protocol, it does not alter any of the core functions of Bitcoin. Thus, the imperfections concerning mining, energy consumption, scalability, 51% attacks and the like will

---

170 c.p. Hopkins et al. (2014), http://siliconangle.com/blog/2014/04/21/bitcoin-sidechains/, 01.08.2014

171 c.p. Bradbury (2014), http://www.coindesk.com/bitcoin-core-developers-bitcoin-side-chains/, 28.07.2014

remain present even if side chains lead the cryptocurrency market increasingly to concentrate on and within Bitcoin. In fact, a positive network effect achieved through side chains could potentially worsen some of these issues further. However, it is not clear at this point how Bitcoin will evolve in the future and what features might be changed and adapted to future. A system of verifiably two-way pegging could be utilized to create a Bitcoin 2.0 at some point in the future and link ownership of original bitcoins to the new Bitcoin technology.

It can be speculated that if side chains within Bitcoin or an updated Bitcoin 2.0 equivalent will be present and successfully integrate innovations that are currently developed within the cryptocurrency ecosystem, the result could be very well a significant market share of decentralized financial innovation within the global financial infrastructure. Decentralization of finance implies that loans could be made without banks, contracts without lawyers, stocks could be exchanged without brokers, and microtransactions be conducted with almost no transaction fees.

# 8 Conclusion

The alternative cryptocurrency market has been analyzed and explored in order to answer the question of whether a genuine Bitcoin 2.0 can already be identified. Courtois (2014) argued that the shortcomings of Bitcoin will be self-defeating and result into the loss of its dominant position at some time in the future. This notion is in fact echoed by many, both supporters and opponents of the cryptocurrency. We have analyzed key weaknesses concerning mining, network delay, transaction fee policy, volatility, non-reversible transactions, energy consumption, anonymity and scalability. Furthermore, we have discussed promising second-generation cryptocurrencies that specifically address these weaknesses and shortcomings of Bitcoin. Our analysis showed that Bitcoin is by no means a cutting-edge technology and there are a number of more sophisticated approaches or alternative methods that provide higher utility to the cryptocurrency technology.

In spite of this, due to Bitcoin's nature as an open-source protocol and the potential that side chains offer to the protocol, it can very well be assumed that the search for a genuine Bitcoin 2.0 is not reasonable. Similar to the development of the Internet, there may be no need for a "2.0" version of a concept that has enough capabilities to be improved and extended in order to address shortcomings and adapt to new innovations. Flexible open source technology implies that Bitcoin development can address many known shortcomings by adapting the technology. The side chain proposal can transform the cryptocurrency market and concentrate efforts and innovation into Bitcoin, instead of dispersing the ecosystem by a large number of cryptocurrencies. By doing so, the combined efforts could result into a long term market share of decentralized financial infrastructures within the global financial sector.

In short:

- Bitcoin is disruptive. Until cryptocurrencies were invented, there was no practical way of transmitting value from any point on the globe without a third party intermediate.
- Bitcoin is innovative. The block chain technology could offer a variety of additional implementations and serve as a secure information propagation and verification method.

- Bitcoin technology has a future: Future implementations go beyond payment transactions. New developments allow various additions to the network technology and could evolve into a system for smart contracts, micropayments, store of information, information propagation, etc.

Nevertheless, in its current form, Bitcoin does in fact suffer from a number of shortcomings and impediments that need to be addressed. Some of them can be alleviated by technological innovation, but others, such as high volatility and highly skewed distribution of bitcoin holdings among users, may remain very persistent over longer time periods and impede the future of Bitcoin. In addition, whereas it is an innovative and promising invention, it is not a state-of-the-art technology. It is reasonable to assume that sooner or later a competing cryptocurrency could emerge that offers significant advantages over Bitcoin. This thesis showed that Bitcoin's open source protocol nature and the potential that side chains offer to it, could both be factors that may make the emergence of such a "Bitcoin 2.0" unnecessary. While there are certainly a number of projects that can be classified as Bitcoin 2.0 projects, the potential of the side chain proposal supports the notion that Bitcoin could become the dominant cryptocurrency that integrates the innovative power of currently dispersed cryptocurrency market into one major protocol. The development of a meta-Bitcoin opens a wide array of applications for a future, technologically sophisticated, non-institutional financial platform that could obtain a major share of the global financial infrastructure.

Bitcoin is about to transform from a mere cryptocurrency to a decentralized, peer-to-peer finance system with an integrated secure data storage and verification process. Its true potential is not found within its capacity as a virtual currency but is located within the block chain technology. This innovation enables secure mathematical data verification and processing mechanism in a decentralized manner. Thus it eliminates the need for trusted third parties. Its range of applications goes beyond a mere monetary function of a virtual currency. The block chain protocol can be the base for an entirely new class of financial innovation – decentralized finance.

Decentralization of finance implies that loans could be made without banks, contracts without lawyers, stocks could be exchanged without brokers, remittances without obstacles and excessive transaction costs, and microtransactions be conducted with almost no transaction fees. Bitcoin could be the first step towards creating such an alternative decentralized financial market. Moreover, decentralized and openly available financial services could benefit the 2.5 billion adults world-wide that currently do not have access to formal financial services or are outright unbanked. Almost 88% of this unbanked and underbanked population live in poorer parts of the world, such as Africa, Asia, Latin America, and the Middle East.[172] That number is evermore dwarfed by the human population that does only have limited global banking access.

[172] c.p. Chaia et al. (2009), p.19-20

## Bibliography

Ahamad, S., & Varghese, M. N. B. (2013). A Survey on Crypto Currencies. In Int. Conf. on Advances in Civil Engineering, AETACE.

Albrecht, R. (2013). Bitcoin Money Supply and Money Creation. DGC Magazine. Available at: http://www.dgcmagazine.com/bitcoin-money-supply-and-money-creation/, Retrieved: 22.07.2014.

Andresen, G. (2013). Back-of-the-Envelope Calculations for Marginal Cost of Transactions. GitHub Gist. Available at: https://gist.github.com/gavinandresen/5044482, Retrieved: 03.09.2014.

Andresen, G. (2014a). Centralized Mining. Bitcoin Foundation. Available at: https://bitcoinfoundation.org/2014/06/13/centralized-mining/, Retrieved: 28.05.2014.

Andresen, G. (2014b). A Scalability Roadmap. Bitcoin Foundation. Available at: https://bitcoinfoundation.org/2014/10/a-scalability-roadmap/, Retrieved: 07.10.2014.

Androulaki, E., Karame, G. O., Roeschlin, M., Scherer, T., & Capkun, S. (2013). Evaluating user privacy in bitcoin. In Financial Cryptography and Data Security (pp. 34-51). Springer Berlin Heidelberg.

Ateniese, G., Faonio, A., Magri, B., & de Medeiros, B. (2014). Certified bitcoins. In Applied Cryptography and Network Security (pp. 80-96). Springer International Publishing.

Ax, J. (2014). Bitcoin promoter Shrem indicted in NY for money laundering. Thomson Reuters. Available at: http://www.reuters.com/article/2014/04/14/us-usa-crime-bitcoinidUSBREA3D1RU20140414, Retrieved: 08.10.2014.

Azzano, M. (2014). Ripple Labs Announces Fidor Bank AG as First Bank to Use the Ripple Protocol. Yahoo Finance. Available at: http://finance.yahoo.com/news/ripple-labs-announces-fidor-bank120200943.html, Retrieved: 19.06.2014.

Babaioff, M., Dobzinski, S., Oren, S., & Zohar, A. (2012). On bitcoin and red balloons. In Proceedings of the 13th ACM Conference on Electronic Commerce (pp. 56-73). ACM.

Back, A. (2002). Hashcash-a denial of service counter-measure. Available at: ftp://sunsite.icm.edu.pl/site/replay.old/programs/hashcash/hashcash.pdf, Retrieved: 20.05.2014

Baran, P. (1964). On Distributed Communications Networks. Communications Systems, IEEE Transactions on, 12(1), 1-9. Available at: http://ieeexplore.ieee.org/stamp/stamp.jsp?tp=&arnumber=1088883, Retrieved: 18.07.2014.

Barber, S., Boyen, X., Shi, E., &Uzun, E. (2012). Bitter to better—how to make bitcoin a better currency. In Financial Cryptography and Data Security (pp. 399-414). Springer Berlin Heidelberg.

Becker, G. (2008). Merkle Signature Schemes, Merkle Trees and Their Cryptanalysis, Available at: http://www.emsec.rub.de/media/crypto/attachments/files/2011/04/becker_1.pdf, Retrieved: 02.10.2014.

Bergstra, J. A., & de Leeuw, K. (2013). Bitcoin and beyond: exclusively informational monies. arXiv preprint arXiv:1304.4758.

Bergstra, J. A., & Weijland, P. (2014). Bitcoin: a money-like informational commodity. arXiv preprint arXiv:1402.4778.

Bellare, M., & Rogaway, P. (2005). Introduction to modern cryptography. UCSD CSE, 207, 207.

Benger, N., van de Pol, J., Smart, N. P., & Yarom, Y. (2014). "Ooh Aah... Just a Little Bit": A small amount of side channel can go a long way. IACR Cryptology ePrint Archive, 2014, 161.

Bentov, I., Gabizon, A., & Mizrahi, A. (2014). Cryptocurrencies without Proof of Work. arXiv preprint arXiv:1406.5694.

Biggs, J. (2014). Fools And Their Bitcoin. TechCrunch. Available at: http://techcrunch.com/2014/03/04/fools-and-their-bitcoin/, Retrieved: 28.06.2014.

Bitcoin Foundation (2014). Removing Impediment's to Bitcoin's Success: A Risk Management Study. Research Brief No1. Available at: https://bitcoinfoundation.org/static/2014/04/Bitcoin-RiskManagement-Study-Spring-2014.pdf, Retrieved. 29.07.2014.

Bitcoin Project (n.d.). Some things you need to know. Bitcoin.org. Available at: https://bitcoin.org/en/you-need-to-know, Retrieved: 02.06.2014.

Bitcoin Project (n.d.). Bitcoin Core version history. Bitcoin.org. Available at: https://bitcoin.org/en/version-history, Retrieved: 19.10.2014.

Bitcoin Sipa (2014). Total network hashing rate: Difficulty. Available at: http://bitcoin.sipa.be/, Retrieved: 21.10.2014.

Bitcoin Wiki (2012). Vocabulary. Available at: https://en.bitcoin.it/wiki/Vocabulary, Retrieved: 20.10.2014.

Bitcoin Wiki (2014). Address reuse. Available at: https://en.bitcoin.it/wiki/Address_reuse, Retrieved: 26.04.2014.

Bitcoin Wiki (2014). Block chain. Available at: https://en.bitcoin.it/wiki/Block_chain, Retrieved: 19.04.2014.

Bitcoin Wiki (2014). Block Hashing Algorithm. Available at: https://en.bitcoin.it/wiki/Block_hashing_algorithm, 03.03.2014.

Bitcoin Wiki (2014). Controlled supply. Available at: https://en.bitcoin.it/wiki/Controlled_supply, Retrieved: 26.04.2014.

Bitcoin Wiki (2014). Creating forks. Available at: https://en.bitcoin.it/wiki/Creating_forks, Retrieved: 10.07.2014.

Bitcoin Wiki (2014). Genesis block. Available at: https://en.bitcoin.it/wiki/Genesis_block, Retrieved: 08.04.2014.

Bitcoin Wiki (2014). Difficulty. Available at: https://en.bitcoin.it/wiki/Difficulty, Retrieved: 19.05.2014.

Bitcoin Wiki (2014). Hashcash. Available at: https://en.bitcoin.it/wiki/Hashcash, Retrieved: 09.07.2014.

Bitcoin Wiki (2014). Private key. Available at: https://en.bitcoin.it/wiki/Private_key, Retrieved: 16.06.2014.

Bitcoin Wiki (2014). Proof of Work. Available at: https://en.bitcoin.it/wiki/Proof_of_work, Retrieved: 02.04.2014.

Bitcoin Wiki (2014). Scalability. Available at: https://en.bitcoin.it/wiki/Scalability, Retrieved: 20.10.2014.

Bitcoin Wiki (2014). Target. Available at: https://en.bitcoin.it/wiki/Target, Retrieved: 19.05.2014.

Bitcoin Wiki (2014). Technical background of version 1 Bitcoin addresses. Available at: https://en.bitcoin.it/wiki/Technical_background_of_version_1_Bitcoin_addresses, Retrieved: 29.05.2014.

Bitcoin Wiki (2014). Transaction fees. Available at: https://en.bitcoin.it/wiki/Transaction_fees, Retrieved: 19.05.2014.

Bitcoin Wiki (2014). Units. Available at: https://en.bitcoin.it/wiki/Units, Retrieved: 09.07.2014.

Bitcoin Wiki (2014). Wallet. Available at: https://en.bitcoin.it/wiki/Wallet, Retrieved: 27.04.2014.

Bitcoin Wiki (2014). Weaknesses. Available at: https://en.bitcoin.it/wiki/Weaknesses, Retrieved: 24.04.2014.

Bitcoin Wisdom (2014). Litecoin Hash Rate vs Difficulty (9 Months). Available at: https://bitcoinwisdom.com/litecoin/difficulty, Retrieved: 15.06.2014.

Bitcoin Wisdom (2014). Bitcoin Hash Rate vs Difficulty (9 Months). Available at: https://bitcoinwisdom.com/bitcoin/difficulty, Retrieved: 29.09.2014.

Blockchain (2014). Bitcoin Address: 1Drt3c8pSdrkyjuBiwVcSSixZwQtMZ3Tew. Blockchain.info Available at: https://blockchain.info/address/1Drt3c8pSdrkyjuBiwVcSSixZwQtMZ3Tew, Retrieved: 24.04.2014.

Blockchain (2014). Bitcoin Address: 16VHnxqC9R9j55zgBhmxC92agwBiM8Huu2. Blockchain.info. Available at: https://blockchain.info/address/16VHnxqC9R9j55zgBhmxC92agwBiM8Huu2, Retrieved: 09.06.2014.

Blockchain (2014). Hashrate Distribution. Blockchain.info. Available at: https://blockchain.info/pools, Retrieved: 22.05.2014.

Blockchain (2014). Average Block Size. Blockchain.info. Available at: https://blockchain.info/charts/avg-block-size, Retrieved: 11.10.2014.

Blockchain (2014). Blockchain Size. Blockchain.info. Available at: https://blockchain.info/charts/blocks-size, Retrieved: 11.10.2014.

Blockchain (2014). Market Price (USD). Blockchain.info. Available at: https://blockchain.info/charts/market-price, Retrieved: 12.10.2014.

Blockchain (2014). Total Bitcoins in Circulation. Blockchain.info. Available at: https://blockchain.info/charts/total-bitcoins, Retrieved: 14.10.2014.

Blockchain (2014). Average Transaction Confirmation Time. Blockchain.info. Available at: https://blockchain.info/charts/avg-confirmation-time, Retrieved: 14.10.2014.

Bloomberg (2014). Here's How Bitcoin Is Like the Early '90s Internet. Bloomberg TV. Available at: http://www.bloomberg.com/video/here-s-how-bitcoin-is-like-early-90-s-internetdU0H7ADwTl6arrq122kHPg.html, Retrieved: 23.06.2014.

Bos, J. W., Halderman, J. A., Heninger, N., Moore, J., Naehrig, M., & Wustrow, E. (2013). Elliptic Curve Cryptography in Practice. IACR Cryptology ePrint Archive, 2013, 734.

Brito, J., & Castillo, A. (2013). A Primer for Policymakers, Retrieved: mercatus.org/sites/default/files/Brito_BitcoinPrimer_embargoed.pdf, 01.03.2014.

Bommisetty S. (2014). Elliptic Curve Cryptography: A Case for Mobile Encryption. SecurityLearn Blog. Available at: http://www.securitylearn.net/2014/02/28/elliptic-curve-cryptography-a-case-formobile-encryption/, Retrieved: 14.06.2014.

Bornholdt, S., & Sneppen, K. (2014). Do Bitcoins make the world go round? On the dynamics of competing crypto-currencies. arXiv preprint arXiv:1403.6378.

Bos, J. W., Halderman, J. A., Heninger, N., Moore, J., Naehrig, M., & Wustrow, E. (2013). Elliptic Curve Cryptography in Practice. Microsoft Research. November.

Bradbury, D. (2013). The problem with Bitcoin. Computer Fraud & Security, 2013(11), 5-8.

Bradbury, D. (2014). Bitcoin Core Developers Weigh in on Side Chain Proposal. CoinDesk. Available at: http://www.coindesk.com/bitcoin-core-developers-bitcoin-side-chains/, Retrieved: 28.07.2014.

Bryans, D. (2014). Bitcoin and Money Laundering: Mining for an Effective Solution. Ind. LJ, 89, 441.

Briscoe, B., Odlyzko, A., & Tilly, B. (2006). Metcalfe's Law is Wrong. IEEE Spectrum. Available at: http://spectrum.ieee.org/computing/networks/metcalfes-law-is-wrong, Retrieved: 04.07.2014.

Buterin, V. (2013a) Bitcoin Network Shaken by Blockchain Fork. Bitcoin Magazine. Available at: http://bitcoinmagazine.com/3668/bitcoin-network-shaken-by-blockchain-fork/, Retrieved: 21.8.2014.

Buterin, V. (2013b). Mastercoin: A Second-Generation Protocol on the Bitcoin Blockchain. Bitcoin Magazine. Available at: http://bitcoinmagazine.com/7961/mastercoin-a-second-generationprotocol-on-the-bitcoin-blockchain/, Retrieved: 18.09.2014.

Buterin, V. (2014a). Ethereum White Paper: A Next Generation Smart Contract & Decentralized Application Platform. Available at: https://www.ethereum.org/pdfs/EthereumWhitePaper.pdf, Retrieved: 28.09.2014.

Buterin, V. (2014b). Side Chains: The How, The Challenges and the Potential. Bitcoin Magazine. Available at: http://bitcoinmagazine.com/12349/side-chains-challenges-potential/, Retrieved: 28.07.2014.

Buterin, V. (2014c). On Mining. Bitcoin Magazine. Available at: http://bitcoin-magazine.com/14282/mining-2/, Retrieved: 07.07.2014.

Campbell, S. (2014). Bitcoin exchange MtGox 'faced 150,000 hack attacks every second'. The Telegraph. Available at: http://www.telegraph.co.uk/finance/currency/10686698/Bitcoin-exchangeMtGox-faced-150000-hack-attacks-every-second.html, Retrieved: 08.06.2014.

Cawrey, D. (2014a). How Dogetipbot Turned a Spoof Altcoin into a Tipping Phenomenon. CoinDesk. Available at: http://www.coindesk.com/dogetipbot-turned-spoof-altcoin-tipping-phenomenon/, Retrieved: 24.10.2014.

Cawrey, D. (2014b). How Bitcoin's Technology Could Revolutionize Intellectual Property Rights. CoinDesk. Available at: http://www.coindesk.com/how-block-chain-technology-is-working-totransform-intellectual-property/, Retrieved: 28.06.2014.

Cawrey, D. (2014c). What Are Bitcoin Nodes and Why Do We Need Them? CoinDesk, Available at: http://www.coindesk.com/bitcoin-nodes-need/, Retrieved: 25.05.2014.

Chaia, A., Dalal, A., Goland, T., Gonzalez, M. J., Morduch, J., & Schiff, R. (2010). Half the World is Unbanked. Financial Access Initiative. Available at: http://www.microfinancegateway.org/gm/document-1.9.40671/25.pdf, Retrieved: 20.05.2014.

Channer, W. (2014). Winklevoss twins: Bitcoin will be bigger than Facebook. The Guardian. Available at: http://www.theguardian.com/technology/2014/may/19/winklevoss-twins-bitcoin-bigger-thanfacebook-investors, Retrieved: 05.06.2014.

Chen, C. (2014). Warning: Litecoin Miners Need To Leave Coinotron. Cryptocoin News. Available at: https://www.cryptocoinsnews.com/warning-litecoin-miners-need-leave-coinotron/, Retrieved: 25.05.2014.

Christin, N. (2013). Traveling the Silk Road: A measurement analysis of a large anonymous online marketplace. In Proceedings of the 22nd international conference on World Wide Web (pp. 213224). International World Wide Web Conferences Steering Committee.

Cipher, N.N. (2014). The Rise of Darkcoin. DeepDotWeb. Available at: http://www.deepdotweb.com/2014/05/20/the-rise-of-darkcoin/, Retrieved: 06.06.2014.

Citigroup (2014). Disruptive Innovations II: Ten More Things to Stop and Think About. Available at: https://ir.citi.com/RZh%2B9GHcy3eQvegHG9vuU3r5%2FxkjXBMM-fUnULRTyibawadNFQ RrrFA%3D%3D, Retrieved: 02.05.2014.

CNBC (2014). Bitcoin to $1 million? Why it could happen. CNBC. Available at: http://www.cnbc.com/id/101552753, Retrieved: 05.06.2014.

Coblee (2011). [ANN] Litecoin - a lite version of Bitcoin. Launched! Bitcoin Talk Forum, Available at: https://bitcointalk.org/index.php?topic=47417.0, Retrieved: 08.09.2014.

Cohen, B. (2014). United States to Monitor Canadian Border for Illicit Drug-Related Bitcoin Transactions. Let's Talk Bitcoin. Available at: http://letstalkbitcoin.com/blog/post/united-states-to-monitorcanadian-border-for-illicit-drug-related-bitcoin-transactions, Retrieved: 03.10.2014.

Coinbase (2014). I's bits. Coinbase Blog. Available at: http://blog.coinbase.com/post/89405189782/itsbits, Retrieved: 21.07.2014.

Courtois, N. T., Grajek, M., &Naik, R. (2013). The Unreasonable Fundamental Incertitudes Behind Bitcoin Mining. arXiv preprint arXiv: 1310.7935.

Courtois, N. T. (2014). On The Longest Chain Rule and Programmed Self-Destruction of Crypto Currencies. arXiv preprint arXiv:1405.0534.

Cowley, S. (2013). Bitcoin more powerful than fastest supercomputers. CNN Money. Available at: http://money.cnn.com/2013/05/23/technology/enterprise/bitcoin-supercomputers/, Retrieved: 29.08.2014.

Credit Suisse (2013). Global Wealth Report 2013. Crédit Suisse Zurich. Available at: https://publications.credit-suisse.com/tasks/render/file, Retrieved: 18.08.2014.

Crippen, A. (2014). Buffett blasts bitcoin as 'mirage': 'Stay away!'. Available at: http://www.cnbc.com/id/101494937, Retrieved: 08.10.2014.

Cryptobadger (2013). The Altcoin Explosion... And How To Profit From It. CryptoBadger. Available at: http://www.cryptobadger.com/2013/05/altcoin-explosion-profit/, Retrieved: 05.09.2014.

Davidson, K. (2014). Jamaican Bobsledders Ride Dogecoin Into Olympics. Bloomberg. Available at: http://www.bloombergview.com/articles/2014-02-04/jamaican-bobsledders-ride-dogecoin-intoolympics, Retrieved: 06.09.2014.

Decker, C., & Wattenhofer, R. (2013). Information propagation in the bitcoin network. In Peer-to-Peer Computing (P2P), 2013 IEEE Thirteenth International Conference on (pp. 1-10). IEEE.

Dent, S. (2013). $1.2 million in Bitcoins hijacked in 'social engineering' attack. Engadget. Available at: http://www.engadget.com/2013/11/09/bitcoin-hijack-1-2-million/, Retrieved: 03.06.2014.

DeCola, P. (2014). Redditors Fork Up Cash, Wise To Drive Doge At 'Dega. Nascar. Media. Available at: http://www.nascar.com/en_us/news-media/blogs/Off-Track/doge-reddit-josh-wise-talladegasuperspeedway-aarons-499.html, Retrieved: 12.06.2014.

De la Rouviere, S. (2013). Not actually capped at 100 billion? GitHub Gist. Available at: https://github.com/dogecoin/dogecoin/issues/23, Retrieved: 10.06.2014.

Del Castillo, M. (2013). The Brothers Encrypted: Siblings become crypto currency upstarts. Upstart Business Journal. Available at: http://upstart.bizjournals.com/news/technology/2014/02/03/bobby-and-charles-lee-bitcoinbrothers.html?page=all, Retrieved: 09.06.2014.

Dingledine, R., Mathewson, N., & Syverson, P. (2004). Tor: The second-generation onion router. Naval Research Lab Washington DC.

Dion, D. A. (2013). I'll Gladly Trade You Two Bits on Tuesday for a Byte Today: Bitcoin, Regulating Fraud in the E-Conomy of Hacker-Cash. U. Ill. JL Tech. & Pol'y, 165.

Dogecoin (2013). [ANN][DOGE] Dogecoin - very currency many coin - v1.8. Bitcoin Talk Forum. Available at: Required Updatehttps://bitcointalk.org/index.php?topic=361813.0, Retrieved: 10.06.2014.

Dowd, K. & Greenaway, D. (1993). Currency Competition, Network Externalities, and Switching Costs: Towards an Alternative View of Optimum Currency Areas. The Economic Journal 103(420): 1180–89.

Dree12 (2012). List of Major Bitcoin Heists, Thefts, Hacks, Scams, and Losses [Old]. Bitcoin Talk Forum. Available at: https://bitcointalk.org/index.php?topic=83794.0, Retrieved: 29.06.2014.

Duffield, E. & Hagan, K. (2014). Darkcoin: Peer-to-Peer Crypto-Currency with Anonymous Blockchain Transactions and an Improved Proof-of-Work System. Available at: http://www.darkcoin.io/downloads/DarkcoinWhitepaper.pdf, Retrieved: 06.06.2014.

Duffield, E. (2014). Development Updates - July 15th. Darkcoin Talk Forum. Available at: https://darkcointalk.org/threads/development-updates-july-15th.1788/, Retrieved: 24.10.2014.

Eyal, I., & Sirer, E. G. (2013a). Majority is not enough: Bitcoin mining is vulnerable. arXiv preprint arXiv:1311.0243.

Eyal, I., & Sirer, E. G. (2013b). Bitcoin Is Broken. Hacking, Distributed. Available at: http://hackingdistributed.com/2013/11/04/bitcoin-is-broken/, Retrieved: 21.05.2014.

Fargo, S. (2014). Litecoin Will Not Hard Fork to Fend Off ASICs! Cryptocoin News. Available at: https://www.cryptocoinsnews.com/litecoin-will-hard-fork-fend-asics/, Retrieved: 08.09.2014.

Fienup, M. (2001). Reaching Agreement ("Byzantine Generals Problem"). Lecture notes distributed in Distributed Computing (810:146), Spring 2001 at the University of Northern Iowa. Available at: http://www.cs.uni.edu/~fienup/cs146s01/in-class-overheads-andactivitie/lecture10.lwp/odyframe.htm, Retrieved: 07.04.2014.

Friedman, M. (2009). Capitalism and freedom. University of Chicago press.

European Central Bank (2012). Virtual Currency Schemes. ECB Report, Oct. 2012. Available at: www.ecb.europa.eu/pub/pdf/other/virtualcurrencyschemes201210en.pdf, Retrieved: 20.03.2014.

Gimein, M. (2013). Virtual Bitcoin Mining Is a Real-World Environmental Disaster. Bloomberg. http://www.bloomberg.com/news/2013-04-12/virtual-bitcoin-mining-is-a-real-worldenvironmental-disaster.html, Retrieved: 27.07.2014.

Gill, R. (2014). Moolah Founder Accidentally Donates 20 Million Dogecoin to Sponsor NASCAR Driver. CoinDesk. Available at: http://www.coindesk.com/moolah-founder-accidently-donates-20million-dogecoin-to-sponsor-nascar-driver/, Retrieved: 01.06.2014.

Gillespie, C. M. (2014a). Bitcoin User Accidentally Sends 800 BTC to Old Mt.Gox Address. Coinwrite. Available at: http://coinwrite.org/bitcoin-user-accidently-sends-800-btc-old-mt-gox-address/, Retrieved: 01.06.2014.

Gillespie, C. M. (2014b). BREAKING: Facebook Approves Dogecoin Tipping App. Cryptocoin News. Available at: https://www.cryptocoinsnews.com/facebook-approves-dogecoin-tipping-app/, Retrieved: 24.10.2014.

Goldfeder, S., Bonneau, J., Felten, E. W., Kroll, J. A., & Narayanan, A. (2014). Securing Bitcoin wallets via threshold signatures. Available at: http://www.cs.princeton.edu/~stevenag/bitcoin_threshold_signatures.pdf, Retrieved: 10.10.2014.

Green, M. (2013). Zerocoin: making Bitcoin anonymous. A Few Thoughts on Cryptographic Engineering. Available at: http://blog.cryptographyengineering.com/2013/04/zerocoin-making-bitcoinanonymous.html, Retrieved: 05.05.2014.

GoldmanSachs (2014). All About Bitcoin. Goldman Sachs Global Macro Research. Available at: http://www.paymentlawadvisor.com/files/2014/01/GoldmanSachs-Bit-Coin.pdf, Retrieved: 13.04.2014.

Goodman, L. M. (2014). Tezos: A Self-Amending Crypto-Ledger Position Paper. Available at: http://tezos.com/position_paper.pdf, Retrieved: 06.10.2014.

Gustafsson, B. (2013). Milton Friedman, Land value tax and internet currencies [Video file]. YouTube. Available at: http://www.youtube.com/watch?v=j2mdYX1nF_Y, Retrieved: 02.03.2014.

Gup, B. E. (2014). What Is Money? From Commodities to Virtual Currencies/Bitcoin. From Commodities to Virtual Currencies/Bitcoin (March 14, 2014). Available at: http://ssrn.com/abstract=2409172, Retrieved: 04.03.2014.

Güring, P., & Grigg, I. (2011). Bitcoin & Gresham's Law-the economic inevitability of Collapse. Available at: http://iang.org/papers/BitcoinBreachesGreshamsLaw.pdf, Retrieved: 19.05.2014.

Hajdarbegovic, N. (2014). Why Bitcoin Mining Can No Longer Ignore Moore's Law. CoinDesk. Available at: http://www.coindesk.com/bitcoin-mining-can-longer-ignore-moores-law/, Retrieved: 11.10.2014.

Hanley, B. P. (2013). The False Premises and Promises of Bitcoin. arXiv preprint arXiv:1312.2048.

Harrigan, M. (2014). A Network Analyst's View of the Block Chain. Available at: http://www.coindesk.com/network-analysts-view-block-chain/, Retrieved: 20.05.2014.

Heiko, H. (2014). Dagger. GitHub Gist. Available at: https://github.com/ethereum/wiki/wiki/Dagger, Retrieved: 19.09.2014.

Henderson, J. (2014). How Bitcoin Makes Transactions Cheaper. CoinDesk Available at: http://www.coindesk.com/bitcoin-solving-double-spending-problem/, Retrieved: 20.02.2014.

Hendler, J., & Golbeck, J. (2008). Metcalfe's law, Web 2.0, and the Semantic Web. Web Semantics: Science, Services and Agents on the World Wide Web, 6(1), 14-20.

Hern, A. (2014). A history of bitcoin hacks. The Guardian. Available at: http://www.theguardian.com/technology/2014/mar/18/history-of-bitcoin-hacks-alternativecurrency, Retrieved: 28.06.2014.

Higgins, S. (2014). US Banks Announce Ripple Protocol Integration. CoinDesk. http://www.coindesk.com/us-banks-announce-ripple-protocol-integration/, Retrieved: 06.10.2014.

Holdgaard, L. (2014). An exploration of the Bitcoin ecosystem. http://bitcoin-expert.net/wpcontent/uploads/2014/01/Thesis.pdf, Retrieved: 01.05.2014

Hopkins, S., Wheatley, M., & Tolentino, M. (2014). What are side-chains? SiliconANGLE. Available at: http://siliconangle.com/blog/2014/04/21/bitcoin-sidechains/, Retrieved: 01.08.2014.

IMF (n.d.). Anti-Money Laundering/Combating the Financing of Terrorism (AML/CFT). International Monetary Fund. Available at: http://www.imf.org/external/np/leg/amlcft/eng/, Retrieved: 29.08.2014.

Johnson, B., Laszka, A., Grossklags, J., Vasek, M., & Moore, T. (2014). Game-theoretic analysis of DDoS attacks against Bitcoin mining pools. Available at: http://fc14.ifca.ai/bitcoin/papers/bitcoin14_submission_16.pdf, Retrieved: 02.05.2014.

Jones, R. (2014). PayPal washes its hands of bitcoin scam, The Guardian. Available at: http://www.theguardian.com/money/2014/mar/01/paypal-bitcoin-scam-ebay, Retrieved: 28.06.2014.

Kaminsky, D. (2011). Black Ops of TCP/IP 2011 [Power Point Presentation]. Available at: http://dankaminsky.com/2011/08/05/bo2k11/, Retrieved: 24.05.2014.

Kaminsky, D. (2013). I Tried Hacking Bitcoin And I Failed. Business Insider. Available at: http://www.businessinsider.com/dan-kaminsky-highlights-flaws-bitcoin-2013-4, Retrieved: 29.03.2014.

Karame, G., Androulaki, E., & Capkun, S. (2012). Two Bitcoins at the Price of One? Double-Spending Attacks on Fast Payments in Bitcoin. IACR Cryptology ePrint Archive, 2012, 248.

Kaskaloglu, K. (2014). Near Zero Bitcoin Transaction Fees Cannot Last Forever. In The International Conference on Digital Security and Forensics (DigitalSec2014) (pp. 91-99). The Society of Digital Information and Wireless Communication.

Kelsey, J. (2003). The Denationalization of Money: Embedded Neo-Liberalism and the Risks of Implosion. Social & Legal Studies, 12(2), 155-176.

Kharif, O. (2014). Bitcoin 2.0 Shows Technology Evolving Beyond Use as Money. Bloomberg. Available at: http://www.bloomberg.com/news/2014-03-28/bitcoin-2-0-shows-technology-evolvingbeyond-use-as-money.html, Retrieved: 03.09.2014.

Kimonolabs (2014). Bitcoin correlator: Time-series (Bitcoin) to Time-series (Litecoin). Kimonolabs Inc. Available at: https://www.kimonolabs.com/bitcoin/correlator, Retrieved: 18.10.2014.

King, S., & Nadal, S. (2012). PPCoin: peer-to-peer crypto-currency with proof-of-stake. Available at: http://wallet.peercoin.net/assets/paper/peercoin-paper.pdf, Retrieved: 03.10.2014.

King, S. (2013). Primecoin: Cryptocurrency with prime number proof-of-work. Available at: http://dl.frz.ir/FREE/papers-we-love/digital_currency/primecoin.pdf, Retrieved: 05.10.2014.

Klyubin, A. (2013). Some SecureRandom Thoughts. Android Developers Blog. Available at: http://android-developers.blogspot.co.il/2013/08/some-securerandom-thoughts.html, Retrieved: 03.06.2014.

Koblitz, N. (1987). Elliptic curve cryptosystems. Mathematics of computation, 48(177), 203-209.

Karins K., & Judith Sargentini (2014). Report on the proposal for a directive of the European Parliament and of the Council on the prevention of the use of the financial system for the purpose of money laundering and terrorist financing. European Parliament. Available at: http://www.europarl.europa.eu/sides/getDoc.do?pubRef=-//EP//TEXT+REPORT+A72014-0150+0+DOC+XML+V0//EN, Retrieved: 25.10.2014.

Kroll, J. A., Davey, I. C., & Felten, E. W. (2013). The Economics of Bitcoin Mining, or Bitcoin in the Presence of Adversaries. In Proceedings of WEIS (Vol. 2013).

Krugman, P. (2011). Golden Cyberfetters. The New York Times Available at: http://krugman.blogs.nytimes.com/2011/09/07/golden-cyberfetters/?_r=0, 28.02.2014, Retrieved: 03.03.2014.

Krugman, P. (2013). Bitcoin Is Evil. The New York Times. Available at: http://krugman.blogs.nytimes.com/2013/12/28/bitcoin-is-evil/, Retrieved: 03.03.2014.

Lamport, L., Shostak, R., & Pease, M. (1982). The Byzantine Generals Problem. ACM Transactions on Programming Languages and Systems (TOPLAS), 4(3), 382-401.

LearnCryptography (2014). 51% Attack. Learn Cryptography Blog. Available at: http://learncryptography.com/51-attack/, Retrieved: 19.05.2014.

Levin, J. (2014). Measuring Bitcoin Volatility. Coinometrics. Available at: http://news.coinometrics.com/measuring-bitcoin-volatility/, Retrieved: 29.05.2014.

Litke, P. & Stewart, J. (2014) Enterprise Best Practices for Cryptocurrency Adoption. Dell SecureWorksCounter Threat Unit™ Threat Intelligence. Available at: http://www.secureworks.com/assets/pdf-store/white-papers/wp-enterprise-best-practices-forcryptocurrency-adoption.pdf, Retrieved: 20.05.2014.

Liu, A. (2013a). Who's Building Bitcoin? An Inside Look at Bitcoin's Open Source Development. Motherboard. Available at: http://motherboard.vice.com/blog/whos-building-bitcoin-an-insidelook-at-bitcoins-open-source-development, Retrieved: 08.06.2014.

Liu, A. (2013a). Beyond Bitcoin: A Guide to the Most Promising Cryptocurrencies. Motherboard. Available at: http://motherboard.vice.com/blog/beyond-bitcoin-a-guide-to-the-most-promisingcryptocurrencies, 18.10.2014.

Liu, A. (2014). What Satoshi Said: Understanding Bitcoin Through the Lens of Its Enigmatic Creator. Motherboard. Available at: http://motherboard.vice.com/blog/quotes-from-satoshiunderstanding-bitcoin-through-the-lens-of-its-enigmatic-creator, Retrieved: 21.07.2014.

Lubin, J. (2014). The Issuance Model in Ethereum. Ethereum Blog. Available at: https://blog.ethereum.org/2014/04/10/the-issuance-model-in-ethereum/, Retrieved: 18.09.2014. Luther, W. J. (2013). Cryptocurrencies, Network Effects, and Switching Costs. Available at SSRN 2295134.

Marion, F. (2014). Satoshi Nakamoto Quotes. Crypt Blog. Available at: http://crypt.la/2014/01/06/satoshi-nakamoto-quotes/, 18.04.2014.

Matonis, J. (2011). Why Are Libertarians Against Bitcoin? The Monetary Future. Available at: http://themonetaryfuture.blogspot.co.at/2011/06/why-are-libertarians-against-bitcoin.html, Retrieved: 18.04.2014.

Mayyasi, A. (2013). Are Bitcoins The Future? Priceonomics Blog. Available at: http://blog.priceonomics.com/post/47135650437/are-bitcoins-the-future, Retrieved: 28.04.2014.

McGee, J., & Sammut-Bonnici, T. (2002). Network industries in the new economy. European Business Journal, 14(3), 116-132.

McGuire, P. (2013). Such Weird: The Founders of Dogecoin See the Meme Currency's Tipping Point. Motherboard. Available at: http://motherboard.vice.com/blog/dogecoins-founders-believe-inthe-power-of-meme-currencies, Retrieved: 10.06.2014.

Meiklejohn, S., Pomarole, M., Jordan, G., Levchenko, K., McCoy, D., Voelker, G. M., & Savage, S. (2013). A fistful of bitcoins: characterizing payments among men with no names. In Proceedings of the 2013 conference on Internet measurement conference (pp. 127-140). ACM.

Menezes, A. J., Van Oorschot, P. C., & Vanstone, S. A. (1996). Handbook of applied cryptography. CRC press.

Mick, J. (2011). Inside the Mega-Hack of Bitcoin: the Full Story. DailyTech. Available at: http://www.dailytech.com/Inside+the+Mega-Hack+of+Bitcoin+the+Full+Story/article21942.ht m, 22.08.2014.

Miers, I., Garman, C., Green, M., & Rubin, A. D. (2013). Zerocoin: Anonymous distributed e-cash from bitcoin. In Security and Privacy (SP), 2013 IEEE Symposium on (pp. 397-411). IEEE.

Moore, T., & Christin, N. (2013). Beware the middleman: Empirical analysis of Bitcoin-exchange risk. In Financial Cryptography and Data Security (pp. 25-33). Springer Berlin Heidelberg.

Möser, M., Böhme, R., & Breuker, D. (2013). An inquiry into money laundering tools in the Bitcoin ecosystem. Proceedings of the APWG eCrime Researchers Summit (ECRIME 2013). San Francisco, USA.

Nakamoto, S. (2008). Bitcoin: A peer-to-peer electronic cash system. Consulted, 1(2012), 28. Available at: http://www.bitcoin.org/bitcoin.pdf, Retrieved: 28.02.2014.

Neagle, C. (2013). 10 scary facts about Bitcoin. Network World. Available at: http://www.networkworld.com/article/2167062/software/10-scary-facts-about-bitcoin.html, 21.04.2014.

Neal, R. W. (2013). What Is Silk Road? 4 Things You Need To Know About Underground Black Market Shut Down By FBI. International Business Time. Available at: http://www.ibtimes.com/what-silkroad-4-things-you-need-know-about-underground-black-market-shut-down-fbi-1414042, Retrieved: 23.10.2014.

N.N. (2014). SHA-256 hash calculator, Available at: http://www.xorbin.com/tools/sha256-hashcalculator, Retrieved: 01.06.2014.

N.N. (2014). Why Bitcoin may herald a new era in finance. Available at: http://www.economistinsights.com/technology-innovation/analysis/money-nomiddleman/tab/1, Retrieved: 14.10.2014.

Odlyzko, A. M. (1997). The slow evolution of electronic publishing. In ELPUB. Available at: http://www.dtc.umn.edu/~odlyzko/doc/slow.evolution.pdf, Retrieved: 04.05.2014.

Odlyzko, A. (2003). The case against micropayments. In Financial Cryptography (pp. 77-83). Springer Berlin Heidelberg.

Odlyzko, A., & Tilly, B. (2005). A refutation of Metcalfe's Law and a better estimate for the value of networks and network interconnections. Manuscript, March, 2, 2005.

O'Dwyer, K. J., & Malone, D. (2014). Bitcoin mining and its energy footprint. Irish Signals & Systems Conference 2014 and 2014 China-Ireland International Conference on Information and Communications Technologies (ISSC 2014/CIICT 2014). 25th IET, vol., no., pp.280, 285, 26-27 June 2013.

Pease, M., Shostak, R., & Lamport, L. (1980). Reaching agreement in the presence of faults. Journal of the ACM (JACM), 27(2), 228-234.

Pohjanpalo, K. (2014). Bitcoin Judged Commodity in Finland After Failing Money Test. Bloomberg. Available at: http://www.bloomberg.com/news/2014-01-19/bitcoin-becomes-commodity-infinland-after-failing-currency-test.html, Retrieved: 19.03.2014.

Protiviti (2012). Guide to U.S. Anti-Money Laundering Requirements. Protiviti Inc. Available at: http://www.protiviti.com/en-US/Documents/Resource-Guides/Guide-to-US-AMLRequirements-5thEdition-Protiviti.pdf, Retrieved: 23.10.2014.

Ratha, D., Eigen-Zucchi, C., Plaza, S., Wyss, H., & Yi, S. (2013). Migration and remittance flows: Recent trends and outlook, 2013–2016. Migration and Development Brief, 21, 2.

Ratha, D., & Shaw, W. (2006). South-South migration and remittances. World Bank. Washington, DC. Processed.

Raulo (2011). Optimal pool abuse strategy. Available at: http://bitcoin.atspace.com/poolcheating.pdf, Retrieved: 14.03.2014.

Reid, F., & Harrigan, M. (2013). An analysis of anonymity in the bitcoin system (pp. 197-223). Springer New York.

Ren, L. (2014). Proof of Stake Velocity: Building the Social Currency of the Digital Age. Available at: http://www.reddcoin.com/papers/PoSV.pdf, Retrieved: 29.05.2014.

Ripple Labs (2013). Ripple Market Makers, Ripple Labs Inc. Available at: https://ripple.com/ripple_mm.pdf, Retrieved: 22.06.2014.

Ripple Labs (2014a). Ripple Gateways, Ripple Labs Inc. Available at: https://ripple.com/ripplegateways.pdf, Retrieved: 22.06.2014.

Ripple Labs (2014b). The Ripple Protocol Primer. Ripple Labs Inc. Available at: https://ripple.com/ripple_primer.pdf, Retrieved: 22.06.2014.

Ripple Labs (2014c). The Ripple Protocol: Executive Summary for Financial Institutions. Ripple Lab Inc. Available at: https://ripple.com/files/ripple-FIs.pdf, Retrieved: 22.06.2014.

Ripple Labs (n.d.). Investors. Ripple Labs Inc. Available at: https://www.ripplelabs.com/investors/, Retrieved: 16.10.2014.

Ripple Labs (n.d.). XRP Distribution. Ripple Labs Inc. Available at: https://www.ripplelabs.com/xrpdistribution, Retrieved: 16.10.2014.

Ron, D., & Shamir, A. (2013). Quantitative analysis of the full bitcoin transaction graph. In Financial Cryptography and Data Security (pp. 6-24). Springer Berlin Heidelberg.

Rogojanu, A., & Badea, L. (2014). The issue of competing currencies. Case study–Bitcoin. Theoretical and Applied Economics, 21(1), 103-114.

Rogers, M. (2014). Bitcoin malware: Beware the digital pickpockets. Lookout. Available at: https://blog.lookout.com/blog/2014/03/26/bitcoin-threat-landscape/, Retrieved: 09.07.2014.

Ron, D., & Shamir, A. (2013). Quantitative analysis of the full bitcoin transaction graph. In Financial Cryptography and Data Security (pp. 6-24). Springer Berlin Heidelberg.

Rosenfeld, M. (2011). Analysis of Bitcoin Pooled Mining Reward Systems. Available at: http://arxiv.org/pdf/1112.4980.pdf, Retrieved: 10.05.2014.

Rosenfeld, M. (2014). Analysis of hashrate-based double spending. Available at: http://arxiv.org/pdf/1402.2009.pdf, Retrieved: 04.05.2014.

Ruffing, T., Moreno-Sanchez, P., & Kate, A. (2014). CoinShuffle: Practical Decentralized Coin Mixing for Bitcoin. Available at: http://crypsys.mmci.unisaarland.de/projects/CoinShuffle/coinshuffle.pdf, Retrieved: 12.05.2014.

Ruohonen, K. (2010). Mathematical cryptology. Lecture Notes. Available at: http://math.tut.fi/~ruohonen/MC.pdf, Retrieved: 28.05.2014.

Sardesai, N. (2014). Who Owns All the Bitcoins – An Infographic of Wealth Distribution. Cryptocoin News. Available at: http://www.cryptocoinsnews.com/news/owns-bitcoins-infographic-wealthdistribution/2014/03/21, Retrieved: 22.07.2014.

Schwartz, D., Youngs, N., & Britto, A. (2014). The Ripple Protocol Consensus Algorithm. Available at: https://ripple.com/files/ripple_consensus_whitepaper.pdf, Retrieved: 18.09.2014.

Shubber, K. (2014). The 9 Biggest Screwups in Bitcoin History. CoinDesk. Available at: http://www.coindesk.com/9-biggest-screwups-bitcoin-history/, Retrieved: 09.06.2014.

Siby, S. (2013). Paying your Internet, One Byte at a Time. Available at: ftp://129.132.2.212/pub/students/2013-HS/SA-2013-49.pdf, Retrieved: 22.05.2014.

Skudnov, R. (2012). Bitcoin clients. Bachelor's Thesis. Available at: http://bitcoinmalaysia.com/wpcontent/uploads/2012/12/Bitcoin_Clients_Thesis_Skudnov_Rostislav.pdf, Retrieved: 01.04.2014.

Smith, J. (2014). Bitcoin mining pool GHash.IO is preventing accumulation of 51% of all hashing power, GHash.io, Available at: https://ghash.io/ghashio_press_release.pdf, Retrieved: 28.05.2014.

Sompolinsky, Y., & Zohar, A. (2013). Accelerating Bitcoin's Transaction Processing. Fast Money Grows on Trees, Not Chains. Available at: https://eprint.iacr.org/2013/881.pdf, Retrieved 28.05.2014.

Spagnuolo, M. (2013). BitIodine: Extracting Intelligence from the Bitcoin Network. Doctoral dissertation, Politecnico di Milano, Piazza Leonardo da Vinci 32, Milan. Available at: https://www.politesi.polimi.it/bitstream/10589/88482/3/thesis.pdf, Retrieved. 23.06.2014.

Spaven, E. (2013). Bitcoin Price Soars Over $266 and Hits a New All-Time High. CoinDesk. Available at: www.coindesk.com/bitcoin-price-all-time-high/, Retrieved: 29.05.2014.

Sprankel, S. (2013). Technical Basis of Digital Currencies. Available at: http://www.coderblog.de/wp- http://www.carlsterner.com/research/2009_resilience_and_decentralization.shtmlcontent/uploa ds/technical-basis-of-digital-currencies.pdf, Retrieved: 15.05.2014.

Srinivas, V., Dillon, D., & Zagone, R. (2014). Bitcoin: The new gold rush? Available at: http://www.deloitte.com/assets/Dcom-UnitedStates/Local%20Assets/Documents/FSI/us_fsi_BitcointheNewGoldRush_031814.pdf, Retrieved: 15.08.2014.

Sterner, C. (2013). Resilience and Decentralization. Available at: http://www.carlsterner.com/research/2009_resilience_and_decentralization.shtml, Retrieved: 12.05.2014.

Stokes, R. (2012). Virtual money laundering: The case of Bitcoin and the Linden dollar. Information & Communications Technology Law, 21(3), 221-236.

Szabo, N. (1999). Micropayments and mental transaction costs. In 2nd Berlin Internet Economics Workshop.

Tanaka, T. (1996). Possible economic consequences of digital cash. First Monday, 1(2). Chicago

Techfact (2013). Taking down the Bitcoin, Attacking Silkroad & TOR network. Tech News TechFact. Available at: http://technews.techfact.org/post/63176373302/taking-down-the-bitcoin-attackingsilkroad-tor, Retrieved: 25.06.2014.

Thomas, S. & Schwartz, E. (2013). Ripple Labs' W3C Web Payments Position Paper. Ripple Labs. Available at: http://www.w3.org/2013/10/payments/papers/webpayments2014_submission_25.pdf, Retrieved: 29.10.2014.

Torpey, K. (2014). Adam Back: Sidechains Can Replace Altcoins and 'Bitcoin 2.0' Platforms. Cryptocoin News. Available at: http://www.cryptocoinsnews.com/news/adam-back-sidechains-can-replacealtcoins-bitcoin-2-0-platforms/2014/04/10, Retrieved: 01.08.2014.

Treanor, J., Osborne, H., & Wearden, G. (2014). Bank of England payment system crashes. The Guardian. Available at: http://www.theguardian.com/business/2014/oct/20/bank-of-englandpayment-system-crashes, Retrieved: 20.10.2014.

Tromp, J. (2014). Cuckoo Cycle: a memory-hard proof-of-work system. IACR Cryptology ePrint Archive, 2014, 59.

The Economist (2014). Hidden flipside: How the crypto-currency could become the internet of money. Available at: http://www.economist.com/news/finance-and-economics/21599054-how-cryptocurrency-could-become-internet-money-hidden-flipside, Retrieved: 08.07.2014.

Varian, H. R. & Shapiro, C. (1999). Information rules: a strategic guide to the network economy. Harvard Business School Press, Cambridge.

Villasenor, J., Monk, C., & Bronk, C. (2011). Shadowy Figures: Tracking Illicit Financial Transactions in the Murky World of Digital Currencies, Peer-to-peer Networks, and Mobile Device Payments. Brookings Institution.

Weaver, N. (2013). Once You Use Bitcoin You Can't Go 'Back' — And That's Its Fatal Flaw. Wired. Available at: http://www.wired.com/2013/11/once-you-use-bitcoin-you-cant-go-back-and-thatirreversibility-is-its-fatal-flaw/, Retrieved: 09.06.2014.

Wingfield, N. (2013). Bitcoin Pursues the Mainstream. The New York Times. Available at: http://www.nytimes.com/2013/10/31/technology/bitcoin-pursues-themainstream.html?_r=1&, Retrieved: 07.08.2014.

Wile, R. (2013). 927 People Own Half Of All Bitcoins. Business Insider, Available at: http://www.businessinsider.com/927-people-own-half-of-the-bitcoins-2013-12, Retrieved: 27.06.2014.

Wile, R. (2014). Prices Fall As Bitcoin Confronts Doomsday Scenario. Business Insider. Available at: http://www.businessinsider.com/today-bitcoins-doomsday-scenario-arrived-2014-6, Retrieved: 09.06.2014.

Willett, J. R. (2012). The Second Bitcoin Whitepaper. White paper. Available at: https://e33ec872-a62cb3a1a-s-sites.googlegroups.com/site/2ndbtcw-paper/2ndBitcoinWhitepaper.pdf, Retrieved: 12.10.2014.

Willet, J. R. (2014). The Master Protocol / Mastercoin Complete Specification. GitHub Gist. Available at: https://github.com/mastercoin-MSC/spec/, Retrieved: 12.10.2014.

Wolfram Research, Inc. (n.d.). 256^2. Wolfram|Alpha. Available at: https://www.wolframalpha.com/input/?i=2^256, Retrieved: 16.05.2014.

Woo, D., Gordon, I., Iaralov, V. (2013). Bitcoin: a first assessment. Bank of America Merrill Lynch. FX and Rates Research Report, Available at: https://ciphrex.com/archive/bofa-bitcoin.pdf, Retrieved: 19.07.2014.

Xorbin (2014). SHA-256 hash calculator. www.xorbin.com. Available at: http://www.xorbin.com/tools/sha256-hash-calculator, Retrieved: 01.06.2014.

Zeiler, D. (2014). First U.S. Bitcoin Derivative Reduces Risk for Businesses. Money Morning. Available at: http://moneymorning.com/2014/09/12/first-u-s-bitcoin-derivative-reduces-risk-for-businesses/, Retrieved: 22.10.2014.

Zellkos (2014). I hope so [Reddit forum post]. Reddit. Available at: http://www.reddit.com/r/dogecoin/comments/2kcpkd/1_week_left_for_the_dogecoin_game_ dev_contest_can/clk2lb3, Retrieved: 26.10.2014.

# Appendix

## A1: Bitcoin Vocabulary

**Address**

A Bitcoin address is similar to a physical address or an email. It is the only information you need to provide for someone to pay you with Bitcoin. An important difference, however, is that each address should only be used for a single transaction.

**Altcoins**

Alternative cryptographic currencies based on Bitcoin.

**Bitcoin (abbreviated BTC)**

The name of a revolutionary, decentralized peer-to-peer cryptographic virtual currency.

**Bitcoins**

Applies in the context of using Bitcoin as a means of payment or to refer to an amount of cryptocurrency.

**Block**

Blocks are links in a chain of transaction verifications. Outstanding transactions get bundled into a block and are verified roughly every ten minutes on average. Each subsequent block strengthens the verification of previous blocks. Each block contains one or more transactions.

**Block Chain**

Each block includes the difficult-to-produce verification hash of the previous block. This allows each subsequent block to be linked to all previous blocks. These blocks which are linked together for the purpose of verifying transactions within blocks is called the block chain.

**Branching Point**

The block at which the block chain diverges into multiple chain branches

**BTC**

The decimal unit of Bitcoins. One BTC is equal to 100,000,000satoshis of $10^{-8}$BTC.

### Checkpoint Lockin

Every once in a while, an old block hash is hardcoded into Bitcoin software. Different implementations choose different checkpoint locations. Checkpoints prevent various DOS attacks from nodes flooding unusable chains and attacks involving isolating nodes and giving them fake chains. Satoshi announced the feature here and it was discussed to death here.

### Coinbase

Coinbase is another name for a generation transaction. The input of such a transaction contains some arbitrary data where the scriptSig would go in normal transactions -- this data is sometimes called the "coinbase", as well.

### Confirmation

In order to protect the network against double spending of Bitcoins, a transaction can only be seen as confirmed if a certain number of blocks within the blockchain verified the transaction.

### Cryptography

Cryptography is the branch of mathematics that lets us create mathematical proofs that provide high levels of security. Online commerce and banking already uses cryptography. In the case of Bitcoin, cryptography is used to make it impossible for anybody to spend funds from another user's wallet or to corrupt the block chain. It can also be used to encrypt a wallet, so that it cannot be used without a password.

### Difficulty

Every 2016 blocks, Bitcoin adjusts the difficulty of verifying blocks based on the time it took to verify the previous 2016 blocks. The difficulty is adjusted so that given the average estimated computing power of the whole bitcoin network, only one block will verified on average every ten minutes for the next 2016 blocks. The difficulty is usually expressed as a number, optionally accurate to many decimal places (eg. in block 100,000 it was 14,484.162361. The difficulty is inversely proportional to the hash target, which is expressed as a hex number with around 50 digits, and is the number under which a block's generated hash must be to qualify as an officially verified block. The hash target is equal to ((65535 << 208) / difficulty). Difficulty is also often called block difficulty, hash difficulty, verification difficulty or the difficulty of generating bitcoins.

**Double-Spending**

Attempting to spend coins that have already been spent in another transaction. If a malicious user tries to spend their bitcoins to two different recipients at the same time, this is double spending. Bitcoin mining and the block chain are there to create a consensus on the network about which of the two transactions will confirm and be considered valid.

**Generate Bitcoins**

When a Bitcoin miner finds a block, it receives newly minted bitcoins and the transaction fees which may or may not be included in the block. The amount of bitcoins awarded for verifying a block is 50 BTC for the first 210,000 blocks and half the previous amount of bitcoins for each subsequent 210,000 blocks. On average, 210,000 blocks take about 4 years to verify. The total amount of bitcoins that will ever be minted is roughly 21,000,000 BTC.

**Hash**

The output of a hash function.

**Hash Function**

A computer algorithm which takes an arbitrary amount of input data and deterministically produces fixed length output, known as the data's "hash", that can be used to easily verify that data has not been altered. If you change any single bit of the original data and run the hash algorithm, the hash will completely change. Because the hash is seemingly random, it is prohibitively difficult to try to produce a specific hash by changing the data which is being hashed.

**Hash Rate**

The hash rate is the measuring unit of the processing power of the Bitcoin network. The Bitcoin network must make intensive mathematical operations for security purposes. When the network reached a hash rate of 10 Th/s, it meant it could make 10 trillion calculations per second

**Low Priority**

See Priority.

**Memory pool**

Generators store transactions waiting to get into a block in their memory pool after receiving them. Received transactions are stored even if they are invalid to prevent nodes from constantly requesting transactions that they've already seen. The memory pool is cleared when Bitcoin is shut down, causing the network to gradually forget about transactions that haven't been included in a block.

**Merkle root**

Every transaction has a hash associated with it. In a block, all of the transaction hashes in the block are themselves hashed (sometimes several times -- the exact process is complex), and the result is the Merkle root. In other words, the Merkle root is the hash of all the hashes of all the transactions in the block. The Merkle root is included in the block header. With this scheme, it is possible to securely verify that a transaction has been accepted by the network (and get the number of confirmations) by downloading just the tiny block headers and Merkle tree -- downloading the entire block chain is unnecessary. This feature is currently not used in Bitcoin, but it will be in the future.

**Miner**

Computer software which is designed to repeatedly calculate hashes with the intention to create a successful block and earn coins from transaction fees and new coins created with the block itself. The term references an analogy of gold miners who dig gold out of the ground and thus "discover" new gold that can be used to create new coins with a similar kind of discovery occurring with a successful hash to create new Bitcoins.

**Node**

Each Bitcoin client currently running within the network is referred to as a Node of the system.

**Nonce**

A nonce is an otherwise meaningless number which is used to alter the outcome of a hash. Each time Bitcoin hashes a block, it increments a nonce within the block which it is trying verify. If the numeric value of the effectively random hash is below a certain amount determined by the block generation difficulty, then the block is accepted by other clients and gets added to the chain.

**Orphan Block**

An orphan block is a block that is not in the currently-longest block chain.

**Priority**

A scoring mechanism to help ensure that expensive data storage isn't consumed by lower quality and spam. Low priority transactions will not get included by a miner if the limited space is already filled by higher priority transactions. A transaction fee will affect priority.

**Proof of Work**

A result that can only be obtained through the use of computational resources. Changing the data in the proof of work requires redoing the work.

**P2P**

Peer-to-peer refers to systems that work like an organized collective by allowing each individual to interact directly with the others. In the case of Bitcoin, the network is built in such a way that each user is broadcasting the transactions of other users. And, crucially, no bank is required as a third party.

**Private Key**

A private key is a secret piece of data that proves your right to spend bitcoins from a specific wallet through a cryptographic signature. Your private key(s) are stored in your computer if you use a software wallet; they are stored on some remote servers if you use a web wallet. Private keys must never be revealed as they allow you to spend bitcoins for their respective Bitcoin wallet.

**Reorganize**

A block chain reorganize (or reorg) happens when one chain becomes longer than the one you are currently working on. All of the blocks in the old chain that are not in the new one become orphan blocks, and their generations are invalidated. Transactions that use the newly-invalid generated coins also become invalid, though this is only possible in large chain splits because generations can't be spent for 100 blocks. The number of confirmations for transactions may change after a reorg, and transactions that are not in the new chain will become "0/unconfirmed" again. If a transaction in the old chain conflicts with one in the new chain (as a result of double-spending), the old one becomes invalid.

**Satoshi**

The base unit of Bitcoin (0.00000001 BTC) is sometimes called a Satoshi, after Bitcoin's creator Satoshi Nakamoto.

**Seed Nodes**

Nodes whose IP addresses are included in the Bitcoin client for use during a new installation when the normal bootstrapping process through IRC wasn't possible.

**Signature**

A cryptographic signature is a mathematical mechanism that allows someone to prove ownership. In the case of Bitcoin, a Bitcoin wallet and its private key(s) are linked by some mathematical magic. When your Bitcoin software signs a transaction with the appropriate private key, the whole network can see that the signature matches the bitcoins being spent. However, there is no way for the world to guess your private key to steal your hard-earned bitcoins.

**Subsidy**

The block subsidy is the BTC created for generating a block. The subsidy is halved every four years.

**Super Nodes**

A participant in a p2p network which connects to as many other nodes as possible.

**Tonal Bitcoin (abbreviated TBC)**

Adaptation of Bitcoin to the Tonal System. 1 TBC is defined as 1,0000 (65,536 decimal) base bitcoin units. Not widely used.

**Transaction Fee**

A voluntary fee which can be added to a transaction which is used as an incentive to add the bitcoin transaction to a block. The fee determines the likelihood of inclusion in any given block, where a high fee included with a transaction has a priority over transactions with a lower fee included or no fee at all.

**Virgin Bitcoin**

The reward for generating a block that has not yet been spent, a state which might increase the ability to transact anonymously.

**Wallet**

A Bitcoin wallet is loosely the equivalent of a physical wallet on the Bitcoin network. The wallet actually contains your private key(s) which allow you to spend the bitcoins allocated to it in the block chain. Each Bitcoin wallet can show you the total balance of all bitcoins it controls and lets you pay a specific amount to a specific person, just like a real wallet. This is different to credit cards where you are charged by the merchant.

Source: Bitcoin Wiki. Vocabulary, 20.10.2014

Bitcoin.org. Vocabulary, 20.10.2014

## A2: List of Altcoins

2chcoin
CasinoCoin
FastCoin
JouleCoin
Nybble
SifCoin
21Coin
CatCoin
FateCoin
JunkCoin
OCoin
Skeincoin
42Coin
ChainCoin
FCKBanksCoin
JupiterCoin
OlyimpicCoin
SkyCoin
66Coin
ChinaCoin
Feathercoin
KakaCoin
OneCoin
SmartCoin
AirCoin
ChocoCoin
FederationCredits
KarmaCoin
OnionCoin
SnowCoin
AlcohoCoin
CinnamonCoin
FedoraCoin
KingCoin
OnlineGamingCoin
SochiCoin
AlienCoin
CloudCoin
FerretCoin
KittehCoin
OrbitCoin
SolarCoin
AlphaCoin
Coin2
FireflyCoin
KlingonDarsek
PACCoin
SpainCoin
AlphaOmegaCoin
Coinye
FlappyCoin
KlondikeCoin
PandaCoin
SpotsCoin
AmericanCoin
ColossusCoin
FlashCoin
KrugerCoin
PandaCoin2
StableCoin
AmKoin
CommunityCoin
FlorinCoin
KudosCoin
PanguCoin
StarCoin
AndroidToken
CopperBars
FoxCoin
LeadCoin
PARTICLE
STLCoin
AnimeCoin
Copperlark
FrankoCoin
LeafCoin
PayCoin
StockCoin
AnonCoin
CorgiCoin
FreeCoin
Lebowskis
PeerCoin
StoriesCoin
ApeCoin
CosmosCoin
FreiCoin
LeproCoin
PenguinCoin
SunCoin
AppleCoin
CraftCoin
FrozenCoin
Litebar
Pennies
SuperCoin
Argentum
CrimeCoin
FryCoin
Litecoins
PeopleCoin
SwagCoin
AsicCoin
CryptoBuck
GabenCoin
LiveCoin
PHICoin
SynCoin
AstroCoin
Cryptobits
GalaxyCoin
LottoCoin
Philosopherstone
TagCoin
AtomCoin
CryptogenicBullion
GaltCoin
LoveCoin
PhoenixCoin
TeaCoin
AuroraCoin
CryptoniumCoin
GameCoins
LuckyCoin
PhysicsCoin
TekCoin

BabyCoin
CthulhuCoin
GayCoin
Lucky7Coin
PiggyCoin
TerraCoin
Baconbits
Cubits
GeoCoin
LXCoin
PikaCoin
TeslaCoin
BaseCoin
CureCoin
GiftCoin
MachineCoin
PirateCoin
ThorCoin
BatCoin
DataCoin
GILCoin
Maples
PlatinumToken
Tickets
BattleCoin
DeutcheeMarks
GlobalCoin
MarioBrosCoin
PlayToken
TigerCoin
BBQCoin
DevCoin
GlobeCoin
MarsCoin
PokerCoin
TimeCoin
BeaoCoin
DiamondCoin
GoatCoin
MasterCoin
PotCoin
TittieCoin
BeeCoin
DigitalCoin
GoldCoin
MazaCoin
PowerCoin
TrollCoin
BellaCoin
Digitbyte
GoldFlexibly
MediterraneanCoin
PremineCoin
Troptions
BellsCoin
DobbsCoin
GoldPressedLatinum
MegaCoin
Primecoin
UFOCoin
BenjaminCoin
DogeCoin
GPUCoin
MemeCoin
Protoshares
UnionCoin
BestCoin
DollarPounds
GrainCoin
MemoryCoin
PXLCoin
USDeCoin
BetaCoin
Doubloons
GrandCoin
MetisCoin
PythonCoin
UniteCoin
BillionCoin
DragonCoin
GridCoin
Microcash
Quark
UnitedScryptCoin
BinaryCoin
DubstepCoin
GrowthCoin
MilanCoin
RabbitCoin
Unobtanium
BitGem
DuckDuckCoin
GrumpyCoin
MinCoin
RadioactiveCoin
ValueCoin
Bitbar
EagleCoin
H2OCoin
MintCoin
RapidCoin
VegasCoin
Bitcoin
EarthCoin
HamburgerCoin
MoleculeCoin
RastaCoin
VelocityCoin
Bitcoin 2
EBTCoin
HeroCoin
MonaCoin
RealCoin
VendettaCoin
BitShares
EcoCoin
HiroCoin
MoonCoin
RedCoin
VertCoin
BlackCoin
Ekrona
HobbitCoin
MurrayCoin
ReddCoin
WikiCoin
BladeCoin
ElaCoin
HoboNickelsCoin
Naanayam
RevolutionCoin
WorldCoin

| | | |
|---|---|---|
| BlakeCoin | ICoin | SecondsCoin |
| ElectricCoin | NeoCoin | ZeitCoin |
| HotCoin | SCoin | CNoteCoin |
| Namecoins | YaCoin | ExtremeCoin |
| RichCoin | BrightCoin | ItalyCoin |
| XCoin | Ethereum | Novacoins |
| BlessCoin | I0Coin | SecureCoin |
| ElephantCoin | NetCoin | ZenithCoin |
| Huitong | SaturnCoin | CacheCoin |
| NanoToken | YuanBao | EZCoin |
| RonPaulCoin | ButterflyCoin | IXCoin |
| XenCoin | EuroCoin | NuCoin |
| BossCoin | ImperialCoin | SeedCoin |
| EmeraldCoin | NextCoin | ZetaCoin |
| HunterCoin | SauronRings | CageCoin |
| NBCoin | ZCCoin | FailCoin |
| RoyalCoin | ByteCoin | JCoin |
| XivraCoin | ExileCoin | NutCoin |
| BottleCaps | IncaCoin | SexCoin |
| EMUCoin | NobleCoin | ZeusCoin |
| HyperCoin | SavingCoin | CarbonCoin |
| NEMCoin | ZedCoin | FairCoin |
| RVDCoin | CCoin | JerkyCoin |
| XmasCoin | EXOCoin | NyanCoin |
| BountyCoin | InfiniteCoin | SherlockCoin |
| EternalCoin | Noirbits | ZombieCoin |

Source: http://listofaltcoins.com/index.php/Main_Page, 20.10.2014

You never change things by fighting the existing reality.

To change something, build a new model that makes the existing model obsolete.

Richard Buckminster Fuller

Lightning Source UK Ltd.
Milton Keynes UK
UKHW03f1300200418
321385UK00002B/321/P